The Official Guide to

ancestry.com℠

The Official Guide to

❧ancestry.com℠

by George G. Morgan

❧ancestry publishing

Library of Congress Cataloging-in-Publication Data

Morgan, George G.,
 The official guide to Ancestry.com / by George G. Morgan.
   p. cm.
 Includes bibliographical references and index.
 ISBN-13: 978-1-59331-304-3 (alk. paper)
 ISBN-10: 1-59331-304-7
 1. Ancestry.com (Firm) 2. Genealogy—Computer network resources—Handbooks,
manuals, etc. 3. United States—Genealogy—Computer network resources—Handbooks,
manuals, etc. I. Title.

CS21.5.M67 2007
025.06'9291—dc22   2007005530

Published by
Ancestry Publishing, a The Generations Network™ division
360 West 4800 North
Provo, Utah 84604
www.ancestry.com

First Printing 2007
10 9 8 7 6 5 4 3 2

ISBN-13: 978-1-59331-304-3
ISBN-10: 1-59331-304-7

Printed in Canada

Contents

Contents

Chapter 3
Working with Digitized Image Collections..........51

Chapter 4
My Ancestry 69

Chapter 5
Working with Census Records.............................91

Chapter 6
Birth, Marriage, and Death Records 115

Chapter 7
Family Facts 131

Contents

Chapter 11
Immigration Records 185

Chapter 12
Court, Land, and Probate Records 201

Chapter 13
Military Records 211

Chapter 14
Reference and Finding Aids 225

Dedication

This book is dedicated to the tens of thousands of librarians and archivists who serve genealogists around the world. They share their knowledge and expertise in locating information to help us, and celebrate the joy of the search and the thrill of discovery with us. Without their unselfish desire to learn and serve, we would falter in our family history odyssey far more frequently.

I would particularly like to dedicate this book to the memory of the first librarian in my life, in Madison, North Carolina. She was a warm and generous lady who helped shape my love for libraries and for genealogical research. Her love of learning and teaching was contagious, and a part of her lives on in all of my work.

Miss Mary Scott Johnson
1904–1979

Acknowledgments

The sheer size and scope of the contents of Ancestry.com is mind-boggling. There are many people who helped make this ambitious book project come to fruition. I would like to thank the great people at The Generations Network, Inc. and Ancestry Publishing for their faith in my ability to bring the book to life. In particular, Loretto "Lou" Szucs is a warm and inspiring friend whose vision makes all the Ancestry books the *crème de la crème* in the genealogical industry. Jennifer Utley and Matthew Wright epitomize the professionalism of editorial guidance and provided every tool and contact I needed to write the text. Many thanks go to Tana Pedersen Lord for poring over the manuscript and creating a wonderful index. Matthew Rayback for his patient and expert editing.

I would also like to acknowledge the support and encouragement of my family, friends, and the genealogical community who always stand behind me and keep me striving for excellence. I am indeed the most fortunate of writers!

Finally, I would like to thank the users of Ancestry.com for acknowledging its superior content through their continued use of the service. It is my deepest hope that this book will help make you a better researcher and extend your research to new levels.

Introduction

My genealogical research began when I was ten years old.
That was back in the early 1960s when everything a researcher
did involved either visiting a records repository in person or
writing lots of letters. You submitted queries to magazines and
to genealogical society newsletters and journals. You waited for
responses to those letters and queries, which were agonizingly
slow. If you were fortunate, you got something back that
helped further your research; if not, you started over again in
another direction.

As electronic communications came of age, many of us used
slow, dial-up modems to connect to genealogy Bulletin Board
Services (BBSs) and, later, to genealogy groups through early
online services: Compuserve, GENie, Prodigy, and others,
all of which were text-based facilities. The entry of America
Online into the field intensified commercial competition with
its expanded range of electronic resources. The Genealogy
Forum on America Online became a leader in online

genealogy, offering articles, graphical materials, message boards, scheduled online chats, a file cabinet for uploading and downloading of GEDCOM files, and other resources.

With the appearance of what we know as the modern Internet and the introduction of the first Web browsers that supported graphics (first Netscape, then Internet Explorer, and then others), worldwide communications exploded. E-mail and Web pages quickly changed the way we communicated, and it was not long before genealogy became one of the foremost uses of the Internet.

What Is Ancestry.com?

Among the earliest genealogical database resources on the Internet was Ancestry.com^{SM}. I've used Ancestry.com for so long that it has become second nature for me to immediately turn to it for how-to articles and advice, databases, message boards, books and CDs, and much more. Most genealogists are well aware of Ancestry.com and have used it in some way. Ancestry.com is essentially a subscription database service; however, it also happens to contain a wealth of *free* material accessible to anyone.

Ancestry.com is the largest online genealogy database collection in the world. It is one of a large family of genealogy-related companies that make up The Generations Network, Inc., a company located in Provo, Utah (formerly MyFamily. com, Inc.). The Generations Network includes:

- **Ancestry.com**—Ancestry.com is the world's #1 online source for family history information, containing the Web's largest collection of family history records—including databases, message boards, and digitized books and newspapers, to mention just a few—and helping genealogists organize and save their family trees.

- **Ancestry.co.uk**—Ancestry.co.uk is the largest online archive of family history records from the United Kingdom and Ireland, including census records as well as civil, ecclesiastical, and emigration records.

- **Ancestry.ca**—Ancestry.ca is the best place online for Canadians to research their family history and offers the largest collection of family history records available. It is part of the World Deluxe Collection.

- **Ancestry.de**—Ancestry.de is the newest addition to the Ancestry database collection family. It provides access to German database content and is also part of the World Deluxe Collection.

- **Ancestry.au**—Ancestry.au is the database collection of Australian genealogical databases, available to Australians as part of the UK Heritage Collection. It is also part of the World Deluxe Collection.

- **Genealogy.com**—Genealogy.com is a vast collection of family and local histories, vital records, military records, and much more.

- **RootsWeb.com**—RootsWeb.com is a thriving, free genealogy community on the Web, providing a robust worldwide environment for learning, collaborating, and sharing for both the expert and the novice researcher alike.

- **MyFamily.com**—MyFamily.com is a website at that allows anyone to easily create and maintain a private, unique family website and strengthen family relationships.

- *Family Tree Maker*—*Family Tree Maker* Version 16 is the number-one-selling genealogical database software on the market, providing the user with everything needed to create, grow, and publish his or her family tree.

- **Ancestry Publishing**—Ancestry Publishing is the publishing imprint of The Generations Network, Inc. With more than fifty books in its catalog—including such landmark titles as *The Source: A Guidebook to American Genealogy* and *Red Book: American State, County, and Town Sources*, both in their third edition—Ancestry Publishing is the most prestigious publisher in the genealogy marketplace. In addition, it publishes *Ancestry* Magazine and numerous databases on CD-ROM.

These subsidiaries complement one another by providing a comprehensive collection of family history resources for learning, researching, documenting, collaborating, and sharing genealogical information.

Working with the Databases

The term "database" can be intimidating to many people the first time they encounter it. *Merriam-Webster's Collegiate Dictionary*, 11th edition, defines a database as a "large collection of data organized especially for rapid search and retrieval (as by a computer)." That sounds pretty straightforward, and, with the technological advances of the last twenty years or so, working with databases has become as simple as using an online library catalog.

Not every database is the same, however. Each one varies, depending upon its content and on the way it is searched. That means that the search template—the online form that allows you to define your search criteria—will also vary, as will your list of search results. As an example, if you searched the Social Security Death Index database, the information you input and the search results will certainly be different than if you were searching in the Georgia Cherokee Land Lottery Records of 1832.

As Ancestry.com has grown, and with the introduction of the various worldwide sister sites, there are now more than 23,000 databases and titles of varying types and sizes available, as of April 2007. New content is added every month and the user interface continues to be examined, improved, and streamlined. So many databases and different types of browse and search capabilities exist that it can be confusing to move from one database or resource or another.

What This Book Will Do for You

The purpose of this book is to help you access the power of the many Ancestry.com databases. You will learn how to navigate the entire site, how to browse, and how to use all of the search functionalities to maximize your use of the entire site. You will learn how each of the major content areas are organized and presented and what is included in each area. Sample searches will be described, the appropriate database search templates and search results will be illustrated, and practical suggestions will be offered for using the results to continue and further your research.

This book focuses on the experience of a user in the United States and works with the Ancestry.com database offerings, including both free and subscription content.

In addition to access to all the databases, Ancestry.com provides a powerful and dynamic Family Tree tool that allows you to build one or more of your own family trees online, add photographs and stories, and invite other authorized people to view and comment on it. The Ancestry Community contains the largest genealogical message board facility in the world, and it allows you to search for and connect with other researchers working on the same family lines that you are. Further, the Learning Center provides access to a whole library of published articles, columns, how-to materials, and more to help you become a savvy genealogical researcher.

This book is not intended as a guide to doing your family history. Though I give tips and suggestions throughout, you should consult a guide to genealogy if you have any questions about methodology. For example, you might consider my own book on the subject:

Morgan, George G. *How to Do Everything with Your Genealogy*. Emeryville, CA: McGraw-Hill/Osborne, 2004.

It is important to remember that Ancestry.com is a dynamic resource that is constantly changing. While it is impossible for a book like this to accurately reflect all aspects of the site into the future, the fundamentals contained therein will remain valuable, even as the site changes. Some of the screens may look different than those shown here, but you can still use those examples to help you learn.

This guide will coach you through using the full range of the Ancestry.com international family of databases and other electronic resources. In no time at all, you will have become a pro in making the online content at Ancestry.com an essential part of all of your research. You will be navigating and searching the data quickly and effectively, *and* you will be better prepared to apply what you find to improve the quality and efficiency of your research at Ancestry.com and across the Internet.

Happy Hunting!

George G. Morgan
Odessa, Florida
April 2007

Chapter 1

Getting Around the Site

Ancestry.com is easy to use once you learn the ropes for navigating the site and using the various search tools. In this chapter, you will learn these essential skills. Even though the site contains more than 23,000 databases and titles with different record types and content, the search templates will essentially look and act the same, regardless of the database.

I urge you to enter the examples shown in the figures of the chapter, and then practice each one with one of your own ancestors. Doing so will help you become more comfortable with using Ancestry.com.

Getting Started

Ancestry.com is a fabulous tool for doing your family history. Before we begin working with it, however, you may want to organize the information you already know about your family so that you can readily access as you learn to use the site. When you're ready, go to <www.ancestry.com>.

Figure 1-1: "Member Login" fields.

Logging In

At the top, notice the fields under "Member Login" (see figure 1-1). If you already have a subscription to Ancestry.com, this is where you log in. Enter your username and password, and click the **Login** button. Figure 1-2 is an example of what the homepage looks like after you've logged in. Note that it changes frequently so this image may look diferent to you.

If you have forgotten your username or password, you can click the "Forgot?" link and a page will appear that allows you

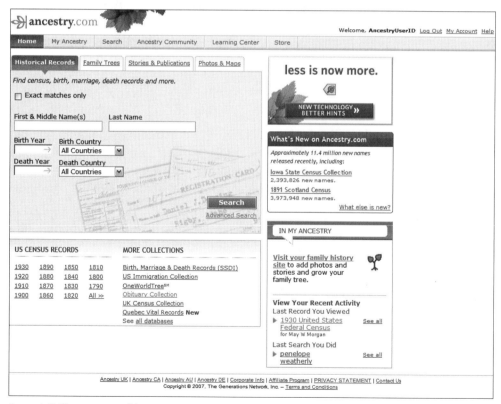

Figure 1-2: The main page of Ancestry.com.

to enter the e-mail address associated with your account. Your username and password will be e-mailed to you.

My Account

Welcome, **AncestryUserID** Log Out My Account Help

You should now see your username in the upper right corner (see figure 1-3), followed by links that allow

Figure 1-3: Top of homepage after login.

you to "Log Out" of Ancestry.com, view and work with "My Account" settings, and access the "Help" facility online. (We will discuss "Help" later in this chapter.) If you have a subscription other than World Deluxe, you will also see an "Upgrade" link. Click the "My Account" link.

On the subsequent "My Account Options" page, you will see your current subscriptions, as well as the option to upgrade your subscription, if applicable. In the "My Account Information" section on the right side of the page are links to additional pages that allow you to manage your account settings (see figure 1-4):

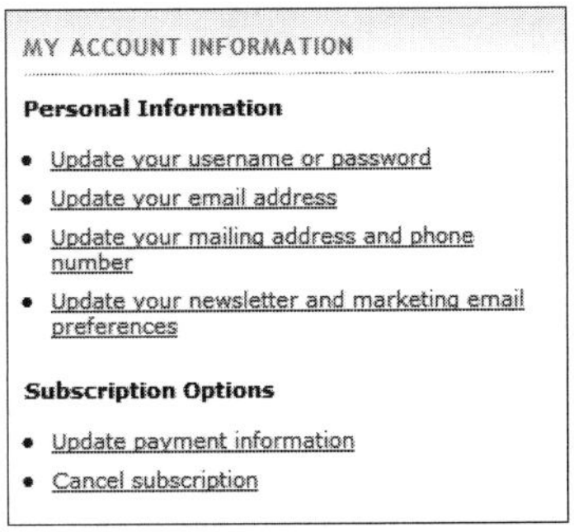

MY ACCOUNT INFORMATION

Personal Information
- Update your username or password
- Update your email address
- Update your mailing address and phone number
- Update your newsletter and marketing email preferences

Subscription Options
- Update payment information
- Cancel subscription

Figure 1-4: The "My Account Information" section on the "My Account Options" page.

- **Update your username or password**—You may change your username and password at any time. Be certain that you write them down and store them in a safe place for future reference.

- **Update your email address**—It is important to maintain your correct e-mail address for your account so that Ancestry.com administrative staff can contact you. The e-mail address is also used in other areas of Ancestry.com to provide a means for other members researching the same ancestral lines to contact you.

- **Update your mailing address and phone number**—Your personal contact information is essential for maintaining a current account profile.

Registering

As Ancestry.com grows, more and more features will be available to users for free by following a simple registration procedure. This will give you a username and a password with which you can sign in on return visits.

Changes to "My Account"

Earlier versions of this page contained options for maintaining your Public Profile, communications preferences, alerts, and other settings. These have now been relocated to the **My Ancestry** tab.

- **Update your newsletter and marketing email preferences**—This page allows you to select the types of information you receive from Ancestry.com. There are some excellent options available here:

  - *Ancestry Newsletter Subscriptions*—Subscribe to the monthly newsletter, the weekly, or both.

  - *Ancestry Product Watch*—Request regular updates about Ancestry products, promotional offers, and discounts on family history books, software, and other items.

  - *Special Offers*— Select "From Ancestry" or "From Ancestry's Trusted Partners."

  - *Email Format*—Specify whether the e-mails sent to you are formatted in HTML with pictures and text or as text-only messages.

- **Update payment information**—This area allows you to update your credit card information for subscription billing purposes.

- **Cancel Subscription**—You can now cancel your subscription online.

The "Help" section contains several frequently asked questions, also known as FAQs, concerning your Ancestry.com account. If you click the "more…" link, you'll come to the Ancestry.com Knowledge Base of help questions and answers.

Using Quick Links to Move Backwards

One method of moving quickly to previous pages is using Quick Links, located below the main toolbar on most pages (see figure 1-5).

The Quick Link shown in figure 1-5 indicates that you have moved from the Ancestry.com homepage to another

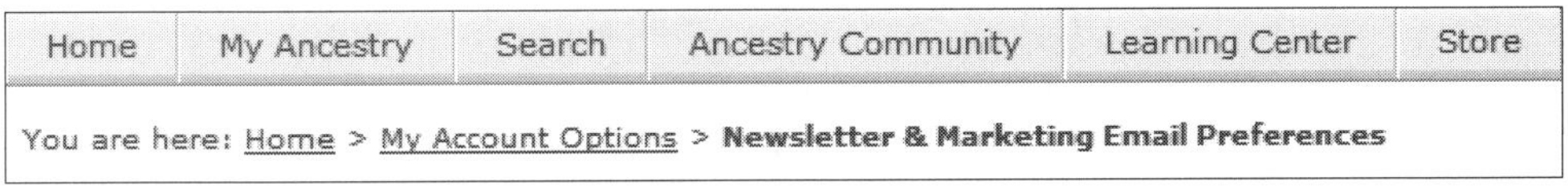

| Home | My Ancestry | Search | Ancestry Community | Learning Center | Store |

You are here: Home > My Account Options > **Newsletter & Marketing Email Preferences**

Figure 1-5: Quick Links.

page titled "My Account Options" and then to another page titled "Newsletter & Marketing Email Preferences." The last link is the page you are currently on. It is bold. If you had landed on the "Update your newsletter and marketing email preferences" page following the route described by the Quick Link shown in figure 1-5, you could simply click the "My Account Options" link to move back to that page. Likewise, if you click the "Home" link, you will move to the Ancestry.com homepage. This can be very convenient when you are working in other areas of Ancestry.com. For example, I searched the 1850 census for my great-great-grandfather Jesse Holder in Gwinnett County, Georgia. When I got to the image that I wanted, there was a line of Quick Links (see figure 1-6).

Quick Links

Quick Links are often called "bread crumbs."

Search > Census > U.S. Census > 1850 United States Federal Census > Georgia > Gwinnett > **Cates**

Figure 1-6: "Quick Link" list from 1850 census image page.

I could click on any of the underlined links to move backwards or leap back to "Census" and begin another general census search. In other words, these Quick Links make it simpler and faster to move around the Ancestry.com site.

Also, from just about anywhere in the site, you can click the Ancestry.com logo in the upper left corner of the page, and this will take you back to the Ancestry.com homepage.

Navigating the Site

The first thing you will notice on Ancestry.com is the logical organization of the information into categories. We are going to study each area of this page and navigate around the entire site, so settle back and enjoy the tour. Follow along as I show you examples of how to get the most out of the site so that you get the experience of physically moving through the site and working with the features discussed. After each example, you may want to try a similar search, using someone from your own family tree.

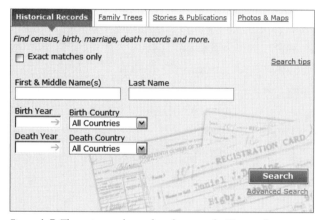

Figure 1-7: The main search template shown on the **Home** *tab.*

The Tabs and What You Will Find There

The gray toolbar across the top of the page consists of tab buttons. The area in which you are located is always the bright green button. As you move your mouse cursor over the other buttons, they change color from grey to green, and you can click on any of the buttons to visit that area. Let's move through each of the tabs as shown in figure 1-7. Later, we'll go back through each area in detail. For now, however, let's get a sense of the overall organization of the site.

The Home Tab

The **Home** tab is the homepage at Ancestry.com (see figure 1-2). This page consists of several sections. The first is the main search template. This basic template, shown in figure 1-7, has tabs as well: **Historical Records, Family Trees, Stories & Publications**, and **Photos & Maps**. These tabs divide the vast number of databases into categories. This makes it easier for you to search specific genres of record types. We will discuss each of these categories in detail later in this chapter and in the next chapter. Later, when you have become more comfortable with the search process, you can choose to use either these search tabs or the "Advanced Search" (see page 44).

Don't overlook the "Search tips" link in the search template; it will provide guidance for more effectively using the features under each of the tabs.

The following are the types of records you can search for on each tab. Please note that the search criteria for each of these four templates is a little different, based on the type of records for which they are used to search.

- **Historical Records**—Search for census, vital, and military records; immigration records and passenger lists; city directories and other finding aids; land and property records; wills and probate records; and other historical materials.

- **Family Trees**—Search for family trees submitted by other members of the Ancestry.com community.

- **Stories & Publications**—Access the site's wealth of historical newspapers, books, and family and local histories.

- **Photos & Maps**—Search historical photographs (including those submitted by users), maps, postcards, and other media.

Below the main search template on the **Home** tab, in the "US Census Records" and "More Collections" sections, you will find links to specialized search templates for each of the most commonly used databases at Ancestry.com, including the U.S. federal census records (see figure 1-8). Ancestry.com is the

US CENSUS RECORDS				MORE COLLECTIONS
1930	1890	1850	1810	Birth, Marriage & Death Records (SSDI)
1920	1880	1840	1800	US Immigration Collection
1910	1870	1830	1790	OneWorldTree℠
1900	1860	1820	All ≫	Obituary Collection
				UK Census Collection
				See all databases

*Figure 1-8: "US Census Records" and "More Collections" sections on the **Home** tab.*

only online service that provides completely indexed, searchable, digitized indexes of all of the U.S. federal census population schedule records from 1790 through 1930 (currently the most recently available U.S. census records), as well as the Slave Schedules from the 1850 and 1860 censuses, the Mortality Schedules from the 1850 through 1880 censuses, the 1890 census population schedule fragments, the Veterans and Widows Schedules, and the 1930 Merchant Seamen Schedules.

Other important collections listed in these sections include the following:

- **Birth, Marriage & Death Records**—This collection includes birth, marriage, divorce, and death records, as well as the Social Security Death Index (SSDI), cemetery records and inscriptions, obituary collections and indexes, parish and probate records, baptismal records, church records, Bible records, and newspaper indexes.

- **U.S. Immigration Collection**—This indexed and digitized collection of ships' passenger lists from 1820 forward is the most complete online compilation of its kind, and includes other databases of immigration, naturalization, and emigration records from many areas of Europe.

- **OneWorldTree**[SM]—OneWorldTree takes family trees submitted by Ancestry members and "stitches" them together with family trees and historical records from other sources. OneWorldTree identifies probable name matches between these sources and displays consolidated results in a worldwide family tree that can help you with your family history research. Your personal privacy is always protected. OneWorldTree never shares information about living family members born after 1930. Any information in your family tree regarding living people born after 1930 will show up on your personal family tree but will remain hidden from other Ancestry members.

- **Obituary Collection**—One of the best tools for locating obituaries is the Obituary Collection. Using this collection with the Historical Newspapers Collection, you can locate otherwise difficult or previously impossible death notices.

- **UK Census Collection**—This collection contains the entirely indexed and digitized population censuses for England, Wales, the Isle of Man, and the Channel Islands from 1841 to 190, plus the 1841 Scotland census.

The "See all databases" link takes you to the Ancestry. com Database Card Catalog, where you can either search for specific databases by title, keyword, record type, year, and other criteria, or you can browse one of two lists of databases. One of those lists is in alphabetical order by title; the other is a categorized list of databases by type (census records, military records, family and local histories, and so on). We will discuss and explore this tool in chapter 2.

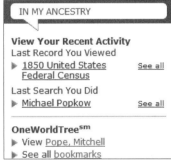

*Figure 1-9: "In My Ancestry" section on the **Home** tab.*

The section of the **Home** tab labeled "In My Ancestry" contains the last record you viewed and the last search you did (see figure 1-9). These allow you to pick up where you left off the last time you were logged into Ancestry.com. By clicking on the link labeled "See all," you can view all of your recent browsing and searches. In effect, your personal research history is saved from session to session, and this makes picking up where you left off a simple task.

You can also go directly to the last person you viewed or edited in OneWorldTree, or to a page listing people you have

What's New on Ancestry.com

Approximately 4.5 million new names released recently, including:

Hamburg Passenger List, 1850-1934
2,547,135 new names.
Public Member Photos
300,000 new names.

What else is new?

Figure 1-10: "What's New on Ancestry.com" section on the Home tab.

User Feedback

You've probably already noticed that there is overlap between features that appear on some pages and links that take you to other major areas. This was not done by chance. The developers and programmers at Ancestry.com have solicited and used a tremendous amount of user feedback and testing with experienced genealogists to determine the common workflows of typical genealogical research.

bookmarked in that tool. (For more information about One World Tree, see page 26).

The "What's New on Ancestry.com?" section gives you a brief summary of recent additions to Ancestry.com (see figure 1-10). Clicking the "What else is new?" link leads you to the "What's new on Ancestry.com" page. Here you will find announcements and descriptions of new databases, articles by genealogical experts to help you get the most from your research, announcements of upcoming changes and improvements, Ancestry products, and more.

Visit this page on a regular basis in order to make sure you haven't missed any new databases *and* to see announcements of what's coming so you can plan your research agenda. The direct links to the recent database additions make working with them quick and easy.

The My Ancestry Tab

The information found on the **My Ancestry** tab is primarily generated as a result of your own personal research. That includes mainly Family History Sites, which include family trees you've created, and links to the records that have been part of your recent activity.

The personalization that Ancestry.com performs and saves for you in the **My Ancestry** tab helps you keep track of much of your primary research. It allows you to continue with people, places, and records that you've already been researching from one online session to another. This feature is, without doubt, one of the most convenient sets of tools available, and only Ancestry.com subscribers have the benefit of this offering. Even before you begin active searching, you can set up and keep track of people and places that you want to research.

We will explore each of the areas on the **My Ancestry** tab in detail in chapter 4.

The Search Tab

The primary reason you have subscribed to Ancestry.com is most likely to search the wealth of database resources that are available there and that are growing every month. The **Search** tab is the main place on the site for conducting such a search.

Here you have the ability to search for specific individuals *or* browse the databases. We will concentrate on search strategies for locating records of your ancestors using this page in chapter 2. In the meantime, however, let's look at the different areas on this tab.

The "Search Records" template is the main feature of the **Search** tab. It looks and works the same as the search template on the **Home** tab (see page 6).

In the upper right-hand corner of the **Search** tab main page is a section labeled "Search Resources" (see figure 1-11). It includes two links. One is the "Advanced Search" link, which allows you to provide many more criteria for your searches. The other link is labeled "Card Catalog" and takes you to a page titled "Ancestry Database Card Catalog." The Card Catalog allows you to search for a specific database by name, if you know it, or by keyword. Additional search options help you narrow your search as well. We'll talk about both of these excellent features in chapter 2 as well.

> **SEARCH RESOURCES**
>
> - Card Catalog
> - Advanced Search

Figure 1-11: "Search Resources" section on the Search tab.

The **Search** tab also provides you with different ways to browse the wealth of databases. One particularly effective way, especially if you're not sure where to start, is to browse for records based on where your family came from. Note the geographical location links in the section labeled "Browse

Browse the Entire Collection

1. Select Region:

United States   UK & Ireland   Europe   Canada
Australia

2. Select State:

- Alabama
- Alaska
- Arizona
- Arkansas
- California
- Colorado
- Connecticut
- Delaware
- Florida
- Georgia
- Hawaii
- Idaho

- Illinois
- Indiana
- Iowa
- Kansas
- Kentucky
- Louisiana
- Maine
- Maryland
- Massachusetts
- Michigan
- Minnesota
- Mississippi
- Missouri

- Montana
- Nebraska
- Nevada
- New Hampshire
- New Jersey
- New Mexico
- New York
- North Carolina
- North Dakota
- Ohio
- Oklahoma
- Oregon
- Pennsylvania

- Rhode Island
- South Carolina
- South Dakota
- Tennessee
- Texas
- Utah
- Vermont
- Virginia
- Washington
- Washington, D.C.
- West Virginia
- Wisconsin
- Wyoming

*Figure 1-12: "Browse Entire Collection" section on the **Search** tab.*

the Entire Collection" (see figure 1-12). You can browse the databases related to a specific area by 1) selecting a region and 2) selecting a state, country, or province, as appropriate. For example, if you select the United States, its map will be displayed (this is the default). Each state is a hotlink. By clicking on a state, another page will be displayed that lists every database on Ancestry.com related specifically to that state. Select any state and start looking at the list of databases. In figure 1-13, you can see the state of Iowa's page as an example.

The main section of the page is a list of links. Each leads to a search template for a database in the collection related to Iowa (or for the state you selected). You can use the drop-down list in the upper left-hand corner to select another state. You can also enter a name to search in the collection of Iowa databases in the section called "Search Databases." At the top of the list of databases, you can collapse or expand the entire set of category lists. You can also use the drop-down list labeled "View" to restrict the number of databases displayed by selecting a year range in which your ancestor lived or in which you are interested.

Figure 1-13: A part of the "Iowa Databases List" page.

At the very top of the panel of databases, you will see three tabs labeled **Database**, **Sources**, and **How To's**. These pages default to the **Database** tab. When you click the **Sources** tab, reference information about different record types and a collection of Web links are displayed. The **How To's** tab presents a page with access to a number of book resources. Click a title for an abstract and then on the link labeled "View Full Context" for the entire entry. Only the **Database** tab is available for the UK and Ireland, Europe, Canada, and Germany areas at this time.

Back on the main page of the **Search** tab, find the section called "Browse Records" (see figure 1-14), which contains a categorized list of different databases. Clicking a link takes you to a page with a specialized search template for that record type. If you click one of the category links (such as "Census" or "Immigration"),

*Figure 1-14: A portion of the "Browse Records" section on the **Search** tab.*

you will also find a list of featured databases in that record category, as well as a scrollable list, which includes links to every database of that category. For example, if you click the "Census" link, you will come to a page with a "Search Census Records" template, a list of the featured census records, and a scrollable list of every census database at Ancestry to which your subscription entitles you. Scroll down to the "New York State Census Collection," highlight it, and click it. The resulting page allows you to search just the available digitized state census records created by the State of New York in 1880, 1892, and 1905. You can also click on a link for a specific year to browse counties, districts, and images.

Back on the main page of the **Search** tab, you will find a link labeled "list all databases" at the bottom of the "Browse Records" section. This leads you to the "Ancestry Database Card Catalog," which will be discussed in chapter 2.

The Ancestry Community Tab

The **Ancestry Community** tab is the place at Ancestry.com where you make connections with other researchers. There are three important components of this area: Message Boards, the Member Directory, and Member Connections.

The Message Boards at Ancestry.com combine the power of both the Ancestry.com and RootsWeb message boards into one location where you can post information and queries about surnames, individuals, locations, ethnic and religious groups, international information and locations, institutions, record types and other resources, genealogical software, and many more topics (see figure 1-15). You

*Figure 1-15: "Message Boards" section on the **Ancestry Community** tab.*

post a message to a message board, and other people may read it. If they have something to share, they can either post a reply on the message board or respond to you privately via e-mail. This collaboration with other researchers may give you information and clues to help extend your research.

The message boards provide you the ability to customize your experience by defining your favorites—those message boards that you want to track and read frequently—and to set up notifications to be sent to you via e-mail when someone posts a new message or a reply. We will discuss how to set up your preferences for message boards and how to get the most from them in chapter 16. On the **Ancestry Community** tab, you can conduct a search of the boards in the "Message Boards" section or browse using the links given.

Figure 1-16: "Member Directory" section on the **Ancestry Community** tab.

The Member Directory provides you the opportunity to connect with other people who share your interests in a particular surname or location (see figure 1-16). We will discuss this facility in chapter 16, but you can see that you can search the directory from the **Ancestry Community** tab.

Finally, the "Members Connections" section allows you to make contacts with other people researching the same individuals or lines as you (see figure 1-17). Go exploring in this area with one of your ancestors' names to see what it is like.

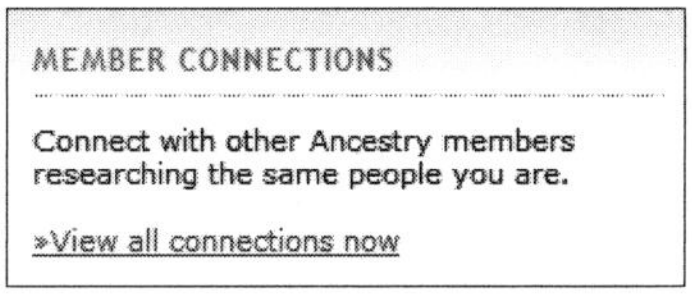

MEMBER CONNECTIONS

Connect with other Ancestry members researching the same people you are.

»View all connections now

Figure 1-17: "Member Connections" section on the **Ancestry Community** tab.

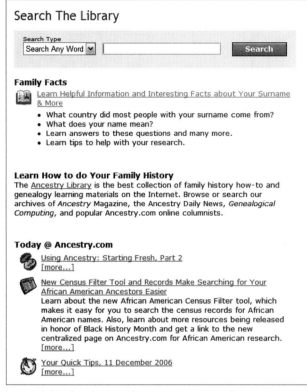

*Figure 1-18: The Library on the **Learning Center** tab.*

The Learning Center Tab

The **Learning Center** tab takes you to the Ancestry.com Learning Center—a tremendous information resource. It is a virtual library providing access to a wealth of reference materials, including every *Ancestry* Magazine article (which are also available at *Ancestry* Magazine's website <www.ancestrymagazine.com>) and the late *Genealogical Computing*, as well as the columns and articles published in the *Ancestry Daily News*, the *Ancestry Weekly Journal*, the *24/7 Family History Circle* blog, and much more (see figure 1-18).

You can use the search field at the top of the page to search the library in a number of ways. You can also click on the links on the right side in the "Learn More About" section for detailed descriptions and links to other articles about various record types and materials.

The section at the lower right side of the page labeled "Browse the Library" allows you to click on a link and see a compendium of links to articles on the subject. If you click on the "more ..." link, a full page with all the categories is listed. From each category, you can view and access the links to all the pertinent articles. Consider the Learning Center your own library for excellent and authoritative information on all things

*Figure 1-19: The homepage of the Ancestry Store on the **Store** tab. The Ancestry Store is also accessible at <www.theancestrystore.com>.*

genealogical. Read chapter 15 to see how to use the Learning Center to your best advantage.

The Store Tab

At the Ancestry Store (on the **Store** tab), you can discover some of the best genealogical publications and software titles (see figure 1-19). Ancestry is a leader in the publication of authoritative genealogical reference books. These include *The Source: A Guidebook to American Genealogy*, *Red Book: American State, County, and Town Resources*, *They Became Americans*, and many more titles. The company also produces *Family Tree Maker*™, a genealogy database program, and a large number of

CD-ROM reference software. We discuss the Ancestry Store in greater detail in chapter 17.

The Ancestry Store is actually a different website <www. theancestrystore.com>. To return to Ancestry.com, click **Back to Ancestry.com**.

Summary

Ancestry.com is, as you have seen, a large site containing many, many resources to assist in your research. The databases comprise the most prolific online genealogical content on the Internet. However, the informational resources, the communication tools, the embedded software, and the ability to customize your own research are very extensive as well.

Now that you know how to navigate the Ancestry.com site and have had an overview of the way it is organized, let's see how to really use the search facilities in chapter 2. Then we'll look at "My Ancestry" data management tools in chapter 3. Then it's on to different record types and a lot of practical examples and research strategies.

Searching for Your Ancestors

You saw in chapter 1 as you explored the main tabs that Ancestry.com is a comprehensive website with many components, functions, and tools. Most users, however, primarily use Ancestry.com to search the more than 23,000 databases and titles and 5 billion names at the site.

The purpose of this chapter is to demonstrate the various search tools and their options so that you can maximize your efficiency in locating records pertaining to your ancestors and their families.

I will use specific examples, and I encourage you to follow along, step by step, and do the searches using the criteria I use in the examples. Please recognize, however, that Ancestry.com is continually adding new content and updating existing databases with new records and indexes. As a result, the search results lists you see when you replicate the search examples may differ from those shown here. Don't let that confuse you. Just take the time to examine the search results and click on

Searching in Other Locations

⋺

This book focuses on Ancestry.com for U.S. users, but we will also explore a number of the databases for other geographies. If you access the UK, Canadian, Australian, and German collections, you should be able to apply what you learn in this chapter to those database collections.

links to view sample records. In this way, you will become familiar with a great many databases and their content.

Database Search Basics

You search for information in a database by entering search criteria, such as first name, surname, location, or time period, to isolate records that may match the person(s) about whom you are seeking information. You will enter your search criteria into fields in online forms, which are referred to as search templates. Your search is often referred to as a query.

Each database is unique and you will find that search templates for various databases will differ depending on the type of records you are searching, the information in them, and the way they are indexed. Consider, for example, that the purpose of the U.S. federal census and the information contained in the census database is completely different than that of the Social Security Death Index (SSDI), the Irish Records Index (1500–1920), or the Baden, Germany Emigration Index (1866–1911). Even the search criteria you enter for a federal census database will differ from that for a state census, just as a U.S. census record will differ from those for the UK and Ireland, Canada, Germany, or other types of census records. While you will certainly always enter names, the other information you may be able to enter into the template may vary significantly. German census database records are in German, so for best results, you should search by using words entered in the German language.

Search Templates

Your use of the Ancestry databases will start with either the main search on the **Home** or **Search** tabs, or with the variety of search tools on the **Search** tab. It is at the latter tab that we will begin your search education.

There are a number of search templates that you will commonly use, and it is important that you understand the differences between them, when and how they are used, and what you can expect in the way of search results.

Your mastery of Ancestry.com will depend on your understanding of searching. Don't be intimidated, however. Take the time to read and re-read the text as necessary, and be sure to follow along and try each of the examples given. These will give you an excellent feel of what is available and how to really succeed with your own research.

The Main Search Template

We will begin our discussion of search strategies by defining each of the main search templates, which can be found on the Home or **Search** tabs. We discussed them briefly in the last chapter, but now we will illustrate just what each tab on the search template can do for you.

To begin, click the **Search** tab.

Historical Records

We will start by searching for one of my great-uncles, Brisco Holder, using the **Historical Records** tab of the main search template (which is the default). I have entered his name in the template shown in figure 2-1.

I could further clarify the search by entering his birth year, if I know it, and country. In figure 2-2, I have selected the United States as his birth

Figure 2-1: Basic search for Brisco Holder through historical records.

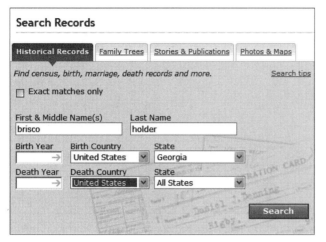

Figure 2-2: Searching with a geographical area selected.

country. In some cases, such as the example in figure 2-2, a drop-down menu appears when you select a country, which allows me to narrow my search further to more specific geographic areas (such as states) if I choose.

I recommend starting simple with your search. Don't specify any geographical area beyond the country; let Ancestry.com search and present you with the broadest set of matches. You can always narrow your search later. Notice that I did not check the "Exact matches only" box. We'll do that later.

Using the search shown in figure 2-2, a search results page is presented to me (see figure 2-3) called "Ranked Search Results."

A ranked search examines all of the criteria you entered into the fields on the search template. It then produces a search results list that displays matches in descending order based on relevance, with the most relevant matches at the top. Relevance is always determined by comparing your search criteria with the information found on a genealogical record. The closer the match, the more relevant that record is to your search.

You will notice on the "Ranked Search Results" page that there are stars to the left of each record entry. A five-star rating indicates the highest relevance match the search engine could possibly have made based on the criteria entered into the template. As you proceed down the list, the number of stars indicating relevance drops in number.

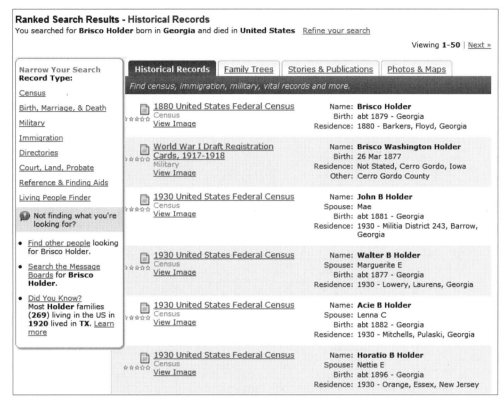

Figure 2-3: "Ranked Search Results" for a historical records search.

Notice that the first two matches shown in figure 2-3, one for a record in the "1880 United States Federal Census" and one in the "World War I Draft Registration Cards, 1917–1918" database, both have three stars beside them. As you proceed down the list, however, you can see results with the last name "Holder" and the letter "B" as a first or middle initial. These results do not match the criteria I entered into the search template as well as the first two, so they appear lower on the page.

Remember, however, that ancestors sometimes spelled their names differently on different occasions and sometimes provided nicknames or initials to record-takers. Record-takers may have also misspelled your ancestors' names or abbeviated them to nicknames or initials. You will want to examine each record individually to determine whether it refers to your ancestor or not.

Beneath each entry, in gray, is a descriptive note as to what kind of record type the entry is.

When I click the link labeled "View Image" under "1880 United States Federal Census" at the top of the list, I see that Brisco is with his family and is one year old. Other information I gave gathered about him tells me that I have the right person. Therefore, I can surmise that he was born by at least 1879.

The other record is a military record, a World War I Draft Registration record from Cerro Gordo County, Iowa. Could this be right? I click the "View Image" link below the record to examine the digitized record, which is shown in figure 2-4. Sure enough, this is my great-uncle a long way from home, in Iowa, when he registered for the draft. The conclusive proof is the listing of his brother, E. E. Holder of Rome, Ga., as his nearest living relative.

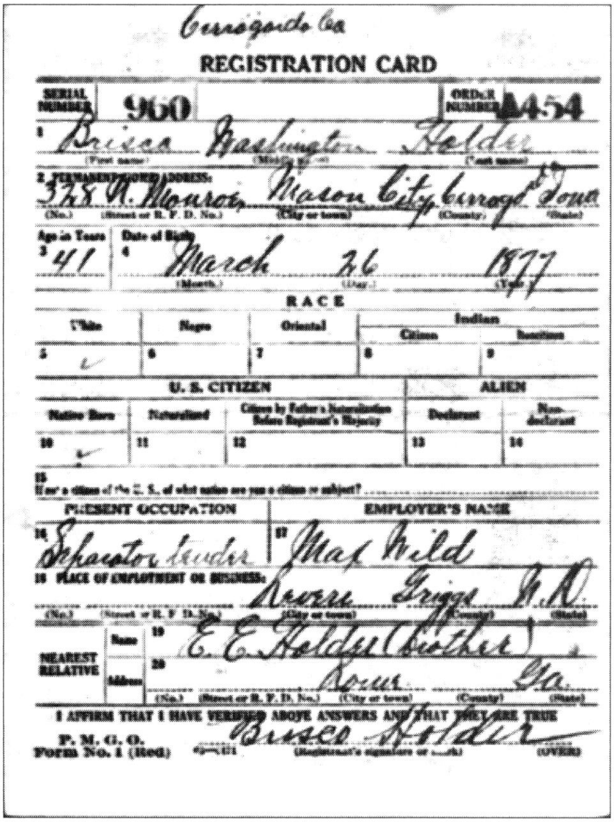
Cerrogordo Co

REGISTRATION CARD

SERIAL NUMBER 960 ORDER NUMBER

1 Brisco Washington Holder
(First name) (Middle name) (Last name)

2 PERMANENT HOME ADDRESS:
328 N. Monroe Mason City Cerrogordo Iowa
(No.) (Street or R. F. D. No.) (City or town) (County) (State)

Age in Years 3 41 Date of Birth 4 March 26 1877
(Month.) (Day.) (Year.)

RACE

White	Negro	Oriental	Indian: Citizen	Indian: Noncitizen
5 ✓	6	7	8	9

U. S. CITIZEN: Native Born	Naturalized	Citizen by Father's Naturalization Before Registrant's Majority	ALIEN: Declarant	Non-declarant
10 ✓	11	12	13	14

15 If not a citizen of the U. S., of what nation are you a citizen or subject?

PRESENT OCCUPATION 16 EMPLOYER'S NAME 17

18 PLACE OF EMPLOYMENT OR BUSINESS:
(No.) (Street or R. F. D. No.) (City or town) (County) (State)

NEAREST RELATIVE Name 19 E. E. Holder (brother)
Address 20 Rome Ga.
(No.) (Street or R. F. D. No.) (City or town) (County) (State)

I AFFIRM THAT I HAVE VERIFIED ABOVE ANSWERS AND THAT THEY ARE TRUE

P. M. G. O. Form No. 1 (Red) Brisco Holder (Registrant's signature or mark) (OVER)

Figure 2-4: Brisco Washington Holder's WWI Draft Registration Card image (front only).

I learned for the first time that he was in Iowa when he registered for the draft, that his middle name was Washington, and that he stated he was born on 26 March 1877 (not 1879, as indicated by the 1880 census), as well as his address and occupation at that time. On the reverse side of the card (not shown) I learn the date of his registration: 12 September 1918.

While on this page, there are three ways that you can narrow your search results. In the "Narrow Your Search" section, lick on a link for any of the record types listed and the search will be performed again, looking this time for only results in that record type. In addition, at the bottom of the search results list are two drop-down lists. The first can be used to adjust the number of search results displayed on the page at one time. The other drop-down can be used to control which relevance-ranked results are displayed. Usually the four- and five-star results are the most likely to be the ones you want. However, it is always best to start with a display of *all* the matches and then narrow the search results list as you feel appropriate.

Note that from any search results page, you can click any of the tabs at the top of the search results section to conduct the same search within each of those categories.

Family Trees Template

There are various kinds of family trees at Ancestry.com, each with different characteristics. Before you start searching them, it's important to recognize these differences. We will cover the creation and maintenance of each of these later in the book.

- **Family Trees**—The most recent addition to the Ancestry. com family trees family is the Family Tree. As an Ancestry. com member, you can build your own family's tree (or multiple ones) online at the Ancestry.com site. You can do this by either entering data manually or by uploading

a GEDCOM file that you have extracted or exported
from your computerized genealogical database program.
These trees are then organized into a personal, mini
website on Ancestry.com where you can keep photos,
stories, records, and so forth. For more on Family Trees,
see chapter 4.

- **OneWorldTree**—OneWorldTree is a powerful research
tool unique to Ancestry.com. It takes family trees submitted
by Ancestry.com members and "stitches" them together
with family trees and historical records from other
sources. OneWorldTree identifies probable name matches
between these sources and displays consolidated results
in a worldwide family tree that can help you with your
family history research. OneWorldTree can give you hints
about your family history—but not necessarily facts. There
are a number of sources consolidated in OneWorldTree,
so it's impossible to know if there are errors in member-
submitted family trees. You are responsible for checking the
information you find on OneWorldTree for accuracy.

- **Ancestry World Tree**—Ancestry World Tree is the oldest
portion of the Ancestry.com Family Trees Collections. It
consists of more than 400 million family names that have
been submitted over the years by members of Ancestry.
com. In addition, the family trees that have been submitted
to the WorldConnect Collection at RootsWeb have been
merged with the original Ancestry World Tree Collection.
Remember that Ancestry.com has accepted all files "as
is" and cannot guarantee the completeness, accuracy, or
timeliness of the information contained in this database.

With all of these family trees in mind, take a look at
the **Family Trees** tab on the main search template (see

figure 2-5). As you can see, there are fields for "First Name" (which can also include a middle name), "Last Name," "Father's First Name," "Father's Last Name," "Mother's First Name," and "Mother's Maiden Name." In addition, just as on the **Historical Records** tab, you may enter birth or death years, and geographic information.

In this example, I entered the name Penelope Weatherly and listed her parents' names as Walton Weatherly and Elizabeth Holder.

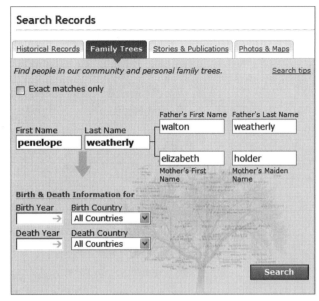

Figure 2-5: Main search template completed for Penelope Weatherly for searching family trees.

The "Ranked Search Results" page is similar to that which we saw for a historical records search (see figure 2-6). Notice

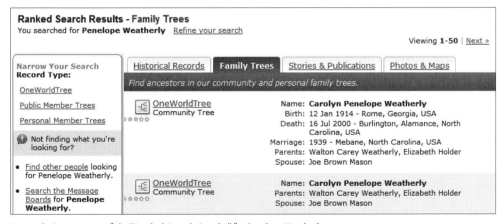

Figure 2-6: A portion of the "Ranked Search Results" for Penelope Weatherly.

that the two most relevant matches for a Carolyn Penelope Weatherly are both in OneWorldTree.

"Exact Matches Only" Search

The "Exact matches only" option on the **Historical Records** and **Family Trees** tabs gives you complete control over your search results because each record that is returned *must* match *all* the search terms you enter. Only matches that exactly meet your criteria are returned in the search results list.

One mistake that many users make and that causes them a significant amount of frustration is jumping right in to use the "Exact matches only" option on the search templates. They assume that they already know the exact name, location, date range, or other criteria and that they will immediately get a match. They are amazed, disappointed, frustrated, or aggravated that their search returns no results. This can be a result of any number of factors: a name is misspelled in an original document; an index is incorrect; a person's initials were used rather than his or her first or middle name; the person lied about a date or age or an informant got the information wrong; the person moved or the boundaries of an area changed and the search location was incorrect.

It is almost always preferable to use a general search first and let Ancestry.com return ranked search results to you for review. You can always narrow your search by entering additional keywords or by entering additional search criteria to your query. You can always opt to search using the "Exact matches only" option later.

To get the most out of an exact search, it is usually best to start with only one or two broad search criteria (a surname and a location, for example). If you get too many results, gradually add more criteria to narrow your search. If you get too few results, drop one or more of your search criteria to broaden your search. You can continue this process until you focus in on the record for which you are searching.

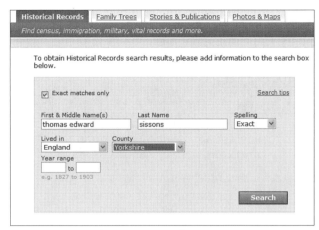

Figure 2-7: Search of historical records for Thomas Edward Sissons in Yorkshire, England with "Exact matches only" selected.

Exact Searching with the Historical Records Template

When you click the "Exact matches only" box on the **Historical Records** tab, an additional drop-down list labeled "Spelling" is displayed after the name (see figure 2-7).

Your options are "Exact" or "Soundex." If you select "Exact," only records containing exactly the information you entered into the template will be returned. Soundex is a sound-alike system used to locate matches of names (primarily surnames) that are spelled differently from one another but sound similar. Perhaps the most obvious example for Americans would be Smith, Smyth, Smythe, or Smithe. To learn more about Soundex, click the "Help" link on the top right-hand corner of any page, enter the word "Soundex" into the "Search for Answers" field, and then click "Definition of Soundex."

In this example, I searched for information about Thomas Edward Sissons, who I know was born in Yorkshire, England. I also am certain of the spelling of his surname. I entered the search criteria in the search template on the **Historical Records** tab, clicking the "Exact matches only" box and specifying England and the county of Yorkshire.

You will notice that, instead of a "Ranked Search Results" page, we get an "Exact Search Results" page, which indicates

Figure 2-8: "Exact Search Results" page for Thomas Edward Sissons.

results in the "Birth, Marriage & Death Records" and "Directories & Membership Lists" categories (see figure 2-8).

After investigating the links under "Birth, Marriage & Death Records," I found the Thomas Edward Sissons I was seeking in the second link, labeled "England & Wales, FreeBMD Birth Index: 1837–1983," an index to births recorded in the October, November, December quarter of 1909. I also found that his grandfather's death was recorded in the April, May, June quarter of 1899 in the "England & Wales, FreeBMD Death Index: 1837–1983."

Since I was searching for exact matches with "Thomas Edward Sissons," I would want to follow it with another exact search for only "Thomas Sissons" and another for "Thos Sissons" and for "Thos Edward Sissons" on the chance that there might be other records I missed.

Exact Searching with the Family Trees Template
The **Family Trees** tab also has the "Exact matches only" option. Remember to start simple and then add more criteria to narrow your search. This really can help alleviate some frustration.

Figure 2-9 shows an exact search for my paternal grandmother, Minnie Wilson. I know she was born in 1873 and died in 1966, both events occurring in North Carolina. These were the only criteria I entered. Her father's surname was automatically added when I entered her name.

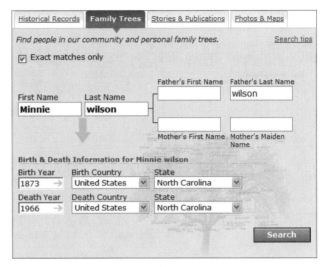

Figure 2-9: Search of family trees for Minnie Wilson with the "Exact matches only" option selected.

The "Exact Search Results" page, which is shown in figure 2-10, has two entries. One is a Personal Member Tree, which I submitted. However, the other entry shows that there are 2,028 matches in Ancestry World Tree.

This number seems highly unlikely and, sure enough, as I review the Exact Search Results list I find many persons with that name with different parents. It is not until I add Minnie's father's first name (or forename) of Joseph and her mother's surname, Patterson, that I narrow the list until there is a listing for her. I also know that "Minnie" was not her given name; it was really Laura. I made changes in the search criteria and

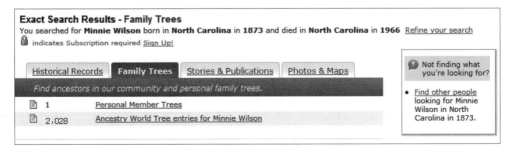

Figure 2-10: "Exact Search Results" page for Minnie Wilson.

Figure 2-11: "Exact Search Results" page for Laura Wilson, a.k.a. Minnie.

obtained the result shown in figure 2-11 in OneWorldTree. This is the result that I wanted!

The yellow triangles that dot the record indicate possible additional or alternative information that has been gleaned from merging records to produce the search results or from information provided by other researchers. By clicking on the link for the name Laura Augusta Wilson, I can view the full record, complete with links to all alternative records, user-submitted trees, and other information.

Stories & Publications Template

There are more than twenty thousand digitized, indexed, and searchable volumes in the Family and Local Histories Collection at Ancestry.com. There also are hundreds of digitized, indexed, and searchable periodicals and historical newspaper collections online. We will examine each of these collections in detail in a later chapter in the book. For now, let's focus on the search process.

Go to the **Stories & Publications** tab.

Type the subject you are searching for in the "Keywords" field. Keep in mind that these searches are exact match searches, so the way you enter the search query will produce different results. Let's say that we are interested in researching the Ball family in Virginia. There are several ways to structure your search to accomplish this, but the search results may be very different depending on the way you enter your search. Let's examine three methods of searching for this family.

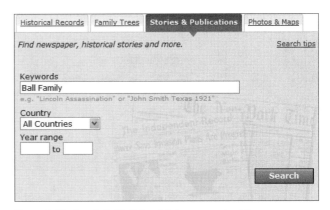

Figure 2-12: Search for "Ball family" in stories and publications.

In the first search, I will simply enter "Ball family" in the "Keywords" field, specifying no country or year range (see figure 2-12). It does not matter whether you enter the data in upper, lower, or mixed case.

On the "Exact Search Results" page, you will note that only a small number of matches in each category of resource materials is listed. They are listed in sequence based on the total number of matches in the source, going from highest to lowest number. You can click the link at the bottom of each list to view all of the results in sequence (see figure 2-13a and b on page 34). I selected the book *150 Years of Freedom, 1811–1961* for the following figure references.

Click the title of the work and the first match from that source will be displayed, or click the number link at the right to display a list of all the matches in that work. A click on the "See more info" link shows a search template specific to that work; detailed source information, notes, subjects included in the work, and locations referenced in the work; and the table of contents with links to the various sections of the work (see figure 2-13c on page 34). Each link in the "Table of Contents" will take you to the first digitized page of that section. You can then read, print, save to a disk, or e-mail that page.

Let's now try another search for the Ball family. This time I have entered the same keywords but have now specified the

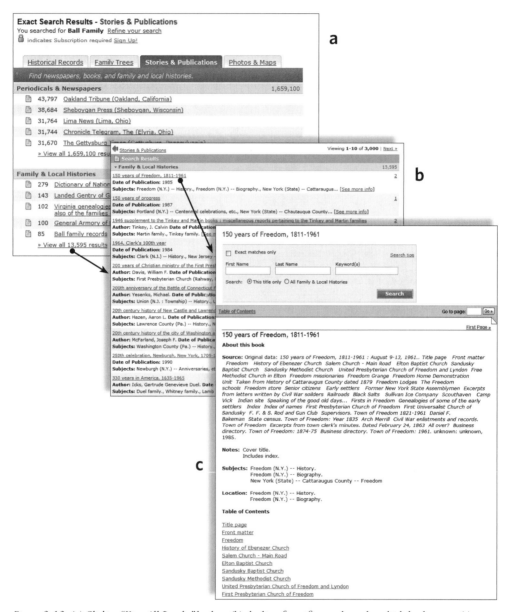

Figure 2-13: (a) Clicking "View All Results" leads to (b) the list of specific search results, which leads you to (c) a database-specific page.

United States in the "Country" drop-down list, and Virginia in the subsequent "State."

As you can see, this results page is very different and much more manageable than the previous example (see figure 2-14). Remember that as you refine your search you may miss a less detailed or more obscure record that would appear in the broader first search.

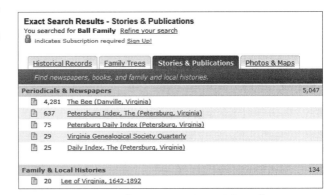

Figure 2-14: A portion of an "Exact Search Results" page for country- and state-specific search.

As a third example, I will use all the same criteria as in the second example but will add a year range of 1600 to 1900.

As you can see, this search limited the search results, perhaps too narrowly (see figure 2-15). There are other keyword combinations I might have used, including the name of the individual for whom I was seeking information, a specific location, and so on. You will have to experiment and explore the options and

Figure 2-15: A portion of an "Exact Search Results" page for country, state, and year range.

search results to insure that you don't miss any potentially important resources.

Photos & Maps Template

Ancestry.com has worked diligently to compile an impressive collection of digitized historical maps over the years. More

Figure 2-16: Search for Mebane, North Carolina, United States in photos and maps.

recently the graphical collection has been expanded to include photographs, postcards, yearbooks, and other materials to help you visualize where your ancestors lived and worked. The **Photo & Maps** tab is a tool you can use to search for those specific resources (see figure 2-16).

As with the searches on the **Stories & Publications** tab, you can enter keywords and then have the option to narrow your search by entering a country, sub-location (when available), or year range. Remember that you can narrow your search too much, so a broad search at the beginning may reveal a wider array of matches. You can then add other criteria to narrow your search as appropriate.

As an example of a search, I have entered the name of a town, Mebane, in the template and have selected the United States and North Carolina from the drop-down lists (see figure 2-16). I decided not to narrow my search to any time period.

The "Exact Search Results—Photos & Maps" page shows results from the "Library of Congress Photo Collection, 1840–2000" and from the "U.S. School Yearbooks" collection (see figure 2-17).

I selected the "Library of Congress Photo Collection, 1840–2000" and was presented with another list that includes thumbnails of the

Exact Search Results - Photos & Maps
You searched for **Mebane** Refine your search
🔒 indicates Subscription required Sign Up!

| Historical Records | Family Trees | Stories & Publications | Photos & Maps |

Find photos, historical maps, and other media.

📄 30 Library of Congress Photo Collection, 1840-2000
📄 5   U.S. School Yearbooks

Figure 2-17: A portion of an "Exact Search Results" page from a search in photos and maps.

images, their titles, and more information about the images
(see figure 2-18a).

If you click either the image's title or the thumbnail, you
are brought to a page showing the full-sized image (see figure
2-18b). This page also contains detailed information about the
image, and the option to save it, either to a Family History
Site or to your "Shoebox" for further evaluation at a later time.
In the "Page Tools" section, you also have the option to add

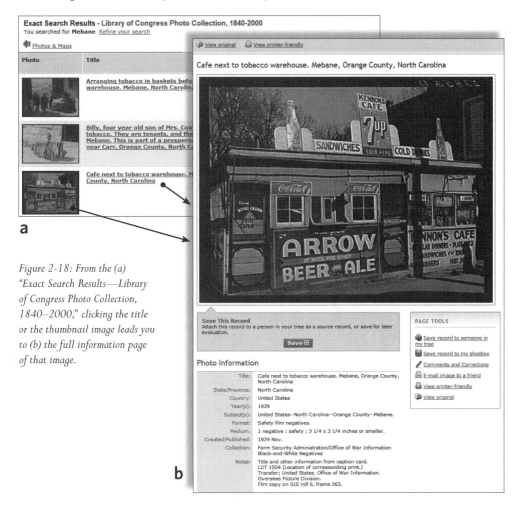

*Figure 2-18: From the (a)
"Exact Search Results—Library
of Congress Photo Collection,
1840–2000," clicking the title
or the thumbnail image leads you
to (b) the full information page
of that image.*

comments or corrections to the record, e-mail the image to someone (including yourself), or view and print this record in a printer-friendly format.

By clicking "View Original," you can see the image in the Ancestry Image Viewer. For more information about using the Image Viewer and working with digitized images, refer to chapter 3.

Database-Specific Search Templates

Some search templates are specific to particular databases, the information they contain, and the way they are indexed. When you browse the databases to locate a particular one you want to search, you'll be presented with the corresponding template. You will see many of these individual templates as you work with different databases. In fact, you've probably already seen different search templates for specific databases as we've explored search results lists and revised searches. We will discuss the details of many of these templates later. For now, let's look at an example.

Go to the **Search** tab on the Ancestry.com homepage. Find the "Browse Records" section on the right side. Let's start with probably the most popular of all the Ancestry.com databases—the United States Federal Census records.

Click "US Federal Census" (see figure 2-19).

You can enter the first and last name as we've seen before. There are also

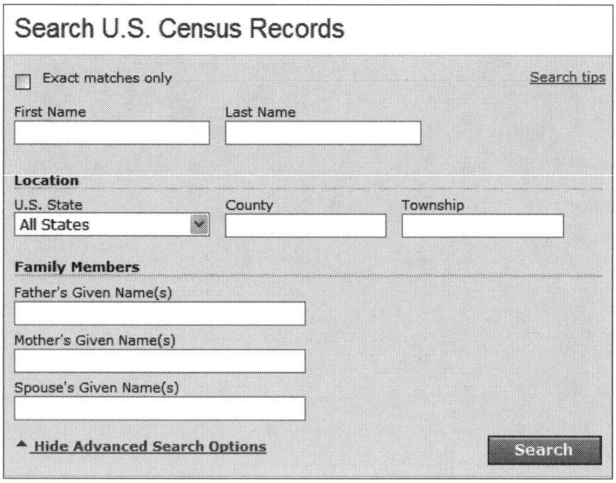

Figure 2-19: The "Search U.S. Census Records" template.

"Advanced Search Options," allowing you to enter "State," "County," and "Township," or the names of various family members. By clicking on the link on any template labeled "Advanced Search Options," you can either hide or show these optional fields. If you select a specific census to search, there are more search criteria fields from which you may choose.

Finding Specific Databases

Let's say that you want to look for specific immigration records. On each of the main search pages of the categories listed in the "Browse Records" section on the **Search** tab, you will find a list of featured records and a scroll box of all records in that category.

Let's look at an example. On the **Search** tab, go to the "Browse Records" section and click on the category link labeled "Immigration Records." A corresponding search template will be displayed on the "Search Immigration Records" page.

However, if you scroll down the same page, you will see additional information, as shown in figure 2-20. Included is a list of featured collections of immigration records, particularly those collections that are most frequently used or which have been recently

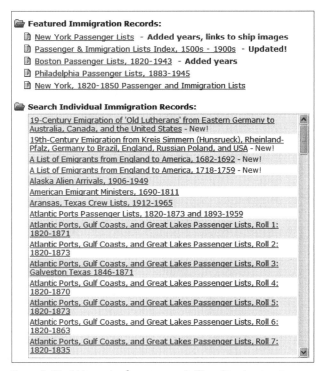

Figure 2-20: Additional information on the "Searching Immigration Records" page.

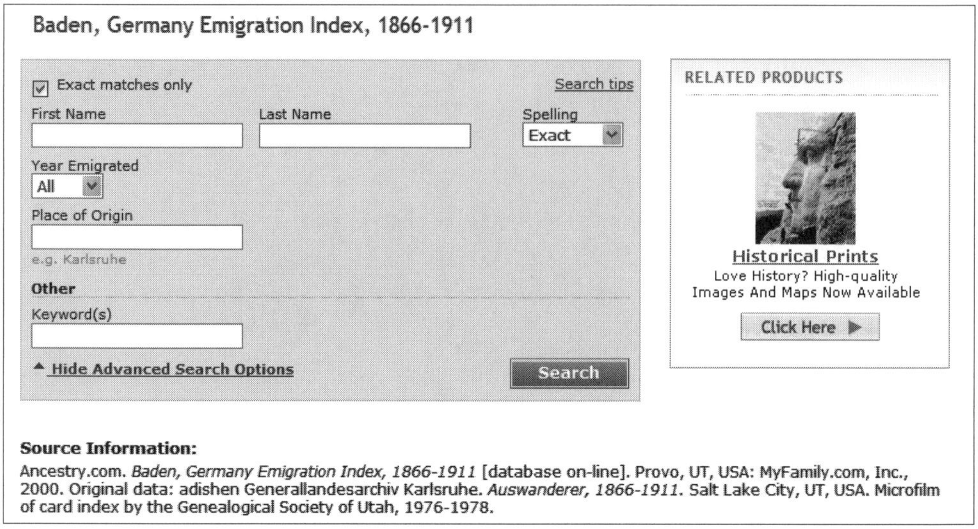

Figure 2-21: A portion of the "Baden, German Emigration Index, 1866–1911" database page.

added or updated. Below that list is a scroll box containing a list of all the databases of immigration records at Ancestry. com. Naturalization records and indexes will also be included in the list as they become available.

Let's say that you have German ancestors who immigrated to the United States in the 1880s. They could have left Germany from one of several German ports, or they could have traveled into the Netherlands and taken a ship from there. They also may have made their way to England, where they booked passage on a ship departing from Liverpool or another port of departure. For the point of this exercise, though, let's say that you have browsed the list of databases and have decided to search the "Baden, Germany Emigration Index, 1866–1911." To search this databases, you must first locate and click the name of the database in the scroll box. The resulting page and specialized search template with the "Hide/Show Advanced Search Options" link should look familiar (see figure 2-21).

Every database search page includes a description of the database, as well as an extended description that may provide some hints for more effective searching. Also, at the bottom of the page is the source information for the database. You can actually copy and paste this into your genealogy database program as part of your source citation and then add the Web address of <www.ancestry.com> and the date on which you accessed the data.

In the examples we've examined, you can see how the templates may vary, depending on the content of the database and how it is indexed, but you should also see that the fundamentals of each search is the same. Remember that almost every template will have a link to search tips, database-specific information, or information to help you construct more effective queries in the database in question.

The Ancestry Database Card Catalog

In the "Search Resources" section on the **Search** tab is a link labeled "Card Catalog" and another labeled "Advanced Search." Both of these offer you some of the most powerful searching at Ancestry.com.

When you click the "Card Catalog" link a search template for the Ancestry Database Card Catalog is displayed (see figure 2-22). This powerful search

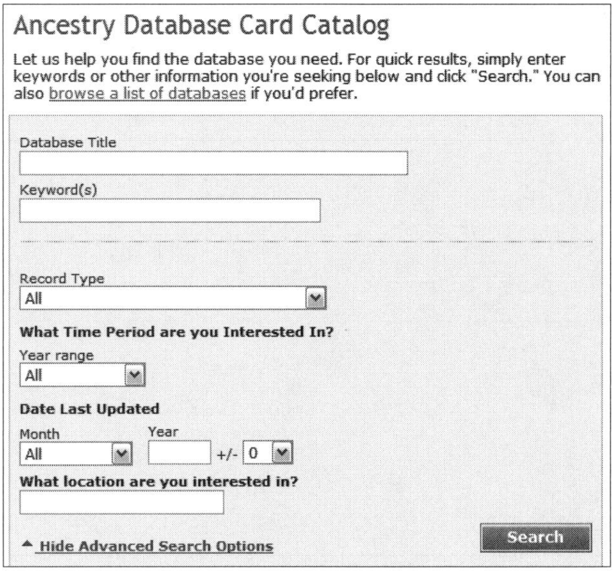

Figure 2-22: The Ancestry Database Card Catalog template.

facility was added in 2006 and provides a fast way to locate any Ancestry.com database that might be pertinent to your research. You may enter the name of a database if you know it or simply enter keywords or other information, such as the type of record or time period you are interested in, and click the **Search** button. Of course, if you aren't really certain about what it is you want to locate, you can always browse the databases alphabetically by name or by category, by clicking the "Browse a list of databases" link at the bottom of the search template page.

Let's say that you want to locate the "Social Security Death Index" database. You could certainly enter the full name in the "Database Title" field. However, if you simply enter "social security" in the field, the search engine will search for all databases that have those words in the title. See the result in figure 2-23.

Exact Search Results - Ancestry Database Card Catalog
You searched for **Database** Refine your search

All Reference & Finding Aids Results

Viewing **1-1 of 1**

View Record	Title	Category	Places	Record Count
View Record	Social Security Death Index	Birth, Marriage, & Death	United States of America	77,759,196

Figure 2-23: The "Exact Search Results" page from an Ancestry Database Card Catalog search.

Simply click the link labeled "Social Security Death Index" and you will come to a page with a search template for the database you have selected.

You would get the same result if you entered "social security" in the "Keyword(s)" field. If, however, you entered only the keyword "social" in the field, you would get close to 300 matches. This is because the word "social" appears in the text description or in the "Subjects" section of each of these three hundred databases.

The "Advanced Search Options" for the Ancestry Database Card Catalog include the following:

- **Record Type**—This drop-down list allows you to narrow your search to major categories of record types, just as on other pages you have already seen and explored.

- **What Time Period Are You Interested In?**—This drop-down list gives you the following options:

  - *All*
  - *1750–1799*
  - *1800–1849*
  - *1850–1899*
  - *1900–1949*
  - *After 1949*
  - *Before 1750*

  Choosing a certain time period allows you to narrow the list of databases for which you are searching. Be aware, however, that some databases may have a publication year included in the textual source information that could cause some unexpected results.

- **Date Last Updated**—Many genealogists keep concise records of when they accessed a database or a website to avoid duplication of their effort if the content has not been updated since they last visited or used the site. These three fields allow you to specify a month and year, or a range of time. The date you specify will be *either* the date it was initially added to the Ancestry Database Card Catalog or the last time the database was updated with new records or new features. If you look at the Source Information at the bottom of the page, you can see the year it was added by

Ancestry.com or the copyright date. All of these are part of this search option's functionality and allow you to keep track of new or updated databases.

- **What Location Are You Interested In?**—You can narrow your search of databases to one specific area.

As you can see, the Ancestry Database Card Catalog is a very powerful search tool with a great deal of flexibility that you can use to effectively locate databases that may be pertinent to your research goals.

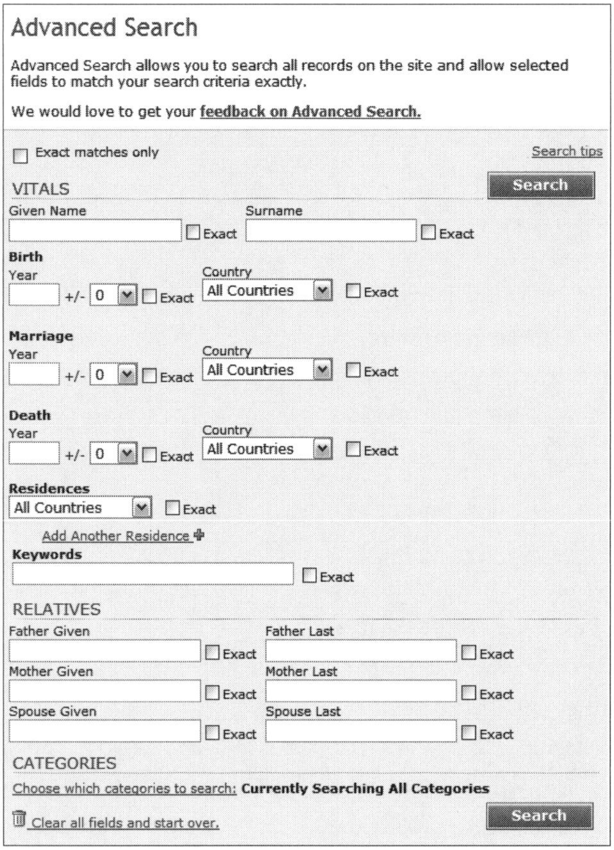

Figure 2-24: The "Advanced Search" template.

The Advanced Search Template

Also in the "Search Resources" section at the upper right-hand corner of the **Search** tab is a link labeled "Advanced Search" (see figure 2-24).

The "Advanced Search" template combines a number of search criteria fields into the same form. These include given name (middle name or initials may also be used here); surname; birth, marriage, and death dates (all with exact or +/- year ranges) and locations; place of residence (you can add multiple residences, if necessary); and keywords. Relatives' names may be used, including father, mother, and spouse.

One thing that makes the Advanced Search tool different and exceptionally flexible is your ability to use the exact search facility in multiple ways. Note on figure 2-24 that there are "Exact" boxes throughout the template. Here are some ways you can use them:

1. Selecting the "Exact matches only" option at the top of the template selects every "Exact" option on the form. When all of the "Exact" options are selected, the search will only return results from records that contain exact matches for all the fields where you entered information.

2. When you deselect the "Exact matches only" box at the top of the search form, all of the "Exact" boxes will be deselected.

3. You can click the "Exact" box by *any* individual field to require the search results to include and match that item exactly. For example, this will allow you to require a location to match exactly, but still find variations of a surname.

4. If an "Exact" box beside a country field is selected and you select a country for which Ancestry.com has records in its databases that pertain to a subdivision, such as state, province, county, parish, town, and so on, the additional fields will be displayed that allow you to enter this data.

With all of these search tools and examples in mind, let's explore some search strategies you can employ that may help you in your research.

Search Strategies

Now that you have seen so many search templates and tools, let's fine-tune your search skills with some very practical strategies. This section includes some proven suggestions

Advanced Search

Advanced Searching is the only way to search all of the databases on Ancestry.com at once.

for adjusting your searches to get by even some of the most difficult problems found in databases. Not only will you be able to apply these strategies at Ancestry.com, but you will find them helpful in other databases you may access in your library, in archives, and on the Internet.

Some Ancestry.com search results may not help you in your research, even though they technically match your query terms. This is especially true if you are researching an ancestor with a common name. You may want to refine your search by locality, keyword, or other options to filter out unwanted results. These are some good search strategies you can employ to increase your success rate at locating ancestors.

Wildcard Searching

Spelling names can sometimes be tricky as well as frustrating. Was your ancestor's surname spelled Gray or Grey in specific records? Did your German ancestor spell his name Wilhelm or William? You could try searching multiple times for various spelling combinations or, for a surname, you could use the "Exact" or "Soundex" spelling options. However, Ancestry.com provides another powerful option for substituting either a single character or multiple characters in a name. It is called wildcard searching.

Wildcard searching is available for all text on the site, in both free and subscription databases. Wildcards are special symbols (the asterisk "*" and the question mark "?"), which are used in place of numbers or unknown letters in your search queries.

Rules for Using the Two Wildcard Characters

1. A single character is represented by a question mark "?" (such as "Sm?th" would find both "Smith" and "Smyth").

2. An asterisk "*" represents zero to six characters (e.g., "john*" might return "john," "johnson," "johnsson," "johnsen," "johnsen," "johnnison," and so on). Any use of the asterisk requires at least the first three letters of a name (you cannot search for "Ad*," but could use "Ada*").

First and Middle Name Search Strategies

Searching for an ancestor in a database by first name can be challenging. Here are some strategies that may help:

1. Learn how to misspell the name. The literacy rate in early times was not what it is today, and names were sometimes spelled phonetically. In other cases, people arbitrarily changed the spelling of their name. To add to the confusion, spelling was not standardized until fairly recently.

2. Try alternate spellings of the name. If you believe your ancestor's name was "Johnathan," also try searching for "Jonathan"; if your ancestor's name was "Harriette," try searching for "Harriett"; if your ancestor's name was "Caroline," also try spelling it as "Carolyn" or "Carol Lynn," and so on.

3. Try searching for diminutive spellings of names. If your ancestor's name was "Andrew," try using "Andy" or "Drew"; if your ancestor's name was "Annabelle," try using diminutives like "Anna," "Annie," "Bell," "Belle," or even "Nancy."

4. Some names are replaced with alternate forms. A notorious example is the name "Elizabeth," for which other names such as "Margaret," "Maggie," "Peg" or "Peggy," "Lizzy," "Beth," and "Betty" are common. As a child, even Queen Elizabeth II of England was known among the British royal family as "Lilibet."

5. When looking for people with a common name, you may want to choose another family member in the same residence with a more unusual name, if you know of one. If you are searching for an individual who has an association with a specific area or region, use the name *and* a geographical place to narrow your search.

6. Substitute a middle name, if known, for the first name.

7. Reverse the first and middle names when searching. One of my great-grandmothers was named Lydia Lenora Patterson, yet there are references to her as Lenora only or as Lenora Lydia.

8. Combine both first *and* middle names. My great-grandfather was named Green Berry Holder, yet I have occasionally found him listed on a record or indexed as Greenberry. Combinations of first and middle names are not that unusual.

9. Substitute initials for a first or middle name. The same great-grandfather mentioned above was also listed in some places as G. B. Holder, and, had I not tried using his initials, I would not have found the record I sought.

Surname Search Strategies

My own cardinal rule is, "Learn how to misspell your family surnames. Your ancestors did it and so did the people who recorded their names." The Soundex system is great for getting past the surname spelling variants and locating the most possible matches, including spelling and indexing errors. Here are some strategies for working with surnames that may improve your chances of success:

1. After trying the surname spelling you expect, click the "Exact matches only" box, if available for the database

you are searching. Enter both the first and last names and specify the use of Soundex to get an idea of what spellings of the surname might exist. You might want to specify the name proximity option of at least "within 1 word" in case there is either the middle initial or middle name included in the indexing of the record. Narrow your search by adding a general location. Start with a country first and, if that doesn't provide as useful a result as you need, add the state/county/province, and so on. It also helps if you can narrow the time frame.

2. If you cannot locate the person in the county or province you expected, remember that boundaries did change over time. Broaden your search to surrounding geopolitical areas.

3. Use wildcards with surnames.

4. Reverse first and last names. Sometimes during a transcription of records or indexing, the scribe might have made a transposition error.

Many databases contain information that extends beyond one geographic location or time period. When this is the case, you may receive results outside the selections you designated in the original search. The search templates allow you to limit a search to a specific locality and thereby filter your results more effectively. You can often increase the number of applicable results you receive. To do this, always include a location when performing a search. Searches that include a location will often provide links to additional reference materials, maps, and any other data related to that location.

Summary

Ancestry.com has put a great deal of thought and skill into producing its database search facilities. When you consider the vast variety of databases, it is impressive to see how robust and effective these search tools are. It is understandable for the first-time user to be overwhelmed or become confused. However, there is a commonality to the way the searches operate. When you understand the difference between a ranked search and an exact search and then factor in the necessary differences in the various search templates, you will access and use the databases more effectively. You may not be an expert just by reading this chapter, but you should now have a strong understanding of what is available to you at Ancestry. com, how to use the search facilities, and what some good search strategies are.

Chapter 3

Working with Digitized Image Collections

When you access a database that includes a digitized image, it is important to be able to view it, analyze the information on it, and have the options to print it, save it, share it, or even connect it to one of your personal family trees.

The purpose of this chapter is to explain how to access images and how to use each of the functions associated with them. By the time you finish reading this chapter and performing all the functions you read about, you should be an expert in working with any of the Ancestry.com collections online. In addition, when we talk about these collections in later chapters, you will already know how to effectively work with them.

How to Access a Digital Image

For the examples in this chapter, I will use the 1850 United States Federal Census database. It includes an every-name index and images of each census population schedule. The object of my query is my second great-grandfather, Isaac Morrison, of Greene County, Georgia, his wife, Rebecca, and their family.

So far, we have learned a number of ways in which we could initiate a search in this database. Let's review them:

- You could start on the **Home** tab and click on the link for the year "1850" in the "US Census Records" section. This will take you to the 1850 census database-specific search template.

- You could go to the **Search** tab and use the "Historical Records" search template.

- Also on the **Search** tab, you could click the "US Federal Census" link in the "Browse Records" section. That will take you to the "Search U.S. Census Records" page, where you can opt to use the simplified search template and search for Isaac Morrison in every census, *or* to click the "1850 US Federal Census" link in the "Search a Specific U.S. Federal Census by Year" section. This will take you to a database-specific search template, limiting your search results to the census database you choose.

- You could use the "Advanced Search" template to perform a global search of all the databases at Ancestry.com and then hone in on the specific census records that interest you.

I chose the third option and completed the "1850 United States Federal Census" search template (see figure 3-1 on the next page). Notice that I did not click the "Exact matches only" option (for more on this option, see page 28).

The search results list shows multiple Isaac Morrisons, as you can see in figure 3-2 (located on the next page). However, only the first one satisfied my search criteria that he 1) live in Greene County, Georgia, in 1850, and that 2) he be born in

Georgia. I think I'm on the right track. Remember that you can narrow the number of matches on the "Ranked Search Results" page by using the "Show" drop-down list. From here you can determine which results you want displayed based on their star ranking. In this case, though, the top match was a 3-star match, as are all the other Isaac Morrisons, so this would not have helped narrow down the individuals.

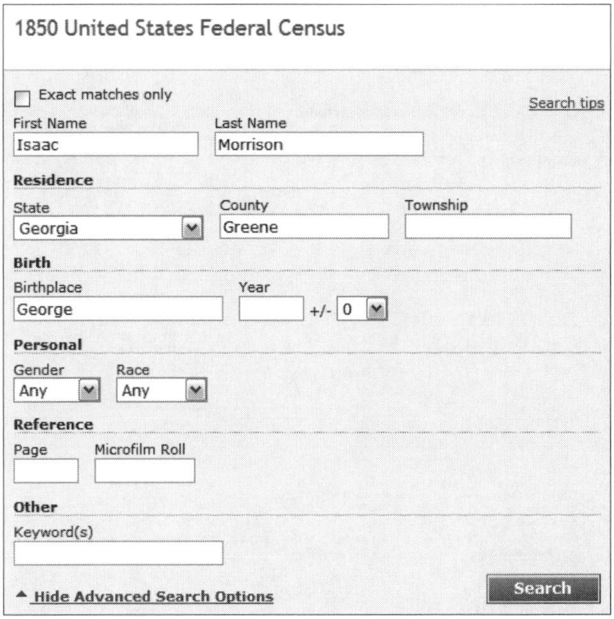

Figure 3-1: Completed search template for the 1850 U.S. Federal Census.

From the search results list, I have two options for accessing the digitized image of the census on which Isaac appears: "View Record" and "View Image." Let's explore the differences.

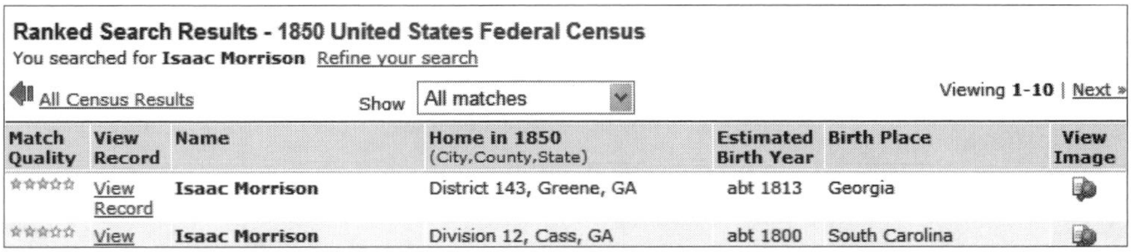

Ranked Search Results - 1850 United States Federal Census
You searched for **Isaac Morrison** Refine your search
All Census Results   Show All matches   Viewing **1-10** | Next »

Match Quality	View Record	Name	Home in 1850 (City,County,State)	Estimated Birth Year	Birth Place	View Image
★★★★★	View Record	**Isaac Morrison**	District 143, Greene, GA	abt 1813	Georgia	
★★★★★	View	**Isaac Morrison**	Division 12, Cass, GA	abt 1800	South Carolina	

Figure 3-2: A portion of the "Ranked Search Results" for Isaac Morrison in the 1850 U.S. Federal Census.

View Record

Click the "View Record" link.

As you can see, it is not the full image of the census document. Instead, this page shows various information.

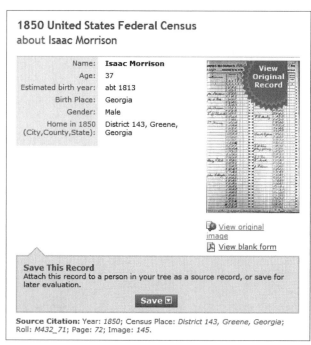

1850 United States Federal Census
about Isaac Morrison

Name:	**Isaac Morrison**
Age:	37
Estimated birth year:	abt 1813
Birth Place:	Georgia
Gender:	Male
Home in 1850 (City,County,State):	District 143, Greene, Georgia

View original image
View blank form

Save This Record
Attach this record to a person in your tree as a source record, or save for later evaluation.

Save

Source Citation: Year: *1850*; Census Place: *District 143, Greene, Georgia*; Roll: *M432_71*; Page: *72*; Image: *145*.

Figure 3-3: Main section of the "View Record" page.

In the main section, you'll find details about Isaac Morrison taken from the actual census population schedule, which we will examine a little later in the chapter (see figure 3-3). There is a link labeled "View original image," which would take you directly to the image itself.

There is also a link labeled "View blank form." If you click this link, assuming that you have the free Adobe *Acrobat Reader* installed on your computer, a PDF file containing a blank transcription form for the 1850 census will open. You may want to print the form so that you can read the column headings more clearly than on the less-than-crisp images of the population schedule itself. It also helps you follow along, column by column, when your ancestors are listed further down on a census page and the column headings are not in view at the time you are readying and analyzing the data.

Below these, you'll find the "Save This Record" section. Clicking the **Save** button allows you to save this record either to one of your trees or to your "Shoebox." The "Shoebox" is a part of the My Ancestry tab and acts like a personal online filing cabinet here at Ancestry.com. We will discuss the My Ancestry tab in detail in chapter 4.

You will find this record's "Source Citation," which can be used for your own citation. Simply copy and paste it into your records. It might look like this:

> Image Source: Year: 1850; Census Place: District 143, Greene, Georgia; Roll: M432_71; Page: 72; Image: 145.

On this page, you will also see "Source Information" for the record and the database description. In the "Description," click "Learn more…" to see a more complete description of the database. The information in the "Source Information" section is also suitable for generating a source citation for your records. My source citation might read as follows:

> Ancestry.com. 1850 United States Federal Census [database online]. Provo, Utah: MyFamily.com, Inc., 2005. Original data: United States. 1850 United States Federal Census. M432, 1009 rolls. National Archives and Records Administration, Washington D.C. <www.ancestry.com>. Accessed 01 November 2006.

Please notice that I included text from the "Source Information" section. However, I also added the Ancestry.com URL, and the date on which I accessed the data. This provides a record for me or for any other researcher as to where and when I accessed the data.

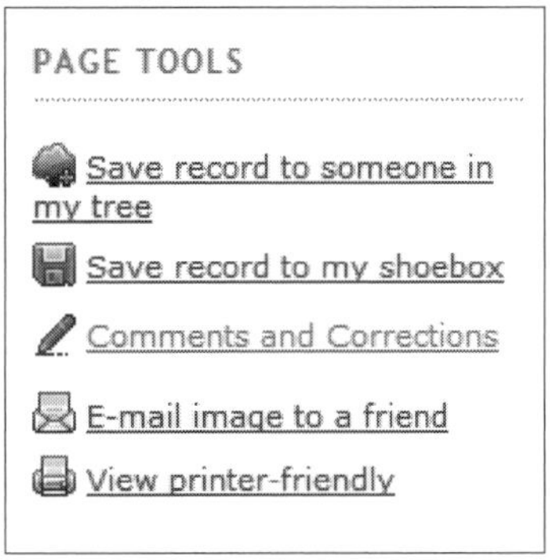

The "Page Tools" section on the right side of the page gives you another way to connect this census record to your personal family tree or to your "Shoebox" (see figure 3-4). The link labeled "Comments and Corrections" takes you to the page shown in figure 3-5 (on page 56).

Here you have three options:

1. You can "Add an Alternate Name" that will appear attached to the record for anyone to see. This may be used to correct or clarify the record. The entry you add is anonymous.

PAGE TOOLS

 Save record to someone in my tree

 Save record to my shoebox

 Comments and Corrections

 E-mail image to a friend

 View printer-friendly

Figure 3-4: The "Page Tools" section of the "View Record" page.

Comments and Corrections
Isaac Morrison
1850 United States Federal Census
<u>**Isaac Morrison Record Page**</u>

Select From The Following Three Options

 Misspelled or Alternate Names

Is the name misspelled? Is there an alternate name for this individual? Help other Ancestry users by providing corrections or additions to our index:

- **Transcription Errors**
- **Nicknames**
- **Birth or Maiden Names**
- **Name Variations**

<u>**Add an Alternate Name**</u>

 Add a Comment

Add a comment to this record. Once posted, other users can respond similar to how they would on a message board.

NOTE: Comments posted to this record may not be viewed elsewhere on the Ancestry site.

<u>**Add a Comment**</u>

 Report an Image Problem

Having technical difficulties? Report the following image problems:
- ***Unreadable Image*** - *The image is blury or I can't read it*
- ***Wrong Image*** - *I was supposed to see a different image*
- ***Missing Image*** - *The image is supposed to be here, but is missing*

<u>**Report an Image Problem**</u>

Figure 3-5: The "Comments and Correction" page.

2. You can "Add a Comment" to this record, to which other researches can respond in a way similar to a message board. This may help other researchers to explain or correct confusing information in their genealogy database.

3. You can "Report an Image Problem" to the technical support team at Ancestry.com for their review.

Back in the "Page Tools" section, you will see another link that allows you to "E-mail the image to a friend." I often use this feature to send interesting documents to family members or researchers. You can also view a printer-friendly version of the record and then easily print it. Note that this is not a printer-friendly version of the census image itself, but of the information shown on this page.

Below the "Page Tools" section is the "Make a Connection" section. This gives you access to the "Member Connection Service," allowing you to make connections with other people who share your interest in researching this person or family.

Finally, if you scroll down the page, you'll see your search template displayed again. Rather than having to go back in your browser to the previous page, you can refine your search and resubmit your query here.

View Image

You may go directly to the record image from the "Ranked Search Results" page (shown in figure 3-2 on page 55) by clicking on the icon of the magnifying glass and document in the "View Image" column at the right side of the entry you wish to view. You are now ready to begin working with the image (see figure 3-6).

You will notice two things at the top of the window. The first is a set of Quick Links (see figure 3-6a). As you will recall,

Loading Images

When the image appears, some browsers will show a small pop-up box that reads, "Press SPACEBAR or ENTER to activate and use this control." This is not a problem; simply press either of the keys.

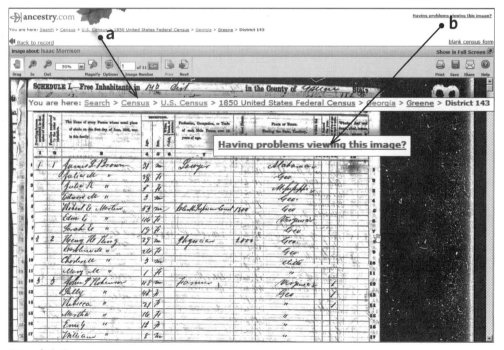

Figure 3-6: Census page.

you can click on any of the underlined links to move backward (for more on Quick Links, see page 4).

There is also a link labeled, "Having trouble viewing the image?" (see figure 3-6b). If you are experiencing problems, click on this link, select the appropriate type of problem, and then provide some descriptive text for the support personnel to locate and attempt to correct the problem. Please note, however, that some of the digitized images may be very faintly written and difficult to read. This is caused by microfilming problems, and Ancestry.com may have produced the most enhanced image possible for visibility.

The Toolbar

We are now going to focus on each of the tools on the toolbar, which is shown in detail in figure 3-7.

Figure 3-7: The toolbar in ImageViewer.

You will find that the control panel is similar in all the image databases, although the **Drag** tool and other settings may not always be available. The intent of this chapter is to show you how *all* the possible controls operate. So let's get going!

View in Full Page Mode

You want to be able to see as much of an image as possible in your Web browser. Ancestry.com has provided a tool to help you do just that. Look on the right side of the blue line that reads, "Image About: Isaac Morrison" and you will see the a link labeled "Show in Full Page." Click on the link and your browser's menu bar, button bar, and every other header bars will be hidden from view. This will provide more room for the page content to be displayed. Click on the same area again to reverse the action and to make your browser's header bars reappear.

Drag

In many of the Ancestry.com image collections, you will see a small hand icon on the toolbar labeled **Drag**. This tool allows you to click and drag the image more efficiently than by using the scroll bars. To activate it, simply click **Drag** and then move your mouse over the document. Your cursor should change from an arrow pointer to the hand icon.

Click-and-hold your left mouse button and the hand changes to a grasping position. If you continue to hold the left mouse button down, you can drag the image on the page in any direction until you see a location on the document that you would like to examine. To "let go" of the image, simply release the left mouse button.

Zoom

If an image is too small for you to read, you can enlarge the document for closer inspection. This is done in two ways.

On the toolbar, to the right of **Drag** button, you will find two buttons: **In** and **Out**. The **In** button has a magnifying glass marked with a "+", while the **Out** button's icon is a magnifying glass marked with a "-". These buttons allow you to zoom in or out on the image. The different digitized image collections have different levels of magnification. Clicking **In** increases the size of the document for easier viewing, all the way up to the highest magnification. Clicking **Out** reduces the size of the image.

For example, when I zoomed in once, I was able to more closely examine the age written down for William Morrison. Comparing the second digit of the number listed by William's name with the fractional age of ½ listed for the youngest child, Jane, I determined that William was twelve years old at the time of the 1850 census. It turned out that the enumerator sometimes made unusual strokes for the number "2" and a comparison on this page helped clarify the entry for William's age.

Image Size

 The second method of changing the size of the image display is to use the drop-down list that contains the standard control settings. All of the image collections online provide settings based on percentage of the original size of the document. Some also include "Fit Image," "Fit Width," and "Fit Height." These cause the image to be displayed to fit the browser window. If the collection you are viewing provides the **Drag** tool, it will not work in the "Fit Image" and "Fit Height" settings because there will be nowhere to move. It does, however, operate on the "Fit Width" setting, where the full width of the original document is displayed, but you can only drag the document up and down.

Magnify

 Sometimes you will want to take an even closer look at a specific area of an online image, just as you would with a physical document. The **Magnify** tool is the answer.

Click **Magnify** in the toolbar. Now move your mouse over the document image. You will see a square box with dotted-line crosshairs. Position the crosshairs over the center of the area you wish to magnify and then press-and-hold the left mouse button. That area will be magnified by about 3×. While holding the left mouse button down, you can move the magnifier around the document page. However, if you want to move the page, you will need to click **Drag** to activate that tool again.

You will find the magnify function exceptionally helpful for examining and analyzing handwriting.

Options

Now that you have a good idea of how to access the images, move them around, change the size, and magnify them, it's time to consider the options for viewing the images in different ways.

Click **Options** on the toolbar and the window shown in figure 3-8 is displayed. This window controls the quality of the digitized images you can view. Once you set the options, they will become the default settings on your account for working with all image collections.

There are four view options settings that you can change. Let's define each one.

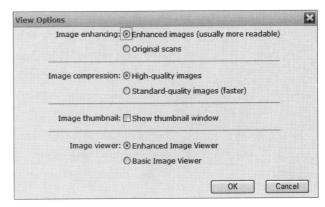

Figure 3-8: "View Options" window.

Image Enhancing

Ancestry.com is responsible for the digitization of a large percentage of the images in its collections. This includes the censuses, ship passenger lists, and World War I draft registration cards, to name a few. Most of the digitization was done using microform images and, during the process, Ancestry.com "cleaned up" the images by adjusting lightness, darkness, and contrast, and by despeckling problem images. The intent was always to make the images more readable and therefore more useful to the researcher.

As a result of all of this diligent work, some of the digitized collections offer you the option of also viewing the original scanned images. In most cases, the enhanced images they produced are superior to the original image. However, you many want to view the original scanned image of a document, particularly if you are having difficulty reading the enhanced image, to see if the original is more legible.

Image Compression

Ancestry.com provides users with "standard quality images" as a default. These are quite crisp and readable and, more important, they are easy and quick to download for users without high-speed connectivity.

There is, however, another version of the images. These higher quality images contain more pixels and are often of a slightly higher resolution. They are more data-intensive and therefore take longer to download, especially for subscribers using dial-up connectivity.

You can experiment with these options and see what works best for you.

Image Thumbnail

A "thumbnail" is a very small version of the full-size image. They are commonly used in graphics software and photographic editing programs. Ancestry.com allows you to turn on or turn off a thumbnail view of the currently displayed document. When this option is turned on, it overlays a small area in the upper right-hand corner of the document displayed in your browser window (see figure 3-9). If you look at the thumbnail view, you will see that a small rectangular area is

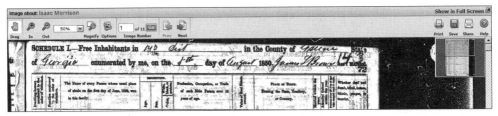

Figure 3-9: Census record in Image Viewer with Thumbnail Image displayed.

highlighted yellow on the thumbnail, which indicates where your browser window is currently located and what area is being viewed.

Click **Drag** and move the hand over the highlighted area in the thumbnail image. Now, click-and-hold the left mouse button and drag the highlighted area over the thumbnail image. You will see that the image in your browser follows right along and is moved just as the highlighted area in the thumbnail moves. This is yet another way to move around the document image.

Image Viewer

Over the years, Ancestry.com has used several types of image viewer software for its digital collections. The viewers are and have always been available to download from Ancestry. com. While some users still use the Basic Image Viewer, Ancestry.com upgraded to an Enhanced Image Viewer quite a while ago. It provides sharper images, faster download speeds through enhanced data compression, and access to some additional features, such as the Thumbnail View and the ability to view both the enhanced and original scans that we discussed above.

You may select which viewer you prefer, but downloading and installing the free Enhanced Image Viewer will insure you have the best experience at Ancestry.com.

Image Number, Previous, and Next

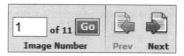

This section of the toolbar allows you to go to and move between images. The white box indicates the number of the image that you are currently viewing. The number to the right indicates the total number of images in this batch. This example of this census document is page 1 of 11. This means that there are a total of 11 documents for Greene County, Georgia, in the 140 District, for the 1850 United States Federal Census. This area allows you to move between document images in two ways.

- Highlight the number of the document in the white box and change it, and then click the **Go** button in order to move to that page. This provides a quick way to move between non-contiguous document pages.

- Use the **Prev** or **Next** buttons. If movement in direction is possible, the arrow will be green. If movement is not possible in one or the other direction, the arrow in that direction will be grayed out.

At this point, you know all about navigating the digitized image collections and how to exercise the options to maximize your experience. Now let's discuss manipulating the images.

Print

Most genealogists will want to print a document for their records. After all, you may want to return to the original document to reexamine it, reverify information, and provide copies to other researchers. Printing the digitized documents from Ancestry.com isn't difficult; you just have to understand what you can and cannot do.

The **Print** button on the toolbar is the only way to ideally print an image from Ancestry.com. If you use your browser's

menu of **File** and **Print**, you
will usually get garbage or,
in the worst case, no image
at all.

When you click **Print**, a
print window will open on
your computer page (see
figure 3-10). Pay attention
to whether a document
is in portrait (vertical)
or landscape (horizontal)
orientation to avoid the
frustration of printing wasted
sheets. Also be aware that

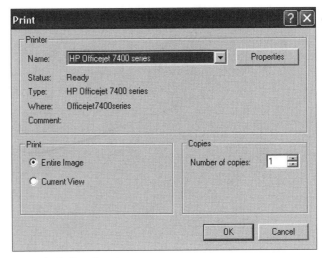

Figure 3-10: "Print" window.

different printers behave in different ways and the options they
offer may influence how you print your document copies.

Note that I have two options in the "Print" window: to print
the entire image or just the current view. The current view
option may be appropriate, for example, if I have zoomed in to
enlarge an area.

If an original document is in landscape orientation,
you will need to change your printer's orientation setting.
Otherwise, you will end up with a truncated image. To change
the orientation of your printer to accommodate original
documents in landscape mode, click the **Properties** button
in the "Print" window and there should be a setting to define
portrait or landscape orientation printing. (Don't forget to
change this back for other print jobs later!)

Save

There will be many times that you will want to save
a copy of the image you have discovered on the site.

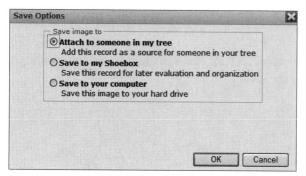

Figure 3-11: "Save Options" window.

You have three methods to do this. Figure 3-11 shows the window that is displayed when you click the **Save** button on the toolbar.

Your first option is to save the file to the record of someone in your personal family tree. Simply click the **Attach to someone in my tree** option.

The second option is to save the record to your "Shoebox" on Ancestry.com. To do this, click the **Save to my Shoebox** option. (For more on the "Shoebox," see page 86 in chapter 4.)

The third option is **Save to your computer**. Many genealogists save a copy of the image and link to a multimedia/photo area on their computer. Others save the file and then e-mail it to others at a later date.

After you have selected your option, click **OK**. If you have opted to save the record to your computer, you will be prompted to supply a name for the file and location for it to be saved. The image will, by default, be saved as a JPEG file.

Share

If you are like me, you get excited when you make a find. I am likely to send a copy of the record to another member or two of my family. You can also send a copy of the record to someone else who is researching the same family line or specific members.

Sharing a record with someone else is very simple. All you have to do is click the **Share** button and a window appears that is similar to the one shown in figure 3-12.

Enter an e-mail address and, if you like, edit or add text to your message. The image will be e-mailed as an attachment with your name and return e-mail address (as shown in your account profile).

Help

The **Help** button on the toolbar provides access to some helpful information about using the Enhanced Image Viewer. When you click the button, a new window opens that includes a number of Frequently Asked Questions and a list of each of the tools we have discussed in this chapter with some descriptive information about them. This is a good place to get refresher information.

*Figure 3-12: The message window generated by the **Share** button.*

Summary

We have covered a great deal so far. By now you should be an expert in searching for information in databases and, if the content includes digital images, you should know exactly how to work with them.

In the next chapter we will discuss **My Ancestry**, your personal data management tool at Ancestry.com. I know you will be impressed. Once we have that under our belts, then we will explore each of the major record groups and discuss the practical application of that data.

Chapter 4

My Ancestry

As you use Ancestry.com, you will find records and information that you want to keep track of. The **My Ancestry** tab makes it possible for you to store and organize the information you find and share it with others.

The information on the **My Ancestry** tab is specifically linked to your account so that, when you log in, the data about your personal research is available to you. That means that lists of recently viewed records, recent searches, and items you have added to your family trees are immediately available to remind you of what you have been working on. This makes it easy to pick up where you left off. There's even a storage area called the "Shoebox" that you can use to store records for people who might be related to you but whose connection to your family you may not have been able to establish yet.

These are wonderful personal tools for managing your research at Ancestry.com and they are unique in the online genealogy community. As we explore the **My Ancestry** tab's component areas, you are sure to appreciate the way the system was designed. You will get ideas for just how to use it to further your own research. And so, with all that said, let's get started.

Family Trees

The most important feature of the **My Ancestry** tab is the ability to create and manage your own family trees. Family trees have been a part of Ancestry.com for a long time, and today they are an active and vibrant feature of the site.

Creating a Family Tree allows you to organize your research, share it with others, and create a dynamic, interesting mini-site for your family or the family you are researching. In addition, Ancestry.com uses the information you enter into your family trees to help you further your research.

Until recently, you could work with your family trees on both the **My Ancestry** tab and the **Family Trees** tab. In order to simplify things, the **Family Trees** tab has been removed; now, the creation and management of your trees will take place on the **My Ancestry** tab.

Click the **My Ancestry** tab. Depending on whether or not you have created your own Family Tree, the main section of the **My Ancestry** tab will look different. Once you have created a tree, it will be labeled "My Family Trees" and will be the place where you manage the sites you've created. We'll discuss the "My Family Trees" section in more detail later in this chapter, but first, let's look at how you start your first tree.

Starting Your First Tree

The first time you click the **My Ancestry** tab (or any other time you do not have any Family Trees), the main section will be labeled "Start Your Family Tree" (see figure 4-1 on page 73).

What Is a Family Tree?

A Family Tree is a personal website hosted by Ancestry.com and dedicated to helping you record, work on, and share your family history. Each site is built around a specific family tree, allowing you to gather records, photos, stories, and other memorabilia to a central location on the Web and organize them in a way to tell the story of that family tree.

Family Trees are the perfect way to take the results of your research on Ancestry.com and turn them into a dynamic and interesting project. As Ancestry.com continues to expand and improve the Family Trees, your options will grow as well. For example, Ancestry.com recently released the beta version of Ancestry Press, which allows you to take the information on your Family Tree, combine it with photos, text, and other features, and create a professional-looking book that you can print. Later this year, you will be able to buy bound copies of your books to distribute to your friends or family. Ancestry Press is just one example of the exciting ways in which Family Trees are going to continue to improve.

You are presented with two options: you can either start a new tree from scratch, or you can start one from an existing GEDCOM file.

Create a New Family Tree

If you are starting from the beginning and don't already have a family tree in some other form (in *Family Tree Maker* or another family tree software, for instance), you will need to create a tree from scratch. To do this, click the "Create a new family tree" option and then click **Start Your Family Tree**.

The process of starting a new tree is easy. Simply follow

*Figure 4-1: "Start Your Family Tree" section on the **My Ancestry** page.*

A History of Trees

Throughout its history, Ancestry.com has tried various kinds of online family trees. Ancestry World Tree is a collection of GEDCOMs submitted by users. OneWorldTree also includes uploaded information from users, but it also includes a search functionality that compares submitted information with information in other submitted trees and online databases to help users enhance their research.

For all intents and purposes, the information from these trees is now treated like any other database on Ancestry.com. For more information about Ancestry World Tree and OneWorldTree as searchable databases, see chapter 2.

the prompts, beginning on the "Start Your FREE Family Tree" page (see figure 4-2). Enter your name, gender, birth date and place, and then click **Next**.

You don't have to start with yourself when creating a new tree. To start with someone other than yourself, simply enter that person's information in the first step of the creation process instead of your own. As the process continues, use that person's father and mother as well. If you do this, make sure the "I'm starting with myself" option is deselected.

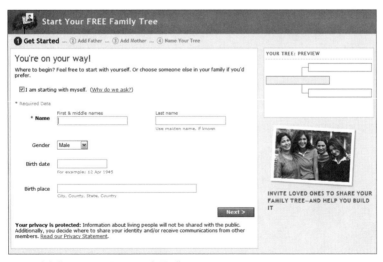

Figure 4-2: "Start Your FREE Family Tree" page.

Once you have entered your own information, you will be asked for the information of your father (Step 2) and your mother (Step 3), including information on their death, if applicable. If you don't have some or all of this information at the time you create the tree, don't worry. You can click **Next** even if the form isn't entirely filled out, or you can click the "Skip this page" link at the top to move to the next page.

In the last step, you will be prompted to name your Family Tree. In addition, you are given the option to make your Family Tree public or personal.

The decision whether to make your Family Tree public or personal ultimately determines how effective your tree is as a research tool. If you set your tree as personal (by deselecting the "Allow others to see my tree" option), no one can see all the details of your tree except people you invite. Others searching on Ancestry.com will be able to see basic information (such as a birth date) about the member of your tree they are searching for, as well as the contact information you have provided in your Member Profile. They can then contact you to view more of your tree. In addition, information about living individuals will never be shown to others without your explicit permission.

If you set your tree as public (by selecting the "Allow others to see my tree" option), it will be available to anyone searching the Family Trees database to view. Remember that even if you set your tree as public, only you and people you invite can contribute or change information on your tree. Once you have made this decision, click **Done**.

Next you will be given the chance to send an e-mail to family members or friends inviting them to your tree (see figure 4-3 on page 74). For each person you want to invite, provide a name and e-mail address, and decide what role you

Subsequent Trees

Once you have created a tree, you can start a new one by clicking the "Create a new family tree" link at the bottom of the "My Family Trees" section. The process is the same as described in the "Create a New Family Tree" section of this book.

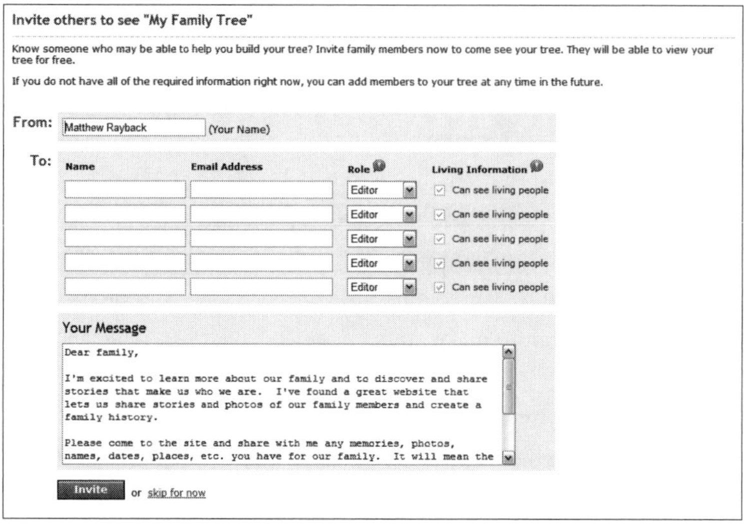

Figure 4-3: The "Invite others to see" page.

want them to have and whether or not they can see living people in your tree.

A person's role on your tree determines what actions they can take in your tree. You can see a chart detailing which role can perform which functions by clicking the blue "I" above the word "Role" (see figure 4-4).

You can either invite people using the pre-written message shown in the "Your Message" section, or you can edit the letter to fit your own needs. Once your invitation is ready, click **Invite** and your new tree will be complete.

Living Relatives

A person in a tree is considered living if there is no death date indicated and he or she is younger than eighty-five years old.

Upload a GEDCOM

The other way to start your first tree is to upload an existing GEDCOM file from your favorite family tree software. On the "Start Your Family Tree" section of the **My Ancestry** tab, click

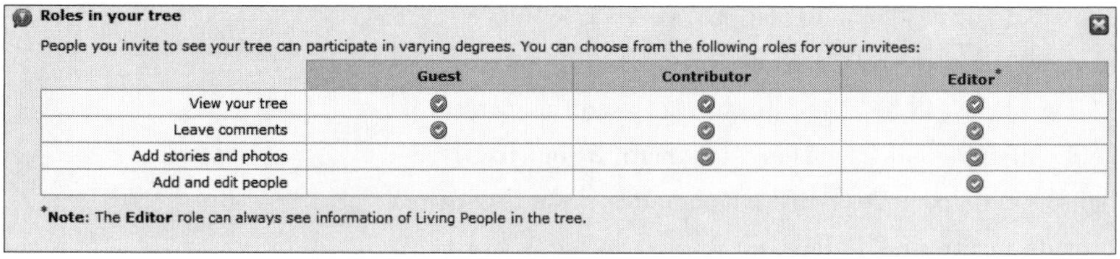

Figure 4-4: An explanation of the various roles available to members of your tree.

the "Upload an existing family tree file" option and then click **Start Your Tree**.

In the "Choose file" field on the resulting page (see figure 4-5), enter a file name or click **Browse** to locate a GEDCOM (.ged) file on your hard drive. Enter a name in the "Tree Name" field and decide whether your want your tree to be public or not.

Upload a Family Tree

When you upload a GEDCOM file, all of the people in it are placed into a new tree on Ancestry. The name you choose to give your tree will be visible to your guests and other Ancestry members. How do I upload my tree?

Choose file	[ ] Browse...
	Find the GEDCOM file on your computer.
	Maximum file size is 100MB.
Tree Name	[ ]
	Give your new tree a name
	☑ Allow others to see my tree as a public member tree and allow my tree information to be compiled into OneWorldTree
	What does this mean?
Description	[ ]
	Enter surnames, years, etc., to help people understand what your tree is about. (optional)
	☐ I accept the Submission Agreement
	[Upload] or Cancel

Figure 4-5: The "Upload a Family Tree" page.

Enter a description in the "Description" field if you want. For example, you could use this field to list specific surnames on your tree.

Once you have finished making the decisions about the file you are about to upload, click the "Submission Agreement" link. If you agree with the submission agreement, click the "I accept the Submission Agreement" check box; then click **Upload**. You can now begin to manage your new tree.

Working with Your Family Trees

Once you have created your first tree, the main section of the **My Ancestry** tab is labeled "My Family Trees." You can see mine in figure 4-6. Notice that I have two personal trees there. The first, labeled "ggm—100406," was created by uploading a GEDCOM file on that date. Since that time, I have added to and edited data. The second, labeled "Holder Tree," consists of individual

Uploading Additional GEDCOMS
❧

Once you have created a tree, you can start a new one by clicking the "Upload a GEDCOM" link at the bottom of the "My Family Trees" section. The process is the same as that described on this page.

My Family History Sites			What's New
Name	Last Modified	Role	Tools
ggm - 100406 View Tree	3/19/2007	**Owner** Invite Family	
Export GEDCOM			
Holder Tree View Tree	12/11/2006	**Owner** Invite Family	
Export GEDCOM			
		🌱 Create a new Family History Site	📋 Upload a GEDCOM

*Figure 4-6: The "My Family Trees" section on the **My Ancestry** tab.*

Figure 4-7: The welcome page of the "ggm-100406" Family Tree.

records I input, and then data I have added, records I linked, and other editing I did.

You can think of each Family Tree you create as a personal Web page for that family. When you click the name of a tree in the "My Family Trees" section, you are brought to a page that acts as a "homepage" for that tree. This is the "Welcome" page. Figure 4-7 shows this page for the first tree in my list, "GGM—100406."

You will notice that the "Welcome" page of your Family Tree is different from other areas of Ancestry.com. The normal Ancestry.com toolbar with the tabs has been replaced with a header indicating the name of your Family Tree and links that correspond with the normal Ancestry.com tabs.

From this "Welcome" page, you can easily manage and navigate through your Family Tree. Just as with the homepage of Ancestry.com, the easiest way to navigate your Family Tree is by using the tabs at the top of the main section.

Home

The **Home** tab is the default page of your tree. It gives you an overview of your tree and lets you manage its various features.

On it, you can perform many of the most useful actions to manage your tree, as well as review recent additions and changes, members, and more. Let's take a look.

In the main section of the **Home** tab, you will find the following options:

- **Add a description or welcome message**—Including a welcome message or an introductory description on your tree helps others who visit understand what they will find on your tree. You might include a list of surnames of people included in your tree, a brief history or the family, or other welcome.

- **Add a photo to the tree**—Here you can include a photograph of your family, or any kind of graphic to represent your tree.

- **View my tree**—You can navigate to a view of your tree here. We will explore the tree itself in greater detail when we discuss the **Family Tree** tab (see page 82).

- **Invite Family**—One of the most exciting features of the Family Trees is your ability to collaborate on it with your family. The Home tab allows you to invite members to your tree in two different ways. First, you can click the "Invite Family" link in the main section (beneath the "View my tree" link). Alternately, you could click the link of the same name in the "Invite Family Members" section on the right side of the page.

  Clicking either of these links brings you to same "Invite others to see" page described on pages 73–74 (see figure 4-3). Fill out the form as described before and click **Invite**.

- **Add a photo**—Your Family Tree can include photos and images to enrich your tree and better tell the story of your family. We will discuss the process of adding photos in greater detail when we examine the **All Photos** tab (see page 84). Note that you can also add a photo from the **Home** tab in the "Recent Photos" section.

- **Add a story**—You can also include family stories and anecdotes with your tree. We will discuss adding stories in greater detail when we talk about the **All Stories** tab. Note that you can also add a story from the **Home** tab in the "Recent Stories" section.

There are a few more actions you can take on the **Home** tab. In the "People in this tree" section, you can view people attached to the family tree. You will see the tree's "Home Person" and the "Last Viewed" person on your tree. You can even see an alphabetical list of everyone on the tree by clicking "See full list of people."

Figure 4-8: "Tools" section on the **Home** *tab.*

In the "Tools" section are three links that help you control the settings of your Family Tree (see figure 4-8):

- **Change tree privacy**—If you want to change your tree from public to personal or vice versa, you can do so by clicking this link. Select the option that is best for you, using the information in the "What does this mean?" sections to help you decide, then click **Save**.

- **Change home person**—The home person of your tree is the person around which the tree is built. In other words, the tree starts with the home person. Generally your home person should be you, but if you are working on a tree that doesn't include you, you can use this feature to decide which person should be the home person.

After clicking the "Change home person" link, enter the name of the person you want to be the home person into the field, indicate if you are the home person or not, and click **Select** (see figure 4-9 on the next page).

- **Manage my tree**—This
  link leads to a page (see
  figure 4-10) that lets
  you take many actions
  to manage your tree,
  including deleting it.

Figure 4-9: The "Select a Home Person for this family tree" page.

People

The **People** tab is where you
see more detailed information
about members of your tree.
When you click on a person's
name in most places on your
Family Tree, you are brought
to his or her page on the
People tab (see figure 4-11).

Figure 4-10: The "Manage" page.

The features on the **People**
tab allow you to view and
modify people in your tree.
In the main section, you'll see
information about the person
in question, as well as about
his or her parents (provided
this information has been

*Figure 4-11: The main section of the **People** tab on "ggm-100406."*

entered onto your tree). From
here, you can add photos (either by clicking the silhouette
shaped link or the "Add a photo" link below it) or stories (with
the "Add a story" link). Refer to the sections on the **All Photos**
tab and the **All Stories** tab for more information on this (see
pages 84–85).

In this main section, you can also search for records in
the Ancestry.com databases that relate to this person and

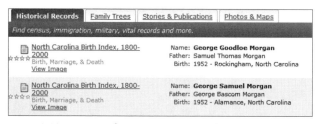

Figure 4-12: A portion of the search results page for a search done from a Family Tree.

add them to your Family Tree. If you click "Search for historical records," you will be presented with a search results page (see figure 4-12). You can go through the list and determine which of the results, if any, are connected to your family member, and then add that record to your tree as documentation in the same way you would if you had found that record in a normal search.

Another way to search Ancestry.com from your Family Tree is to click the leaf icon that may be next to the name of the person you are viewing. When you mouse over the leaf, you will see an indication of the number of records Ancestry.com has found that might enrich your tree. If you click one of the possibilities (such as "1 possible Source Records found"), you will come to a search results page showing those records.

You'll see the leaf icon again in the **Tree** tab and other places in your Family Tree. It functions in those places as it does here.

You can also add comments to the person you are viewing on the **People** tab by clicking "Add a comment." You might want to add a comment to give other viewers more information about this person, explain your research, or for a variety of other reasons.

Another main feature of the **People** tab is the "Timeline" section, which helps you outline major events in the life of that person. To add an event, click "Add event" in the "Timeline" section. Select an event from the drop-down list, then fill in the subsequent fields and click **Submit**. Possible events include "Arrival," "Description," "Residence," and more.

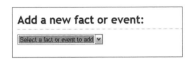
Once an event is included in the "Timeline," you can modify it by simply clicking the title of the event. On the resulting page, you can change information as necessary, add records to support this event, provide alternative information, and so on (see figure 4-13).

Add a new fact or event:

Select a fact or event to add ▼

Figure 4-13: "Add a new fact or event" drop-down list to add to your Timeline.

The sections on the right side of the **People** tab provide a variety of options. These include the following:

- **Family Members**—This section allows you to view and navigate to members of the person's immediate family. Click on any of the names shown and you will be taken to that person's "People" page. You can also click "View more family information" to go to a family group sheet–type page (see figure 4-14).

- **Tools**—The links in this section provide you with a number of familiar options, including searching for source records and inviting family members to contribute. The link "Find Famous Relatives" lets you search Ancestry.com for famous

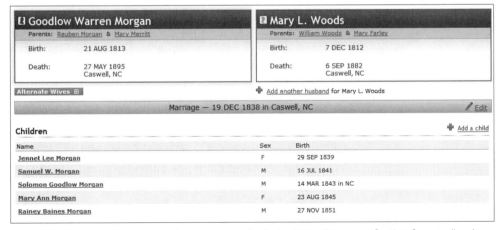

Figure 4-14: You can see family group sheet-type pages like this by clicking "View more family information" on the ***People*** *tab.*

people who might be related to you. You can also review research notes compiled by you and others about this person by clicking "View research note."

- **Source Records**—In this section, you can see how many sources are associated with this person. If you click the "View all source citations" link, you can view each of these sources. In this section, you can add additional sources or learn more about sourcing in general.

- **Community**—As you might expect, this section provides a link to the **Ancestry Community** and helps you find other people who are interested in this person.

Anywhere on your Family Tree, you can move to the "People" page for anyone on your tree. Click "Home Person," or enter a name in the "Find a person in tree" field. Notice that as you enter a name in this field, Ancestry.com tries to anticipate who you might be searching for and provides a list of people in the tree who might match your query.

Family Tree

If you want to view your family tree, click the **Family Tree** tab (see figure 4-15 on the next page). Here you will find five generations of your family organized in a pedigree chart. If this is your first time to the **Family Tree** tab, the person in the first position will be your home person (probably you). If you are returning to your Family Tree, the person in the first position will be whoever it was last time you visited. If you go to the **Family Tree** tab directly from the **Person** tab, the person in the first position will be the person whose page you were just viewing.

To view information about any member of the tree, roll your mouse over that person's name and his or her full birth and death dates will appear, as well as the option to search for

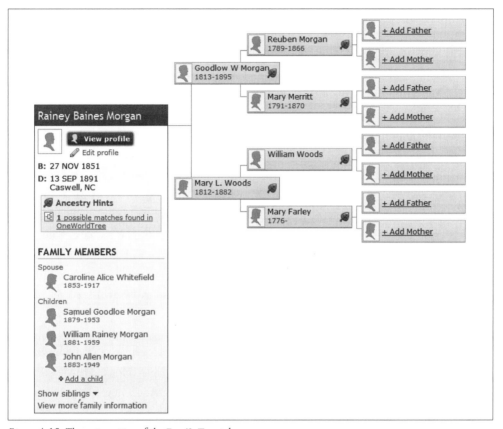

Figure 4-15: The main section of the Family Tree tab.

records for that person or view them from the **Person** tab, or to move this person to the primary position. If you want to add information to a person, you must do it from the **Person** tab. Note also the leaf icon beside some or all of your family members' names. This leaf icon functions the same as it does on the **People** tab, allowing you to search Ancestry.com for ways to grow your tree (see page 80 for more information).

If your tree is larger than five generations, use the arrows to the right of the page to navigate through the generations. If you want to move forward in time, move your mouse over the

Figure 4-16: Moving Caroline Alice
Whitefield into the primary position.

Figure 4-17: The "Upload a Photo" page.

spouse or child you would like to see in the primary position, then click the arrow that appears (see figure 4-16).

On the **Family Tree** tab, you can also edit the information of the person in the first position by clicking the "Edit person" link beneath the tabs. You can click through the various tabs and fill in information as necessary, clicking **Save Changes** when you are finished.

Finally, you can print a copy of your five-generation pedigree chart on the **Family Tree** tab by clicking the "Print" link beside the "Edit person" link. A new window will open, giving you a preview of what the printed copy will look like . If you are satisfied with how it will look on paper, click **Print this page**.

All Photos

As the name suggests, the **All Photos** tab allows you to view all of the photos you have uploaded to your Family Tree. To add a photo, click "Add a new photo," either on this tab, or on any of the other tabs.

Next, enter the location on your computer where the photo is saved, or click **Browse** to search for it on your hard drive (see figure 4-17). Click the "Content Submission Agreement" link. If you agree with the submission agreement, select the "I accept" option and then click **Upload**.

You will be prompted to give the photo a title and

description, as well as to indicate where and when it was taken (see figure 4-18). You can also declare what type of photo it is and attach the photo to someone on your tree. When you have finished, click **Save**. If you want, you can save your photo without attaching it to someone.

Once you have uploaded your photo, you can view it by

Figure 4-18: The "Photo Information" page.

simply clicking it on the **All Photos** tab. This will give you an expanded view of the photograph, as well as allow you to add or review comments made about the image. From this view, you can also print the picture or remove it from your tree using the buttons at the top.

All Stories

Every family has stories. Stories can enhance your family history by preserving memories and anecdotes related to your family members, which helps you understand your family better. You can add stories to your family tree from the **All Stories** tab, or by clicking any of the "Add a new story" links on the other tabs.

Next, decide whether you want to compose the story on Ancestry.com or upload it from your computer, and select the appropriate option.

Figure 4-19: When you choose to compose your story on Ancestry.com or upload it, the appropriate fields appear as Step 2.

Give your story a name, then compose it in the browser (see figure 4-19) or follow the instructions to upload it from your hard drive. Then add a description, location, and date for your story. As with photos, you can now attach this story to a specific member of your family. When you have finished, click **Save**.

You can view and modify your story in exactly the same way you view and modify photos (see page 84).

The Shoebox

The "Shoebox" is a convenient place to store records about people who *might* be related to your family but about which you are unsure (see figure 4-20). Perhaps you just haven't made the connection yet, but you don't want to lose the possible relative and his or her record(s). The "Shoebox" is the perfect place to store the electronic record links, and you

*Figure 4-20: The "Shoebox" section of the **My Ancestry** page.*

can click on those links at any time. Let me use an example.

Let's say that I was searching for one May Wren Morgan and that I found a search result indicating that she was listed in the 1930 U.S. Federal Census in East Orange, Essex County, New Jersey. I can click on two places in the search result shown to add this record to my "Shoebox."

First, I could click **Save**. This gives me the option of saving the record to a Family Tree, or to my "Shoebox." I can also click the "Save this record to my Shoebox" link in the "Page Tools" section. For more on the options on search results, see chapter 3.

Once a record is saved to your "Shoebox," you can open it again at any time by clicking the link.

Recent Activity

On the right-hand panel on the **My Ancestry** tab is the "Recent Activity" section (see figure 4-21). Here you will find links to your most recent online research activity at Ancestry.com. Included are the last fifteen databases you most recently viewed, the last fifteen most recent searches you performed, and the most recently viewed people in OneWorldTree.

Member Connections

Finally, there is one more section on the My Ancestry tab. It is labeled "Member Connections" and it allows you to make use of the Ancestry community (see figure 4-22). While we will discuss communications with other members in more detail in chapter 16, let's look at the options presented here.

Here in the "Member Connections" section you will find two links. The first is labeled "Find Ancestry members" and you can use this to locate other members who are researching the same people that you are seeking. Click that link (see figure 4-23 on page 88).

On the resulting page, you can click one of the names in your personal lists displayed, or you can enter a name, date(s), and location(s) in the search template. The "Site Preferences" we discussed in chapter 1 will determine whether

RECENT ACTIVITY

Recently Viewed Records
- 1930 United States Federal Census for May W Morgan
- World War I Draft Registration Cards, 1917-1918 for Brisco Washington Holder

  » See the 15 most Recently Viewed Records

Recent Searches
- George Goodloe Morgan born in 1952
- penelope weatherly

  » See the 15 most Recent Searches

OneWorldTree^{SM}
- Weatherly, Carolyn Penelope (1914-2000)
- Morgan, Samuel Goodloe (1879-1953)
- Wilson, Laura Augusta (1873-1966)

Figure 4-21: The "Recent Activity" section of the My Ancestry page.

MEMBER CONNECTIONS

- Find Ancestry members who are researching the same ancestors as you are
- Search the Member Directory for people like you

Figure 4-22: The "Member Connections" section of the My Ancestry page.

Figure 4-23: The "Find Members Researching One of These People" page.

Figure 4-24: The "Member Directory" page.

your communication is handled showing your e-mail address or via an anonymous communication.

The other link in the "Member Connections" section is labeled "Search the Member Directory." When you click here, the page shown in figure 4-24 is displayed. You will note that there are tabs along the top of the template for "Interests," "Location/Age," "Experience," "Lineage," "Languages Spoken," and "Faith." You can click any of these tabs to complete the template for that information and click the **Find** button. This will search the public profiles of all Ancestry.com members and present a list of matches to other members who completed their own profile with those data criteria.

Summary

The **My Ancestry** tab helps you move forward with your research. Family Trees are an exciting way for you to organize and save information about your family history, as well as offering you a way to collaborate with others in your family to enrich and expand your family experience. As we proceed to discuss various database types throughout the tree, keep your Family Tree in mind. Look for ways to use it, whether it is by attaching a record to an individual in your tree, or by helping you decide who to research next. If you are not making use of your Family Tree, you are not taking advantage of the full power of Ancestry.com.

Chapter 5

Working with Census Records

Census records are the most frequently-used records among genealogists. This has been proved again and again by statistics gathered by the National Archives and Records Administration (NARA) in the United States, The National Archives (TNA) in the United Kingdom, other countries' archives, the LDS Family History Library in Salt Lake City, and Ancestry.com.

Census documents are a strong resource for locating a person at a specific geographical location at a given point in time. Based on that information, it is then possible to search for other records and evidence in the same geographic area.

Ancestry.com databases include many census documents. The focus of this chapter is on the census collections for the United States, the United Kingdom, and Canada. The vast majority of these collections include full indexes and digitized images. There are additional databases that consist of indexes only, including many of the American state and county censuses, the 1841 Scotland census, and certain areas of Germany. We will discuss the census materials that are available as we address some of the large geographical census collections available at Ancestry.com.

United States Federal Census Records

The United States has taken a population census every ten years, beginning in 1790 and continuing to present times. From 1790 through 1840, the censuses only list the name of the head of household, with some information about others in the household. In 1850, the first every-name census was taken, and in 1880, the census started including the relationship of every individual to the head of household. At various times, additional census documents, or schedules, have been completed to provide detailed information about certain population and economic trends.

The United States federal government's Privacy Act dictates that census information not be released to the public for seventy-two years from the date of the census enumeration. Thus, the most currently available federal census data is that of the 1930 census. Ancestry.com has digitized and completely indexed by name all the available microfilmed federal census records from 1790 to 1930. These record include the following:

- **Population Schedules**—1790 to 1930, including the few surviving fragments of the 1890 census, which was destroyed in the Commerce Department fire in Washington, D.C., on 10 January 1921.

- **Mortality Schedules**—1850 to 1880.

- **Slave Schedules**—1850 and 1860.

- **Veterans Schedules**—1890 (Surviving Soldiers, Sailors, and Marines, and Widows, and so on).

- **Census of Merchant Seamen**—1930.

Ancestry.com has not digitized some of the other United States federal census schedules, such as Agricultural Schedules; Industry/Manufacturing Schedules; Social Statistics: Delinquent, Dependent and Delinquent Classes Schedules; Indian (or Native American) Schedules; or the Enumeration District (ED) Maps.

Listed below are four excellent books that provide in-depth information about the United States federal censuses. You can also use the Ancestry.com Library to locate other reference materials and articles that may aid your research.

Dollarhide, William. *The Census Book: A Genealogist's Guide to Federal Census Facts, Schedules and Indexes.* Bountiful, UT: Heritage Quest, 2000.

Hinckley, Kathleen W. *Your Guide to the Federal Census.* Cincinnati, OH: Betterway Books, 2002.

Morgan, George G. *How to Do Everything with Your Genealogy.* Emeryville, CA: McGraw-Hill/Osborne, 2004.

Szucs, Loretto Dennis and Matthew Wright. *Finding Answers in U.S. Census Records.* Orem, UT: Ancestry, 2001.

Searching the Census Records

You have already seen several ways to access the search templates for United States federal census records. If you are not comfortable with searching these databases, go back and reread chapter 2. For now, here is a quick review of four ways you can search the U.S. federal census:

- On the **Home** tab, click a specific year *or* on the link labeled "All>>".

- On the **Search** tab, click on either the category labeled "Census" or on the link labeled "US Federal Census" in the "Browse Records" section.

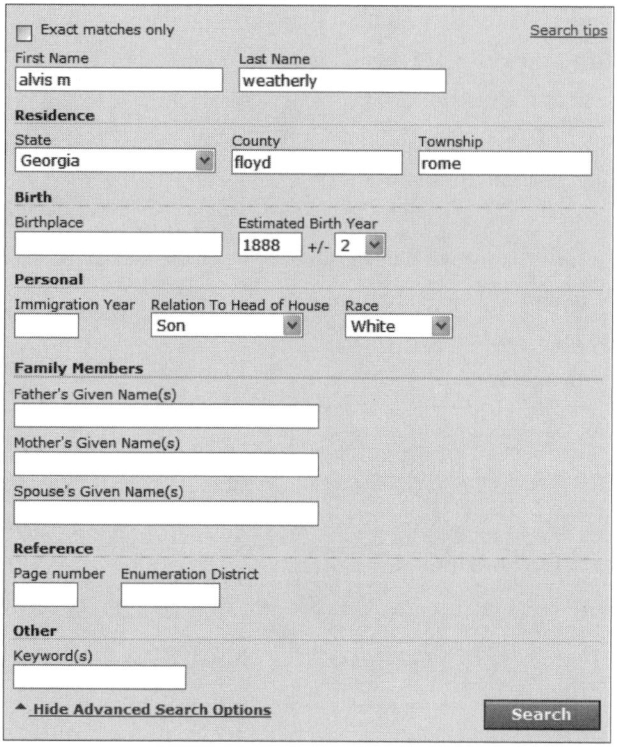

Figure 5-1: Completed template to search "1900 United States Federal Census."

• On the same tab, you can scroll down to the maps and click the one labeled "United States." From there, you can browse the databases for the census form you want, by state.

• Search the "Ancestry Database Card Catalog" for "census" or browse the Ancestry.com databases, clicking a census to explore.

Once you have selected the search template you want to use and decide whether or not to use the "Exact matches only" option, you can fill in the fields with your search criteria and then click **Search**. Figure 5-1 shows a template I completed to search for a family member, Alvis M. Weatherly, in the 1900 census. As you work with each census template, you will note that there are different fields available. These reflect the information on the actual census form, and the options in drop-down lists will represent the options the census enumerators could choose. Remember that you can start with simple search criteria and later narrow your search by completing other data fields on the search template. I began with the general search.

I had to use several search criteria combinations before this one in order to get Alvis's name to come up so high on the "Ranked Search Results" list (see figure 5-2 on the next page).

Match Quality	View Record	Name	Parent or spouse names	Home in 1900 (City, County, State)	Birth Year	Birthplace	Race	Relation	View Image
★★★★★	View Record	**Alvis M Weatherley** 🔖	Amos M, Hallie	Rome, Floyd, Georgia	abt 1888	Georgia	White	Son	📷
★★★★☆	View Record	**Colin M Weatherly**		Bennettsville, Marlboro, South Carolina	abt 1888	South Carolina	White	Son	📷
★★★★☆	View Record	**Charlie M Weatherly Jr.**	C N, J S	Athens Ward 1, Clarke, Georgia	abt 1896	Georgia	White	Son	📷
★★★★☆	View Record	**Addie M Weatherly**	C N, J S	Athens Ward 1, Clarke, Georgia	abt 1886	Georgia	White	Daughter	📷
★★★★☆	View Record	**Cordie M Weatherly**	Andrew, Lizzie M	Greensboro Ward 6, Guilford, North Carolina	abt 1888	North Carolina	White	Daughter	📷

Figure 5-2: A portion of the "Ranked Search Results" page.

On examination of the results, I see that while my search
included the spelling of his surname as "weatherly," the index
for him spelled the surname as "Weatherley," with an extra "e"
near the end. In addition, I see an Amos M. and a Hallie listed
under the "Parent or spouse name" column. These made no
sense! However, on examination of the actual image, I found
an easy explanation (see figure 5-3).

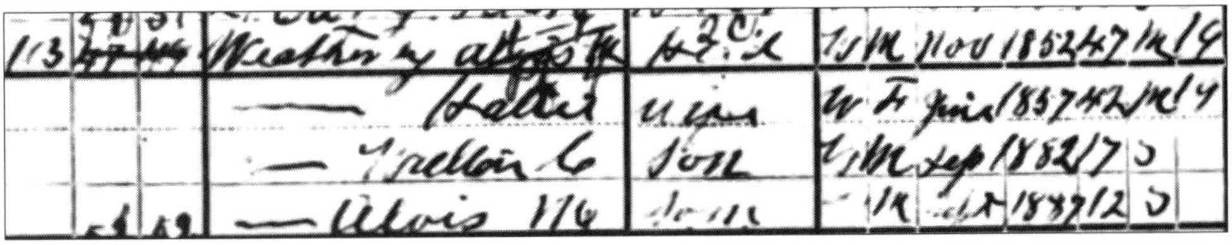

Figure 5-3: Selection from the "1900 United States Federal Census" image.

The enumerator's handwriting is very poor indeed.
Weatherly's surname is not quite legible and his first name
is an unreadable mess. His wife's name does appear to be
"Hallie," but is, in fact, Hattie (short for Harriette), and one
son's name is spelled as "Welton" when it should have been
"Walton." You can see a combination of reasons why there are
problems with the index: the enumerator's writing is very
sloppy, the microfilmed image is faint in an area of the surname
entry for the family, and there are spelling errors. This is an

excellent example of why it is important to use the general search first. A ranked search may reveal the alternate spellings and indexing problems that might never appear in an exact search.

You may have noticed another icon beside the surname in the search results list and on the "View Record" page. If you move your mouse pointer to the icon and pause over it, a small pop-up comment window appears (see figure 5-4).

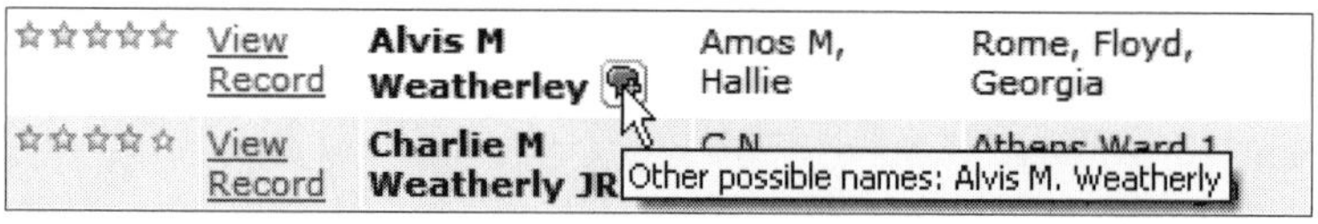

At some point, someone has viewed the record for the index entry and has entered a

Figure 5-4: The comment/correction icon on the "Ranked Search Results" page.

comment or correction for the name. This helps you and other researchers locate the correct record because this new information can be considered in the search process.

The "View Record" page, shown in figure 5-5 on the next page, was discussed in chapters 2 and 3, but now let's look at it in greater depth. I can click the **Save** button to attach the record to someone in a family trees in one of my Family Trees or save the record to my "Shoebox."

I can also use the "Page Tools" to perform these tasks, as well as make additional comments and corrections. (These take a few days to be added to the index and records.) And if I click on the link labeled "View printer-friendly," I am presented with a clean copy of the record that I can send to my printer.

Since the surname on this family was misspelled in the index, I wanted to make some changes and corrections, so I clicked the "Comments and Corrections" link in the "Page Tools" section.

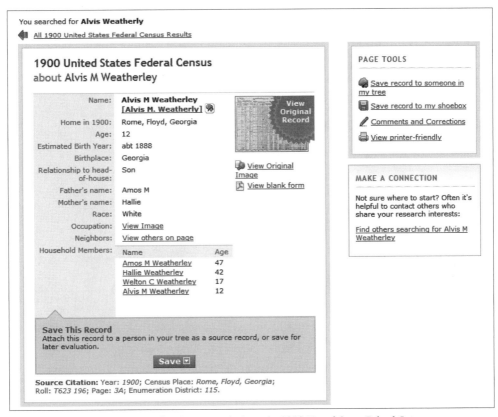

Figure 5-5: The "View Record" page for Alvis M.Weatherly in the 1900 United States Federal Census.

I clicked on the link labeled "Add an Alternate Name," filled in the appropriate information, selected a reason for my submission from the drop-down list, and clicked the **Submit Correction** button (see figure 5-6 on page 98). If you submit a correction, it will be posted to the Ancestry.com index for that database. In addition, if you submit an alternate name, a link will also appear that reads "View Alternative Names."

You may want to add a comment about a record. Click on the link labeled "Add a comment," complete the form, and click one of the buttons: **Post Comment**, **Preview Comment**, or **Cancel** (see figure 5-7 on page 98).

Alvis M Weatherley - 1900 United States Federal Census   Back to Record Correction List

Add A Correction Form

Original Information:

Given Name:	**Alvis M**
Surname:	**Weatherley**
Database Collection:	**1900 United States Federal Census**

Correction Information: Provide an alternate name, reason, and brief explanation of how you know the information you are submitting.

NOTE: Currently we can only accept submissions for alternate names. We will soon add fields for alternate places, dates, and more. For now, please enter **ALTERNATE NAMES ONLY.** Other information will **NOT** be searchable!

Given Name: Alvis Martin

Surname: We ath erly

Reason: Birth/Maiden Name

Explanation: This was his full name and the correct spelling of the surname.

Contributed By: RabidGenealogist

Your username will be displayed in the list of corrections for this record. If you would like to change your Ancestry username, click here.

Submit Correction   **Cancel**

Figure 5-6: Completed template to submit an alternative name correction.

If you experience a problem with the image itself—it is illegible, missing, or the index links to a wrong image, and so on—you can report this on the "Comments and Corrections" page by clicking on the link labeled "Report an Image Error." Complete the form with a description of the problem and as much information as possible, including the Quick Link for the image page and the image number, and click **Submit**. You will see a confirmation message, and the error can then be corrected.

Post Comment

Items marked with • are required.

Name:	George G. Morgan
E-Mail:	MorganWriter@ahaseminars.com
Subject: •	Alvis M. Weatherly
Comment: •	The surname of the family of Alvis M. Weatherly in the 1910 census in Georgia, Floyd County, Rome, District 115 is misspelled as 'Weatherly'. I have submitted a correction.
Source:	Family Bible; Baptismal Record, 1880 U.S. Federal Census
Comment Type:	Contradiction
Attachments:	[Add]

Post Comment   **Preview Comment**   **Cancel**

Figure 5-7: Completed template to add a comment.

As you can see, you can do much more with a record on Ancestry.com than simply look at it. You can print, make comments and corrections, and contact other researchers to share and collaborate.

U.S. State and County Census Records

Ancestry.com also has databases of United States' state and county records, and even a few local census records. There were censuses performed in 1885 in Colorado, the Dakota Territory, Florida, Nebraska, and the New Mexico Territory that were jointly funded by the federal and state governments. Copies of the surviving census schedules became part of the NARA collection and were therefore microfilmed. These documents have also been digitized, with every-name indexes made available by Ancestry.com. You will work with these just as you have with the other federal census images we have already discussed.

Other state, county, and local censuses, as well as other pertinent census-related records, have been collected into databases and are available to search at Ancestry.com. There are even some pre-federal, colonial census record collections. Most of these consist not of digitized images but of transcribed records from other indexes.

You will find the nonfederal census databases listed in the scroll box in the "Census" category. Highlight the database you wish to search and then click **Go**. Let's examine two collections and the different types of records you may see.

The Nebraska Census, 1854–1870 Records

The Nebraska Territory began taking territorial censuses when it first became a territory in 1854 as a result of the Kansas-Nebraska Act by Congress. Nebraska was admitted as a state on 1 March 1867. However, there were censuses taken in

1854, 1855, 1856, and then a few county censuses were taken in 1867, 1874, 1875, and 1878–1879. This database covers the years 1854 to 1870.

When you arrive at the search template for this database, select the "Exact matches only," enter the first name "conrad" and the last name of "smith," and then click "View Record" for any result. In this case, the database is only an index, and there is no digitized record to access, though you still have all the options of other "View Record" pages available here (see figure 5-8). Please notice the index entry that refers to Conrad Smith in Otoe County and Nebraska City in the 1856 NE Nebraska Territorial Census; he appears on page 15.

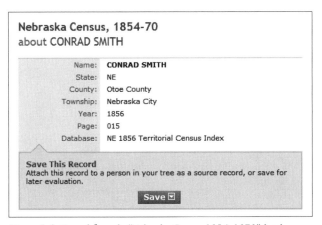

Nebraska Census, 1854-70
about CONRAD SMITH

Name:	**CONRAD SMITH**
State:	NE
County:	Otoe County
Township:	Nebraska City
Year:	1856
Page:	015
Database:	NE 1856 Territorial Census Index

Save This Record
Attach this record to a person in your tree as a source record, or save for later evaluation.

Save ☑

Figure 5-8: Record from the "Nebraska Census, 1854-1870" database.

If you are looking for any information about the status or location of any state census, the best reference book on the subject is the following:

Lainhart, Ann S. *State Census Records*. Baltimore, MD: Genealogical Publishing Co., 1992.

Let's look at another example in which the search results may look different to you. This time, return to the **Search** tab and click the "Card Catalog" link in the "Search Resources" section. On the next page, enter "maryland records" into the "Database Title" field and click **Search**. Locate and click on the one titled "Maryland Records Colonial, Revolutionary, County, and Church from Original Sources Vol. I." The next page contains a search template, source information, and a link at

Exact Search Results - Maryland Records Colonial, Revolutionary, County, and Church from Original Sources Vol. I

You searched for **Rachel Alexander**   Refine your search

◀ All Census Results   Viewing **1-2 of 2**

Maryland Records Colonial, Revolutionary, County and Church from Original Sources
 Marriage Licenses Issued at Upper Marlborough, Prince George's County, Maryland--1777 to 1801.*

Name: Rachel Alexander
Spouse: William Hayes
Marriage Date: 05 Sep 1795
Comment:
View Full Context

Maryland Records Colonial, Revolutionary, County and Church from Original Sources
 Marriage Licenses Issued at Upper Marlborough, Prince George's County, Maryland--1777 to 1801.*

Name: William Hayes
Spouse: Rachel Alexander
Marriage Date: 05 Sep 1795
Comment:
View Full Context

You are here: Historical Records > Census > **Maryland Records Colonial, Revolutionary, County, and Church from Original Sources Vol.**
Results per page 10 ▾   Viewing **1-2 of 2**

Figure 5-9: "Exact Search Results" for the Maryland records database.

the bottom of the page that you can click to learn more about the database. Click that link for a complete list of the contents of the database.

Return to the template and enter "rachel" in the "First Name" field, "alexander" in the "Last Name" field, and click **Search** (see figure 5-9).

What you have found is a printed book that includes "Marriage Licenses Issued at Upper Marlborough, Prince George's County, Maryland—1777 to 1801." There are two entries: one is from the bride index and the other is from the groom index. Note the asterisk following the name of the type of records on the page and click on it. An additional Quick Reference window opens that includes some additional information about the transcriber and source (see figure 5-10).

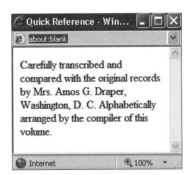

Figure 5-10: Additional "Quick Reference" window.

The two search results reflect the same marriage entry data for Rachel Alexander and William Hayes, who were wed on 5 September 1795. Click on the link labeled "View Full Content" to view a full list, in alphabetical order by surname and then first name of the bride or groom, of marriages.

As you can see, there are different types of materials in these databases, and their format and content differ, one from another. However, all of these materials help place your ancestor into a geographical context at a specific point in history.

Let's move overseas to the United Kingdom and examine their censuses.

UK Census Records

Great Britain began taking the census in 1801 and individual censuses were taken for England, Wales, the Isle of Man, and the Channel Islands. The census was taken on one specific date, known as "census night." All persons spending the night under that roof were recorded as of that date. The forms were typically collected the next day and any missing residences or information were actively collected. The data was then compiled onto the census forms we see today.

The UK censuses were taken, as in the United States, every ten years. The earlier censuses from 1801, 1811, 1821, and 1831 were statistical in nature and listed only the name of the head of household and the number of males and females. It was not until 1841 that an every-name census was created, and since that time, it has become much more useful for tracing one's ancestors.

If you are looking for someone before 1841, it is possible to trace members of families through several other document types. These include the following records:

- **Civil Registrations of Birth, Marriages, and Deaths**—
  Civil registration began on 1 July 1837. You may be able to
  locate records to help you document these events and tie
  family members together that way. (Ancestry.com has the
  civil registration indexes online as image database records.
  We will discuss them in more detail in chapter 6.)

- **Church and Parish Records**—The Church of England,
  established by King Henry VIII, was directed to begin
  recording marriages and christenings in 1538, and birth and
  deaths were recorded in the parish registers in the 1640s,
  with some earlier entries in existence. Nonconformists
  (non-Church of England protestants), Catholics, Quakers,
  and Jews have records dating from various time periods.

- **Land and Property Records**—Land, property, and
  manorial records, along with a wide variety of tax records
  exist. While plentiful, they require some knowledge of
  their history and effective periods; experience with reading
  old handwriting; and sometimes some facility with Latin, as
  the earlier records were handled by ecclesiastical courts.

- **Wills and Probate Records**—Rich in family details and
  highly indicative of the testator's station in life, wills and
  testaments, along with court probate records, can help you
  connect family members together. They, too, were handled
  by ecclesiastical courts until they were replaced with a civil
  court system.

Parliamentary law protecting the privacy of individuals'
information dictates that the United Kingdom's census images
may not be released for 100 years. Several bills introduced into
Parliament in 2005 and 2006 attempted to amend the time
to 90 years so the 1911 census could be released, but each of
these bills was struck down.

There are a number of excellent books that address these topics:

Bevan, Amanda. *Tracing Your Ancestors in the National Archives: The Website And Beyond*. Kew, London, England: The National Archives. 2006.

Colwell, Stella. *The National Archives: A Practical Guide for Family Historians*. Kew, London, England: Public Record Office Publications. 2006.

Colwell, Stella. *Family Records Centre: A User's Guide (Public Record Office Readers Guide)*. Kew, London, England: Public Record Office Publications, 2002.

Herber, Mark. *Ancestral Trails. The Complete Guide to British Genealogy and Family History*. 2nd ed. Baltimore, MD: Genealogical Publishing Co., 2000. (Note: A more recent edition of this book has been published in the UK but was not available through U.S. booksellers at the time of this writing.)

King, Echo. *Finding Answers in British Isles Census Records*. Provo, UT: Ancestry, 2007.

UK Census Search Template

1. Click the **Search** tab.
2. In the "Browse Records" section, click "UK Census Collection."
3. In the "Search a Specific UK Census by Year," click "1861 England Census."

Searching UK Census Records

Let's search for and examine a specific English census record. Use what you have learned so far to find the search template for the 1861 England Census (or use the "UK Search Template" sidebar if you need a little help).

Let's perform a search of the 1861 England census for James Hyland. I knew that he was born in Ireland and immigrated to England shortly after the Irish Potato Famine. I've already located him in the 1851 census but not in the 1841 census. I suspected that he was still living in the town of Oldbury, so I entered these criteria into the search template.

In this case, the search results lists was too large, so I refined my search by adding a birth year of 1813, as I believed it to have been based on information I obtained in the 1851 census. However, I expanded it by two years +/- to catch any estimate made by the indexer (figure 5-11).

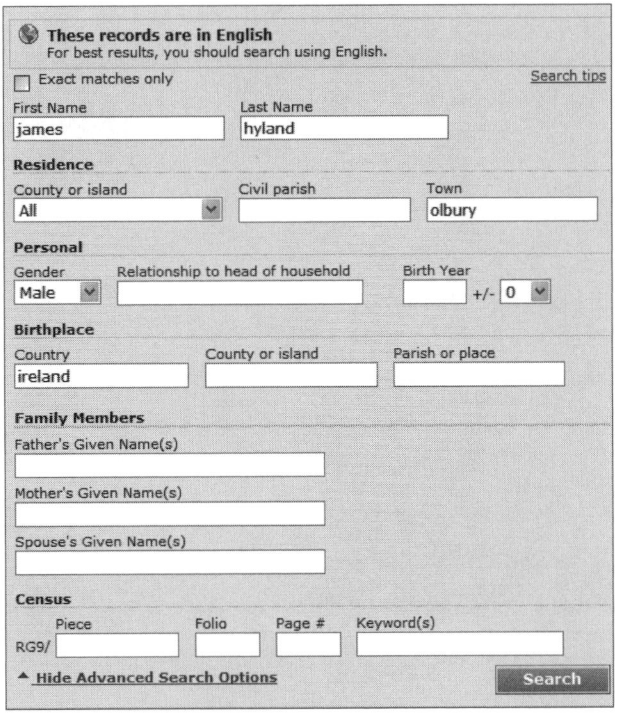

This time I was rewarded with a better search results list; I found James Hyland, born in Ireland and living in Oldbury, Staffordshire. Since his estimated birth year shown in the list is "abt 1814," it was a good idea to add the +/- variable to my search.

Once you get to this point,

Figure 5-11: "1861 England Census" search template.

you can either "View Record" or "View Image." In this case, I wanted to view the record. You'll see why when you look at figure 5-12 on page 106.

The first thing you will notice is that the record is larger than others you may have seen. The same "Page Tools" and "Make a Connection" sections are here, and you still have the option to click on links to view the original document and to view (and print) a blank census form. However, there are other links on the record of special interest.

The most important links are those for the other members of the household. This information has been transcribed from the census document. Like James Hyland's record, the

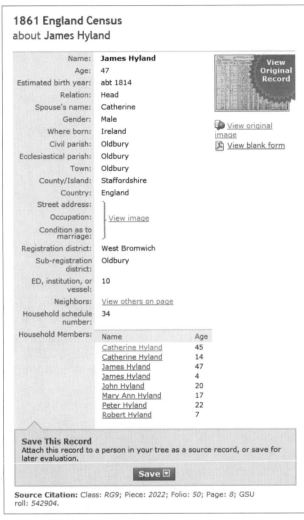

1861 England Census
about James Hyland

Name:	**James Hyland**
Age:	47
Estimated birth year:	abt 1814
Relation:	Head
Spouse's name:	Catherine
Gender:	Male
Where born:	Ireland
Civil parish:	Oldbury
Ecclesiastical parish:	Oldbury
Town:	Oldbury
County/Island:	Staffordshire
Country:	England
Street address:	
Occupation:	View image
Condition as to marriage:	
Registration district:	West Bromwich
Sub-registration district:	Oldbury
ED, institution, or vessel:	10
Neighbors:	View others on page
Household schedule number:	34

Household Members:

Name	Age
Catherine Hyland	45
Catherine Hyland	14
James Hyland	47
James Hyland	4
John Hyland	20
Mary Ann Hyland	17
Peter Hyland	22
Robert Hyland	7

View Original Record

View original image

View blank form

Save This Record
Attach this record to a person in your tree as a source record, or save for later evaluation.

Save ▾

Source Citation: Class: *RG9*; Piece: *2022*; Folio: *50*; Page: *8*; GSU roll: *542904*.

Figure 5-12: "View Record" page for James Hyland.

link takes you to a unique "View Record" page for that person. Another important link is the "View Image" link, which allows you to study the digitized original for yourself. Let's view the original image in the browser. I used the "Full Page" option to view the image (see figure 5-13 on the next page). The paper attached to the image on the right is TNA's reference to the Record Group and Piece Number assigned to this document.

I zoomed in 50% on the census image and captured the details about James Hyland and his family. I now know the names and ages of his wife and his six children. I know that James and two of his sons were employed as labourers at the chemical works while two of his daughters worked as brick makers. Notice, however, the places of birth for each member of the family, and you will see that the parents and all but the last three children were born in Ireland. These last three were born in Worcester Oldbury. This is important information because you may be able to find civil birth registrations as well as parish

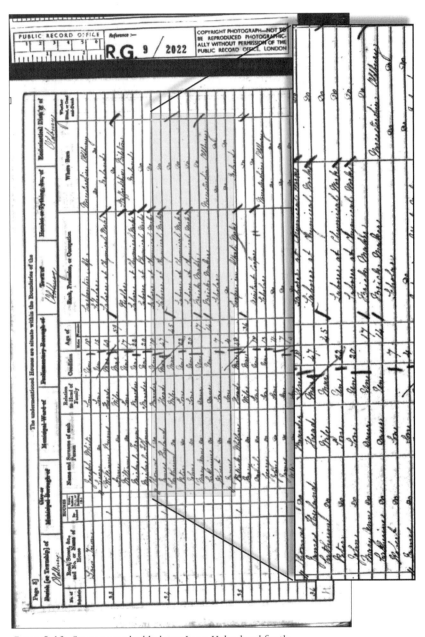

Figure 5-13: Census image highlighting James Hyland and family.

records for their christenings. Daughter Catherine is shown as 14 years old. If we subtract 14 years from 1861, we arrive at an approximate birth date of 1847. This is secondary evidence of the fact that the parents and older children left Ireland between then and the birth of the next oldest child, Mary Ann, who is 17 according to the image. That means that the time of the family's arrival in England can be narrowed down to the approximate period of 1844 and 1847, which happens to be the period of the severe Irish Potato Famine. This is the kind of work that you must do, taking evidence and analyzing it in order to arrive at such hypotheses.

Returning to the "View Record" page, you will see one more link, labeled "View others on page." While you can and should manually read the other persons' entries on the census form, a click on this link produces an "Exact Search List" that shows everyone on that same page. What makes this valuable is that the list is in alphabetical order by surname and then forename, making it easier to view patterns of relatives, friends, old neighbors from Ireland who may have traveled and settled together, and collateral lines. As with the study of any census record, neighbors' information can be extremely useful from one census to another in tracing your own ancestors, their movements, their marriages, and other events.

The Scotland 1841 Census

The 1841 census taken in Scotland is an index and not an image collection. The format of the enumeration districts was slightly different in Scotland because the country took its census independent of its English neighbors. Therefore, the search template is a little different. Look at the database-specific search template I completed for Margaret Alexander of the County of Midlothian (figure 5-14 on the next page).

In the search results list, I found the one in which I was interested. Again, I found it highly ranked, due to the use of a birth year and the +/- variable.

When I clicked the "View Record" link, however, there was no image option (see figure 5-15). Never fear! You can obtain microfilm of the census through your nearest LDS Family History Center. In the meantime, look for a link to a list of other family members and other people who appear on the census page. Even though you do not yet have access to view the actual census page for yourself, you can click on the link labeled "View other family members" and see the whole family group in an "Exact Search Results" list. This can be invaluable in assuring that you have the "correct" Margaret Alexander.

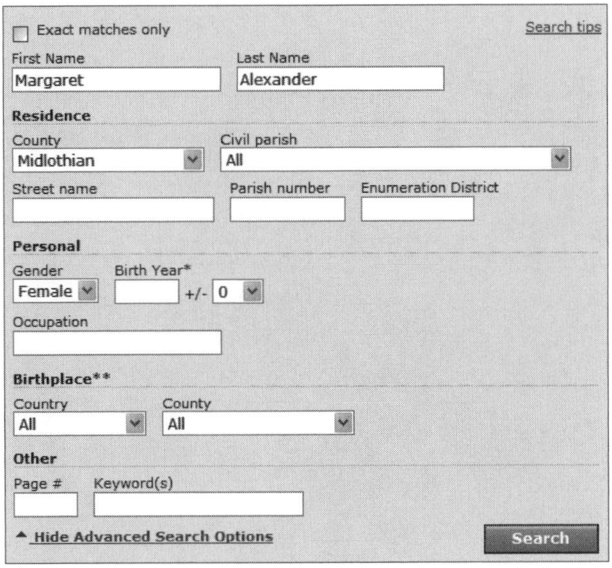

Canadian Census Records

Canada's long and rich history is woven with French

Figure 5-14: The "1841 Scotland Census" search template.

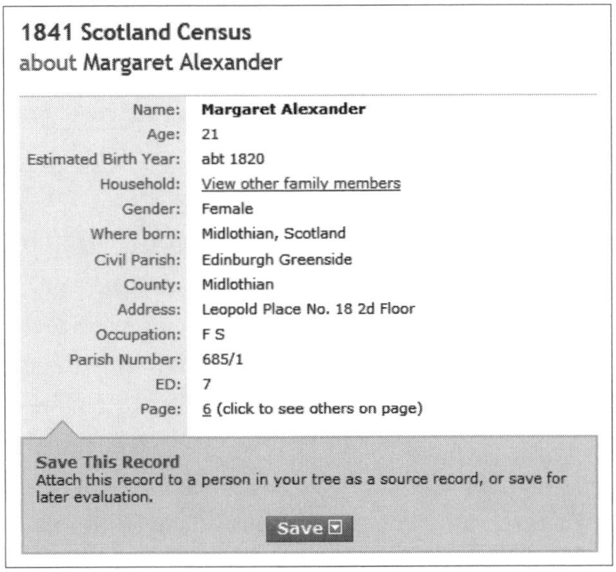

Figure 5-15: "View Record" for Margaret Alexander.

and British influence. It remains, of course, an officially bilingual country. Censuses have been taken in Canada for centuries, with the earliest ordered by Jean Talon in New France (Québec) in 1666. While other censuses were taken in various places, there are no others that survive from before the 19th century. Confederation in 1867 imposed the legal requirement that a census be taken regularly, and the first Dominion census was taken in 1871; it has continued every ten years since that time.

In May 2006, The Generations Network, Inc. (formerly MyFamily.com, Inc.) officially announced the opening of its Canadian equivalent of Ancestry.com and Ancestry.co.uk, known as Ancestry.ca.

There are a number of books that can explain Canadian census history and content in more detail.

Geyh, Patricia Keeney et al. *French-Canadian Sources: A Guide for Genealogists*. Orem, UT: Ancestry, 2002.

Baxter, Angus. *In Search of Your Canadian Roots: Tracing Your Family Tree in Canada*. 4th ed. Baltimore, MD: Genealogical Publishing Co, 2000.

For the purpose of this discussion, we will concentrate on the Canadian census databases available through Ancestry. com. These include the 1901 census, the 1906 census of the Northwest Territories, and the 1911 census.

By this time, you should be completely familiar with how to locate census databases using the "Browse Records" section on the **Search** tab, the "Ancestry Database Card Catalog," and browsing the complete alphabetical database listing.

Go to the search template for the 1901 Census of Canada. Below this template is a list of links to each of the provinces. When you click on a link, you will be prompted to select a district, then a sub-district. When you click on a link to a sub-district, the first page of the census Population Schedule or Tableau (table) will be displayed. You can then browse through the image pages using the tools on the toolbar (see chapter 3). You can also print one or more blank census forms to help you read all the columns or to translate between English and French column headings. (Please note that there are separate census forms for each language where appropriate.)

You will note that there are additional search criteria in the Canadian census than we have encountered in either the United States or United Kingdom templates. These include the fields for "Tribal," "Nationality," "Religion," "Occupation," and "Immigration year." Let's conduct an exact search in the 1901 census.

I searched for Gilbert Flynn, an Irishman who I know was alive in 1901 and lived in the district of Addington in Ontario. I also know that his wife died several years before and that his son, daughter-in-law, and grandchildren shared his home with him. I therefore constructed the search shown in figure 5-16. Since I know so much about him, I clicked "Exact matches only."

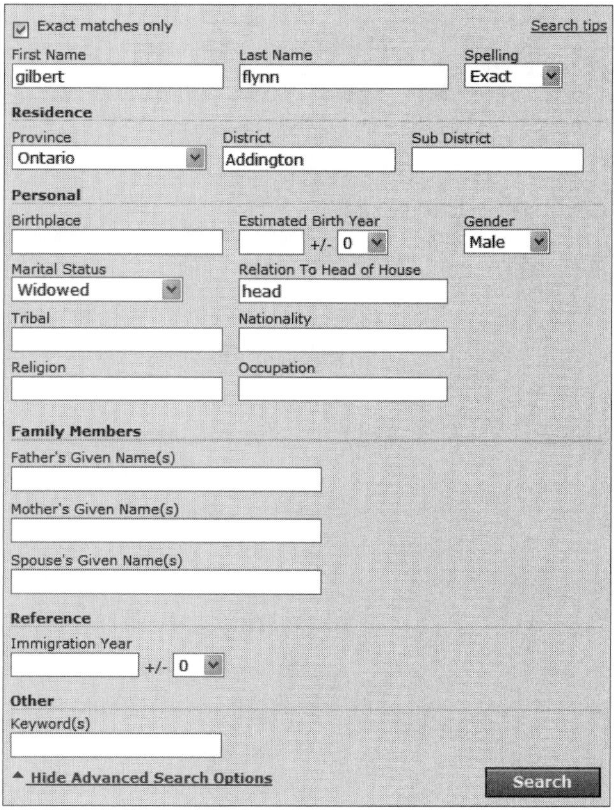

Figure 5-16: Search template for the "1901 Census of Canada."

The search results list contained one listing, and it was the right Gilbert Flynn. The "View Record" page showed a lot of information, including the names and ages of all the members of the household.

The excerpt from the actual census page shows us a few things (see figure 5-17). First, the column headings are printed

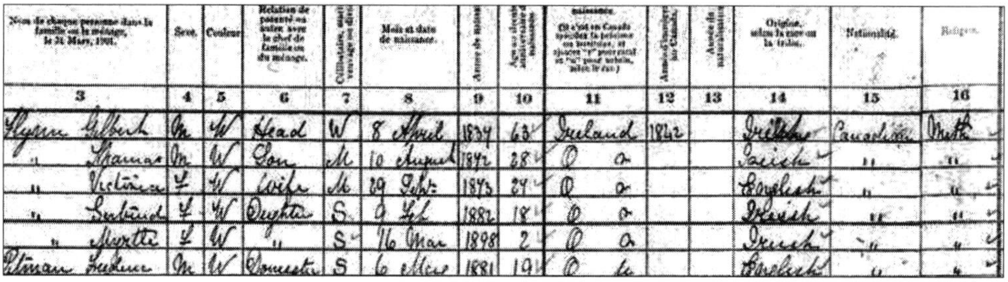

Figure 5-17: Portion of "1901 Census of Canada" image.

twice: first in English and then in French. We learn a great deal about Gilbert Flynn, including the fact that he was born in Ireland on 8 April 1837 and that he arrived in Canada in 1842. He is widowed, and he is a Methodist. His family appears to be living with him, as well as "Ferdine Pitman," who appears to be a live-in servant.

You will find other census databases at the Ancestry.ca site if you visit there, but the 1901, 1906, and 1911 Canadian censuses are as yet the only digitized census collections available.

Summary

The census collections we have explored are impressive. Their availability at Ancestry.com makes your research much simpler, and less expensive, than traveling to an archive to conduct research on-site. Ancestry.com adds more census materials as they become available, and you will see them announced.

In the last several chapters, we have concentrated on how to search for and through databases. We have covered the use of digital collections' images in extensive detail, and you have seen an abundance of page shots. In the following chapters concerning the different categories of records, we will concentrate more on the types of databases, their content, and how to apply it to your research, and less on the "how-to" of locating databases.

If you are still unsure about how to search for databases and records, and how to manipulate the digitized images, you will want to review the previous chapters and practice. Otherwise, we're off to discuss birth, marriage, death, and other related records in chapter 6.

Birth, Marriage, and Death Records

Births, christenings, *bar mitzvahs/bat mitzvahs*, marriages, divorces, adoptions, deaths, and burials—and all the possible evidentiary records and materials that document these important life events—are the keys to building context for our ancestors. We want to know *who* they were; *where* they were born; where they *immigrated* from; what their *full names* were, as well as those of their *parents* and *siblings*; *who* and *when* they married; *where* they lived at every point in their lives; what their *occupation* was; if they performed *military service*; what *religious affiliation* they had; *where* and *when* they died; and *where* are they buried.

In this and the following chapters, we will look at the wide range of records that Ancestry.com provides that can help answer all of these questions. We will focus on birth, marriage, and death records here. Americans refer to these as "vital records" or "vital statistics" and English refer to them as "civil records" or "civil registration records."

You already know how to search for, view, and work with records. Therefore, we will concentrate from this point forward on representative databases in each of the major record categories. We will explore what is available and how these records can be applied to your own research goals. Once you have delved into some of these databases, you should have little or no trouble working with others.

The Major Record Types

The Ancestry.com Birth, Marriage, and Death Records Collection contains a broad variety of records. This section explains some of the types of records you might find:

- **Birth**—Birth records usually show the child's name, gender, date and place born, parents' names, and sometimes other data, such as parents' birthplaces.

- **Marriage**—Marriage records usually show the names of the bride and groom, date and place married, and sometimes other information, such as their ages, place of residence, parents' names, officiating clergy or authorized government official, witnesses' names, and religious affiliation.

- **Death**—In addition to the name of the person, death records usually provide the marital status at the time of death (single, married, widowed, or divorced), cause of death, dates and places of death, name and location of mortuary, burial location or disposition of cremated remains, and sometimes the occupation, date and place of birth, age, parents' names and birthplaces (usually state and country/province/parish), and other useful information. The more recent the death record, the more information you will typically find. Some specific locations have death indexes that may help you pinpoint the date and location of a death, and then you may trace a death certificate and other death- and burial-related records.

- **Church**—Church records contain information about baptisms, marriages, burials, and membership. In addition to the name of the person, church records often provide information about family members.

- **Cemetery**—Some of the cemetery records included in the collection are tombstone inscriptions, burial permits, and death indexes. These records usually show names, birth and death dates, and occasionally additional personal information. Sometimes, they also include information on surviving family members.

- **Social Security Death Index**—The Social Security Death Index (SSDI) is a database that contains the names of deceased persons who applied for and were assigned Social Security numbers and whose deaths were reported to the Social Security Administration (SSA). These records usually include a full name, birth and death dates, and last known residence.

- **Obituaries**—The Obituary Collection contains recent obituaries (2001 to the present) from hundreds of newspapers. In addition to names, dates, places of birth, marriages, and deaths, an obituary often identifies deceased individuals' relationships with other individuals, burial or memorial service details, and other details of people's life events, affiliations, and achievements.

The information that you find in these records can be used as important evidence. Remember, however, that much of what you find in the databases are indexes or transcripts, and that you will want to obtain access to exact facsimile images of each record so that you can personally examine and analyze the data. Ancestry.com provides descriptive information and source citations for each of its databases, as you have already seen. These should provide you with sufficient information to track down the source materials and obtain the copies that you need to perform scholarly research.

Let's now examine some of the Ancestry.com birth, marriage, and death databases that will contribute to your research.

The Social Security Death Index (SSDI)

The SSDI is a compilation of information about deceased persons who filed for and received Social Security numbers, who were paid Social Security benefits at some point in their lives, and whose death was reported to the Social Security Administration (SSA). There are several key points you should bear in mind.

- Usually, a person whose name appears in the SSDI was employed, paid money into Social Security, and, at some time, applied for benefits of some sort. The two most common paid benefits were old age pension or disability benefits. If the person paid into Social Security, but never collected benefits, you will not find him or her in the file.

- The spouses of those who paid into Social Security, but who never worked and contributed to Social Security themselves, will not be included in the file unless they received their spouses' benefits after the spouses' death, and even this is not always true.

- Persons who worked for the railroad exclusively and did not work in another public sector will not be included in the SSDI. Those persons contributed to and collected from Railroad Retirement instead, a separate retirement security fund specifically for railroad workers. Only if the person also worked for a company not affiliated with the railroad will they appear in the SSDI, and they will appear with unique number (beginning with "7") assigned to railroad workers.

- If a person collected benefits at one time, but his or her death was not reported to Social Security, that person will not be included in the SSDI.

The SSDI contains over 80 million records—a number that increases every month—and the information in this database is, for the most part, reliable, and accurate. Remember, though, that information concerning an address or date of death may be incomplete or inaccurate depending on the information supplied by the person who reported the death.

Let's look at an example of a search of the SSDI. I searched for a record for Nora Cunningham, whose year of birth and state of residence I already knew.

Two of the women shown at the top of the "Ranked Search Results" list were born in 1888, but because I know that the family lived near Charlotte, in Mecklenburg County, North Carolina, I chose the second entry in the list (see figure 6-1). You will notice the familiar "View Record" link on the left side of the record. However, on the right you will see a shopping cart icon in a column labeled "Order Record." Let's look at each of these.

Ranked Search Results - Social Security Death Index
You searched for **Nora Cunningham** born in **1888** and died in **North Carolina** Refine your search

All Birth, Marriage, & Death Results   Show [All matches ▾]   Viewing **1-10** | Next »

Match Quality	View Record	Name	Birth Date	Death Date	Last Residence (City, County, State)	Order Record
☆☆☆☆☆	View Record	**Nora Cunningham**	18 Jun 1888	Feb 1975	Como, Hertford, North Carolina	🛒
☆☆☆☆☆	View Record	**Nora Cunningham**	21 Jul 1888	Jun 1980	Charlotte, Mecklenburg, North Carolina	🛒

Figure 6-1: "Ranked Search Results—Social Security Death Index" for Nora Cunningham.

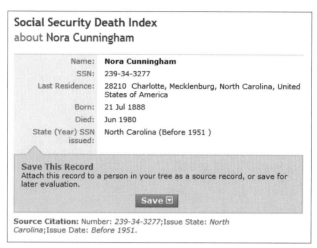

Social Security Death Index
about Nora Cunningham

Name:	**Nora Cunningham**
SSN:	239-34-3277
Last Residence:	28210 Charlotte, Mecklenburg, North Carolina, United States of America
Born:	21 Jul 1888
Died:	Jun 1980
State (Year) SSN issued:	North Carolina (Before 1951)

Save This Record
Attach this record to a person in your tree as a source record, or save for later evaluation.

Save ☑

Source Citation: Number: *239-34-3277;*Issue State: *North Carolina;*Issue Date: *Before 1951.*

Figure 6-2: "View Record" page for the Social Security Death Index.

When you click "View Record," you will see the familiar format of the record page (see figure 6-2). I did not know Nora's exact date of birth, but the record tells me she was born 21 July 1888. I now also know that her death date was in June of 1980. I can save the record to my Family Tree, or, if she was not in the tree, I could add her and the record to it. I also could save the record to my "Shoebox" for later review. There are, however, two important differences in the "Page Tools" section. The first is a link labeled "Order original certificate." In this case, Ancestry.com has formed an agreement with a company named VitalChek that acts as an intermediary to order copies of birth, marriage, divorce, and death certificates for you using your credit card. This is one method of obtaining an original copy of the document. You can also contact the county directly.

The other link in the "Page Tools" section is labeled "Request copy of original application." Clicking this link allows you to write a letter to the SSA to request a copy of the individual's original application for a Social Security number, which was done on a form numbered SS-5 (see figure 6-3 on the next page). The SS-5 contains information supplied by the applicant including name, date of birth, parents' names, place of residence, employer's name and address, and date of application. It can provide details that you may not otherwise have had or that can verify other evidence.

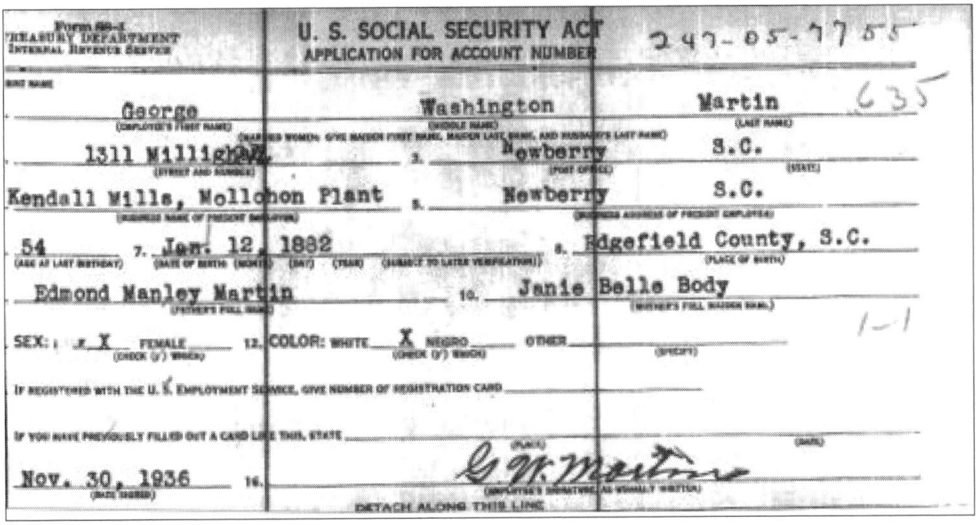

Figure 6-3: Sample SS-5 application form.

Clicking the link labeled "Click here to generate letter" will generate a pre-formatted letter to the Freedom of Information Officer at the SSA requesting a copy of the SS-5 for the individual. There is a cost associated with this request.

As you can see, there are many of components to the SSDI record. Let me suggest some ways to use the SSDI in your research.

- **Request a SS-5 Form**—The most helpful activity is to use the letter-generation facility and send off for the SS-5 form.

- **Locate Lost Relatives**—I have had success locating lost branches of the family and information about them by using the SSDI. For example, I found a letter from my grandmother's brother from the 1940s in which he said he was moving his family to Dayton, OH. An SSDI search of his name and Dayton, OH, located a number of records, and by checking the birth date, I was able to confirm his residence there and his date of death.

- **Confirm Dates**—I have often used the SSDI to search for a person when I was uncertain of a name or place of residence. When you locate his or her record, you can then check the birth date and compare it against what, if anything, you already have. You can also check the death date. If you need corroboration, you can write to the SSA for the SS-5 or write to the vital records agency in the county in which the person lived and seek a copy of a death certificate.

- **Discover Dates of Birth and Death**—You can use these dates to search for birth certificates, death records, obituaries, and other materials. Using the "Residence" and "Last Benefit" (if any listed) will help you focus on specific locations.

- **Locate a Residence**—I have often used the SSDI to locate the last residence of a specific relative, especially if I knew his or her date of birth. I simply enter the surname and given name, along with date or year of birth, and execute a search. This usually provides me with records to help me isolate the last residence address in the SSA's files. If not, I broaden the search. (If you don't get a match the first time, remember that the person may have gone by a middle name. Leave the given name blank and try again. Likewise, try alternate spellings of surnames. "Johansson" may have been spelled "Johanson" or "Johannson" or some other way. Be persistent!) In addition, the residence information may point you to other materials in a specific geographic area, such as land records, tax rolls, voter registration rolls, licenses, court records, newspapers, school records, church records, employment records, probate records, death certificates, obituaries, and a variety of other record types.

• **Find the Place Issued**—The state shown in the SSDI as the one where the SSN was issued may be a surprise to you. A check of the person's SS-5 form will confirm the place where the application was made and the SSN was issued. I have one ancestor whose issued location was shown in the SSDI as PA when I expected it to have been NC. On receipt of his SS-5, I found that he was working in PA in the late 1930s at the time he was required to obtain a SSN. This provided me with more details about his movements and employment history and pointed me toward research in geographical areas I would never have known to check.

A Sample Marriage Database: Maryland 1655–1850

You already know that from the **Search** tab you can click on the main category link and either search all the databases or browse through the scroll box and select a single one to search. I chose the second option and scrolled down to the database Maryland Marriages 1655–1850, highlighted it, and clicked **Search**. I was searching for a woman named Dorcas Alexander who married a man whose surname was McCoy in Cecil County, on the Eastern Shore of Maryland. A general search produced one match at the top of the "Ranked Search Results" page for a woman named Dorcas Alexander in Cecil County who married a Henry McCoy on 8 October 1790. I clicked on that and the record in figure 6-4 was displayed. Now,

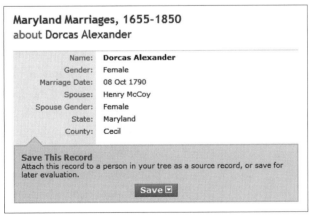

Figure 6-4: "Maryland Marriages 1655–1850" for Dorcas Alexander.

I have the information *and* the source citation information at the bottom of the page. According to the source information, original marriage licenses should be in the county clerk's office. I can now make contact with the courthouse in Cecil County, located in Elkton, Maryland, and request a copy of any marriage record the courthouse has on file.

Under the "Description" is more information about the database. It is important that you always click on any "Learn more …" link that you see because you can often find exceptionally valuable information. In this case, there is much more text, and it includes the Family History Library microfilm reference numbers (FHL # 0013866) for the records in all the counties, including Cecil County, and marriage records referenced in this database. I now also have the option to visit a local LDS Family History Center to view the film and print a copy of the original marriage record. This can save me from writing a letter to the Cecil County, Maryland, county clerk's office, taking a trip there, or going to the FHL in Salt Lake City.

The Ancestry.com Obituary Collection

The Obituary Collection at Ancestry.com is an important resource that gives you access to obituaries from recent years. These obituaries come from hundreds of newspapers. The service scours the Internet daily to find new obituaries and extract the facts into the database. It also provides source information and links to the full obituary text. If you are searching for a recently deceased ancestor, a living relative who might be mentioned in an obituary, or former classmates or neighbors, this is an excellent resource to begin your search.

As an example, I performed a search for Allen C. McSween in Anderson, South Carolina.

The first match in the "Ranked Search Results" page shows the only Allen C. McSween in Anderson, SC (see figure 6-5).

When I click on this record, it shows me the familiar "View Record" page, which includes a great deal of information from Allen's obituary, such as the date of his death, his age (which I can use to estimate a year of birth), the name of the newspaper and publication date, as well as other locations and people mentioned in the obituary. A source citation is also shown under the main box.

I can save the record to my Family Tree or to my "Shoebox." I can also click on the link labeled "View full obituary" (see figure 6-6). The obituary shows a great deal of data. Every reference to the first name is highlighted in blue and every mention of the surname is highlighted in yellow. Allen C. McSween, it turns out, was a Presbyterian minister, and his obituary

Match Quality	Record Type	Information found in record
★★★★★	United States Obituary Collection Birth, Marriage, & Death	Name: **Allen C. McSween** Other: Kathy Dillard "Bebe" McSween Birth: abt 1916 Death: 10 Jan 2000 Publication: 19 Feb 2004 - Anderson, SC, US
★★★★★	United States Obituary Collection Birth, Marriage, & Death	Name: **Allen C. McSween** Birth: abt 1916 Death: 10 Jan 2000 Publication: 9 Nov 2003 - Quincy, MA, US

Figure 6-5: A portion of the "Ranked Search Results" for Allen C. McSween.

Rev. Dr. Allen C. McSween, *Clinton*

The Rev. Dr. Allen C. McSween, age 84, of Frampton Hall, died Monday, January 10, at the Kerr-Johnson Infirmary at Presbyterian Home.

He was born in Dillon, S.C., and was the son of the late Rev. Dr. John and Lina Washington Crews McSween.

Dr. McSween graduated from Presbyterian College in 1938, from which he received a Doctorate of Divinity degree in 1960. He graduated from Union Theological Seminary in Virginia and served as chaplain in World War II in Africa and Italy, where he received the Legion of Merit and Italian Medal of Honor. Dr. McSween served Presbyterian churches in Forest City, Lincolnton, Greensboro, and Mebane, N. C.

He retired in 1977 and served as interim pastor in the Clinton area. He was also the international chaplain of the Civitan Club, a former Kiwanian and a member of Phi Kappa Alpha fraternity.

He is survived by his wife of 59 years, Irene Dillard "Bebe" McSween of the home; three sons, the Rev. Dr. Allen C. McSween Jr. of Greenville, John Dillard McSween of Siler City, N.C., and Larry Dillard McSween of Semmes, Ala.; one daughter, Kathy McSween Ambrose of Knoxville, Tenn.; one sister, Carolyn McSween Webb of Clinton; and five grandchildren.

A private committal service will be held at 10:15 a.m. today in Rosemont Cemetery, followed by a memorial service at 11 a.m. at First Presbyterian Church of Clinton, S.C.

The family will receive friends after the service in the Fellowship Hall.

Figure 6-6: Portion of the obituary for Rev. Allen C. McSween.

provides great details about his education, career, and his family. There are references to the church where the memorial service was held and the cemetery where he was interred. Both of these will potentially point you to other records.

Banffshire, Scotland: Parish and Probate Records

There really are many different record types at Ancestry.com. If you have Scottish ancestors from Banffshire, one database of interest might be the "Banffshire, Scotland: Parish and Probate Records." It is part of a larger collection of historical parish and probate registers from the countries of England, Wales, Scotland, and Ireland. More than 15 million names in this collection come from the early 1500s to the late-1800s.

I selected the Banffshire database and did a search for James Macindoo. The search results list included the parish marriage record information for his marriage on 14 April 1600 to Jonet Paterson (see figure 6-7).

Figure 6-7: Record from the the "Banffshire, Scotland: Parish and Probate Records."

England & Wales, FreeBMD Birth Index: 1837–1983

Civil registration became law on 1 July 1837, shortly after Queen Victoria ascended the throne. It mandated that births,

marriages, and deaths be registered with a civil office in the
area where a person or family lived, but it took some time to
gain full compliance by the population of all of England and
Wales. The ledgers containing registrations of each type of
record are currently held at the Family Records Centre in
London. The original certificates of births, marriages, deaths,
adoptions, and divorces are held by the General Register
Office (GRO) and can be ordered in person at the Family
Records Centre at 1 Myddleton Street in London or at the
GRO website at <www.gro.gov.uk>.

The FreeBMD Indexes for Births, Marriages, and Deaths at
Ancestry.com consist of transcriptions of the hand-written, and
later type-written, alphabetical register ledgers at the GRO.
These were compiled every quarter after all the registry offices
provided copies of the certificates to the GRO. Therefore,
there are separate registers for each type of record, organized
into alphabetical sequence by year and quarter. (For example,
January/February/March is the first quarter.) The FreeBMD
Index database is searchable by name and quarter, district,
county, and other criteria. The search results are presented in
the familiar format with links labeled "View Record" and "View
Image." When you look at the record page, be certain to also
view the image to verify the accuracy of the transcription.

Let's try an example. Scroll to the database titled "England
& Wales, FreeBMD Birth Index: 1837–1983" in the scroll
box, highlight it, and click **Search**. When the search template
appears, perform an exact search for Alice Maud Vinson. That's
all the information you should enter into the template. Click
the **Search** button and then look at the search results list.
You should see two people named Alice Maud Vinson. One
was born in the third quarter of 1872 in St. Thomas, County
Devon, and the other was born in the first quarter of 1880

in Islington in Greater London, London, Middlesex. It is the second entry that we want to study. A click on the "View Record" link shows the data in figure 6-8.

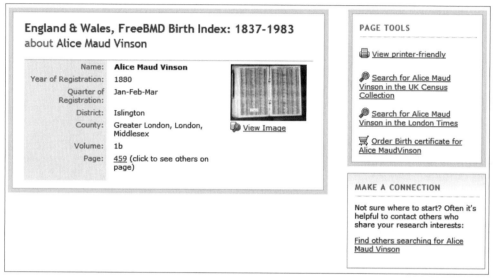

Figure 6-8: FreeBMD Birth Index record for Alice Maud Vinson.

As usual, you see information about Alice's birth. However, this time you see a "Volume 1b" and "Page 459." The year, quarter, district, county, volume, and page number are all essential in order to request a copy of the birth certificate.

Now, take a look at the various options in the "Page Tools" section. There are three new options which you have not seen before.

- **Search for Alice Maud Vinson in the UK Census Collection**—You can click here and the same type of search, ranked or exact, will be used to search the UK Census Collection. Note that if you start with an "Exact matches only" search, Alice will not be located. If you then change to a general search, the search engine will search for all variations of the name, including Alice M Vinson, and you will see that both of the Alice Maud Vinsons who appeared in our search results list are shown in the 1891 census, in Devon.

- **Search for Alice Maud Vinson in the *London Times*—**A click here will provide you with a very lengthy list of links in the *The Times* database. You may then have to search the digitized images of the newspaper to see if our Alice is mentioned in the text.

- **Order Birth Certificate for Alice Maud Vinson—**A click on this link will take you to the General Register Office website where you may order a copy of Alice's birth certificate. (On your first visit to this site, you must set up a free ID and password. After that, you can use that to access your name and address profile for future orders.) Be sure you have all the information mentioned before because you will be prompted to provide specific data in order for the GRO to locate the right record and copy it for you.

Summary

You should have seen as we explored the Birth, Marriage, and Death Records Collection of databases that there is a wealth of information from many geographical areas.

In each database, you've seen that one record may well include information that can lead us to one or many additional records of various types. The more you learn about available record types, the more creative you will become in locating multiple independent source evidences. Additionally, the more exploration you do to see what databases and contents are available for a given area or record type, the more ideas you will get.

Spend some time practicing with different databases, whether you have ancestors in the area or not. This work will continue to build your searching skills and make you familiar with the various search options available to you.

Chapter 7

Family Facts

Placing your ancestors into geographical and historical context is one of the thrills of genealogical research. These people were not isolated, and they should be more to you than just names and dates on a computer page or a printed page. Some of the best clues to help you in your quest are the statistical and contextual leads found in a wide variety of places.

Ancestry.com has compiled a fascinating, searchable Family Facts archive. You can learn about the meaning of your surname, the distribution of people by surname, life expectancy, and much more.

You can access the Family Facts archive from the **Learning Center** tab. You will see the category labeled "Family Facts" just under the "Search the Library" template. When you click there, the page shown in figure 7-1 (on page 132) is displayed.

You can select specific facts to search by either clicking on the fact type in the "Facts" section, which leads to a new page, or by entering a last name in the field shown, selecting a fact

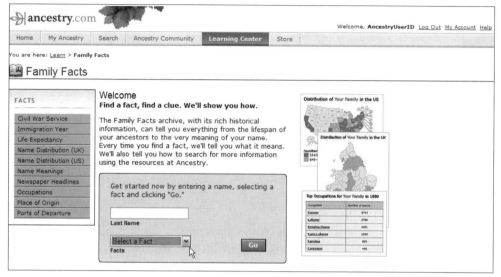

Figure 7-1: The main "Family Facts" page.

type from the drop-down list, and clicking **Go**. We're going to explore each of the individual pages using the surname Adams, just to show you what they look like.

To start, click "Civil War Service" in the "Facts" section and type "adams"; then click **Update**. For each new fact type you click in the "Facts" section, a new page is displayed. Information about each of these, with corresponding page shots, follows.

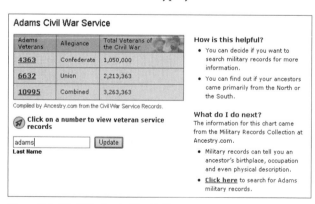

Figure 7-2: "Civil War Service" family facts.

Civil War Service

On the "Civil War Service" page, you can learn about how people with the surname you chose (in this case, "Adams") served in the Civil War (see figure 7-2). Note the number of Adams veterans by allegiance—Confederate, Union, and Combined. Each of the numbers is a link you can click to display a search results list for all persons whose surname is Adams from the Civil War Service database. Each result has a "View Record" link. The "Civil War Service" page also offers suggestions as to why the data on this page might be helpful to your research.

- You can decide if you want to search military records for more information.

- You can find out if your ancestors came primarily from the North or the South.

You may then want to search the Military Records databases for additional records. Military records can tell you an ancestor's birthplace, occupation and even physical description. A link will take you to the "Search Military Records" page.

Immigration Year

Ancestry.com has statistically analyzed the persons whose surname is Adams in their New York Passenger Lists database and a line graph is displayed to indicate its findings (see figure 7-3). You can tell, year by year, how many Adamses immigrated to the United States. This graph can help you to focus your efforts on searching immigration records for a particular period. You can click on one of the year circles

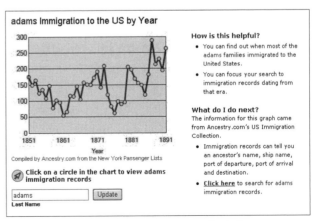

Figure 7-3: "Immigration Year to the US by Year" family facts.

on the graph to display a search results list of all the persons named Adam or Adams, in alphabetical sequence by first name and then in chronological sequence of arrival. Another link in the lower right of the page will take you to the "Search Immigration Records" page.

Life Expectancy

The Life Expectancy page consists of a chart compiled by Ancestry.com from the Social Security Death Index (SSDI) of the age when persons listed in that database died (see figure 7-4). You may click on one of the year circles to see specific search results about persons named Adams, in alphabetical sequence by year of death. This may be a helpful way to view the SSDI data, but you can also click on the link in the lower right of the page to go to the "Search the Social Security Death Index" page.

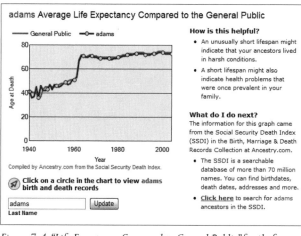

Figure 7-4: "Life Expectancy Compared to General Public" family facts.

Name Distribution (UK and U.S.)

It is always interesting to discover the geographical origins of a particular surname and the density of the name in those areas. Ancestry.com has used both the 1891 England and Wales censuses, and the 1840, 1880, and 1920 United States Federal Census records to perform analyses of the United Kingdom and the United States in those respective years (see figures 7-5 and 7-6 on the next page). (You can select "1840," "1880," or "1920" from the drop-down list on the U.S. page to see the respective maps and surname distributions.)

This may help you focus your search for ancestors and relatives in particular UK counties or U.S. states.

Name Meanings

The origins and meanings of names can be especially interesting. Many of our ancestors used repetitive naming patterns that were traditional in their national or ethnic backgrounds. Others used names that had special meanings to them.

Ancestry.com has produced a Family Facts page for name meanings (see figure 7-7 on page 136). You may enter a first or last name to obtain definitions. The sources of the information are *A Dictionary of First Names* and the *Dictionary of American Family Names*, both published by the Oxford University Press. For this example, I also typed in the first name "Jean."

Not only are the origins of the names provided, but possible alternate names or spellings may be included. You

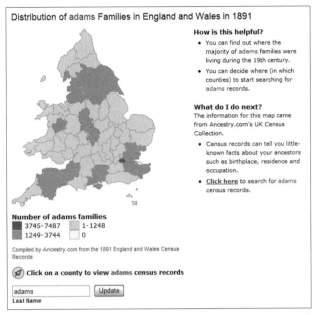

Figure 7-5: "Distribution of Families in the England and Wales in 1891" family facts.

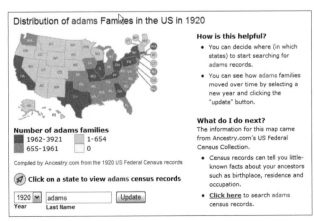

Figure 7-6: "Distribution of Families in the US in 1920" family facts.

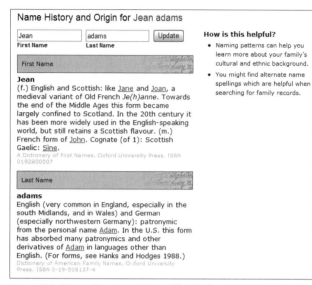

Figure 7-7: "Name History and Origin" family facts.

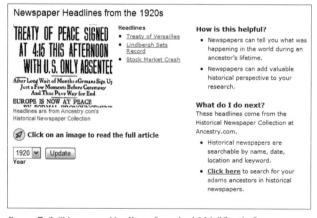

Figure 7-8: "Newspaper Headlines from the 1920s" family facts.

can click on the links to other names to learn more about them as well.

Newspaper Headlines

Placing your ancestors into historical context can be exciting. You probably want to know what was happening on a certain date in your ancestor's lifetime, or about a particularly noteworthy historical event and its potential influence on your ancestor. The "Newspaper Headlines" page, shown in figure 7-8, is a resource for this type of research.

Note that this is not a name-based page. Instead, a drop-down list allows you to select a decade. All of the newspapers are from the Historic Newspaper Collection at Ancestry.com, which we will examine in detail in chapter 10. You can click on a link under the sample newspaper headline to see a specific decade, or you may click on the link in the lower right of the page to go to the "Search Newspaper and Periodical Records" page.

Occupation

What was the number one occupation of heads of households as indicated in the 1880 United States Federal Census population schedules? The answer is not too surprising: farmer. However, Ancestry.com analyzed the 1880 census for the general public *and* for the surname Adams, revealing that 35% of the heads of household were farmers, while 38% of the household heads named Adams

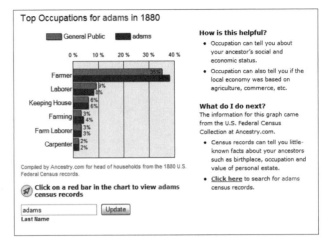

Figure 7-9: *"Top Occupations in 1800" family facts.*

were farmers (see figure 7-9). Knowing something about the occupations of persons with a specific surname in the 1880 census may give you a clue of other places to look for records, such as land and property records or tax records.

Place of Origin

At some point, you'll want to trace your ancestors to their place of nativity. The "Top Places of Origin" page is a great place to start your search (see figure 7-10). You might not know where your Adams ancestor came from, but this analysis of the New York Passenger Lists database indicates that the large majority came from England.

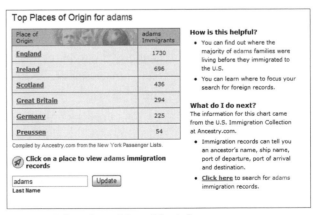

Figure 7-10: *"Top Places of Origin" family facts.*

You can click on any of the locations to view the New York Passenger List search results, which is organized according to surname by the place of origin specified on the manifest.

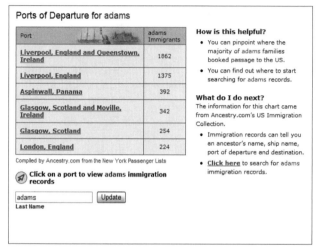

Figure 7-11: "Ports of Departure" family facts.

Ports of Departure

In addition to the place of origin, you will certainly be interested in determining the port from which your ancestors left their homeland to immigrate to America. The "Ports of Departure" page shows a chart representing the primary European ports from which immigrants had departed, as shown in the New York Passenger Lists database (see figure 7-11). Be aware that different groups emigrated from different countries in different concentrations at different times, so the information in this graph may be skewed by using the records of only one port of arrival. However, the data provides an interesting set of places to start your research. Remember, too, that some continental Europeans first went to England or Ireland where they changed ships to continue their immigration to the United States.

You can click on the pie chart to view immigration records for the surname you are searching.

Summary

The Family Facts Collection provides sets of interesting statistics for consideration as you perform your research. You will want to check back here periodically as you perform different types of research. Ancestry.com continues to update and expand this area for your reference.

Chapter 8

Family and Local Histories

Some of the most valuable resources available to you are historical books and manuscripts concerning your family history or that of the local areas in which your ancestors lived. The family histories may have been penned or published by other family members or by historians researching and documenting the area or the family. Local histories can provide geographical and historical context for the places your ancestors lived, and in some cases your ancestors will be mentioned by name. This is especially helpful in determining when they arrived at or departed from the area, as well as how they participated in local events. These publications can, of course, contain errors and omissions and therefore should be used mainly to provide clues and leads for your own personal search for original evidence.

The Family and Local Histories Collection includes more than 20,000 family and local histories, as well as a number of important reference resources.

In this chapter, we will explore both the search and browse functions of this database collection. We will also examine examples of a number of the historical reference works and how they may benefit your research. These include the following:

- A representative family history

- A representative local history

- The Biography and Genealogy Master List

- The American Genealogical-Biographical Index (AGBI)

- Slave narratives

- The Dawes Commission Index (1898–1914)

- The Dictionary of National Biography

While these examples only scratch the surface of the information available, they should give you a sense of the scope of the collection and encourage you to explore it for all of your family lines.

Searching and Browsing the Collection

The most direct way to access the Family and Local Histories Collection is to click the **Search** tab, and then click the link labeled "Family and Local Histories" in the "Browse Records" section. The "Search Family & Local History Records" page is displayed with a search template, a list of featured databases, and a method to browse databases by title. Remember, too, that the "Ancestry Database Card Catalog" facility can also be used to locate databases, including those in this collection.

The search template is already familiar to you. It provides the option to conduct a general or exact search. The Soundex option on the exact search template will help locate alternate spellings of surnames found in both the titles and contents of the histories. As you can imagine, names are often misspelled or alternately spelled in these historical records. Soundex allows you to search for last names that sound like the one you're looking for. Try this even if you think the spelling is obvious. Remember, even Smith can be spelled in a number of ways.

If you wish to browse the collection, scroll down the page to the section labeled "Search Individual Family & Local History Databases," and you will see a link to the "Volume Titles" (see figure 8-1).

Figure 8-1: Search through volume titles.

You may jump to a letter of the alphabet that represents a word in the title of the work. Once you arrive there, you can click on one of the two-letter groups to narrow your browsing, and below that you can click on three- or four-letter groups to further narrow your browse. In the example shown in figure 8-1, I selected "B," then "Ba," and then "Bal" for my browsing. At the bottom of the list is a drop-down menu labeled "Results per page" that allows you to specify 10, 20, or 50 results to be displayed at a time. Every time you browse like this, the total number of records is shown at the top and bottom of the list. In this example, records 1–10 of 133 are displayed in my list, and I can click "Next" to proceed to the next group of 10 (or whatever number I have specified in the drop-down menu).

Each record displayed in the list has two ways to access it. The first is the small page icon at the left, and the second is the underlined hyperlink in the record's name, which is the word in the title that fell within the group of alphabetical browsing that you performed. When you click on either link, a new page is displayed. It contains a template that allows you to search for a specific name within either this title *or* in the entire Family & Local Histories Collection. Simply enter your search criteria and click the **Search** button.

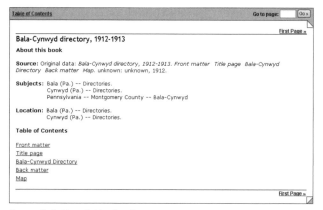

Figure 8-2: Detailed book information.

In this example, I selected the "Bala-Cynwyd directory, 1912–1913," which is a city directory for a community in Pennsylvania (see figure 8-2). (You can also learn about Bala-Cynwyd by searching for it in your favorite search engine. One result of interest is an historical overview at <www.balacynwyd. org/Bala_Cynwyd/History.html>). The "About this book" section includes source information, which can be used to produce your source citation for this resource. Under the Subject and Location categories are key search terms used in your public library's electronic catalog. They are indexed entries that allow you to search more precisely for the best matches.

The links listed under the "Table of Contents" are direct links to areas of the book, which in this case is a city directory. You can click on any of these links to display the digitized image of the page in the Enhanced Image Viewer discussed in chapter 3. You can also click either of the "First Page" links to go to the first page of the book, or you can enter a specific page number in the "Go to page:" field. This is helpful when you have a digitized book with a table of contents or index and you wish to go directly to a referenced page.

Exploring Different Types of Books from the Collection

The Family and Local Histories Collection is fully indexed, with search tools that are very helpful in locating appropriate materials. Some materials consist of digitized images of books or documents, while others are textual representations of the content of the resource. So in order to provide a feeling for the different types of materials, let's look at some examples of the histories contained in this database collection.

A Family History

Published family histories can provide many insights and clues for your research. One of the family lines I am researching is the Ball family of Virginia, which includes Mary Ball, who married Augustine Washington and became the mother of George Washington.

On the "Search Family & Local History Records" page (see page 142), I performed a ranked search for Mary Ball and entered the keyword "Virginia" in order to narrow my search. My search results list is shown in figure 8-3 on page 146.

The familiar "Ranked Search Results" page is displayed, complete with star ratings of relevance. I selected the fourth record, *Virginia Prominent Families, Vol. 1–4*, for my research. When I click on this link, a new page containing an extract from the book is displayed (see figure 8-4 on page 146). My search term, Mary Ball, appears in bold so that I can easily see both instances.

The extract cites "Volume 4." From this page, I can view a printer-friendly version of this item, locate other people who

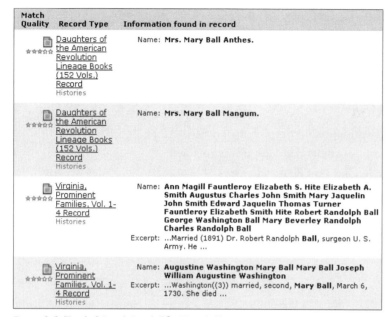

Match Quality	Record Type	Information found in record
★★★★☆	Daughters of the American Revolution Lineage Books (152 Vols.) Record *Histories*	Name: **Mrs. Mary Ball Anthes.**
★★★★☆	Daughters of the American Revolution Lineage Books (152 Vols.) Record *Histories*	Name: **Mrs. Mary Ball Mangum.**
★★★★☆	Virginia, Prominent Families, Vol. 1-4 Record *Histories*	Name: **Ann Magill Fauntleroy Elizabeth S. Hite Elizabeth A. Smith Augustus Charles John Smith Mary Jaquelin John Smith Edward Jaquelin Thomas Turner Fauntleroy Elizabeth Smith Hite Robert Randolph Ball George Washington Ball Mary Beverley Randolph Charles Randolph Ball**
		Excerpt: ...Married (1891) Dr. Robert Randolph **Ball**, surgeon U. S. Army. He ...
★★★★☆	Virginia, Prominent Families, Vol. 1-4 Record *Histories*	Name: **Augustine Washington Mary Ball Mary Ball Joseph William Augustine Washington**
		Excerpt: ...Washington((3)) married, second, **Mary Ball**, March 6, 1730. She died ...

Figure 8-3: "Ranked Search Results" for Mary Ball.

are researching Mary Ball, and learn more about the Ball families and where they lived in 1880. A click on the "Learn more" link will take you to the "Name Distribution" area of the Family Facts databases we discussed in chapter 7.

If you click on the link labeled "View Full Context," you will be presented with a text representation of the contents of that record. I have selected a portion of that from the database, and it is shown in figure 8-5 on the next page.

As you can see, there is a great deal of genealogical information here to review, including Mary Ball's birth, marriage, and death dates, and information about the date

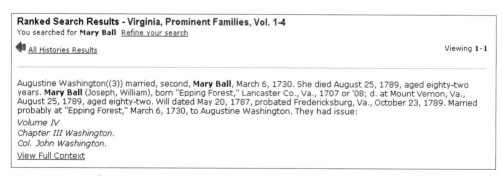

Ranked Search Results - Virginia, Prominent Families, Vol. 1-4
You searched for **Mary Ball** Refine your search

◀ All Histories Results   Viewing **1-1**

Augustine Washington((3)) married, second, **Mary Ball**, March 6, 1730. She died August 25, 1789, aged eighty-two years. **Mary Ball** (Joseph, William), born "Epping Forest," Lancaster Co., Va., 1707 or '08; d. at Mount Vernon, Va., August 25, 1789, aged eighty-two. Will dated May 20, 1787, probated Fredericksburg, Va., October 23, 1789. Married probably at "Epping Forest," March 6, 1730, to Augustine Washington. They had issue:

Volume IV
Chapter III Washington.
Col. John Washington.
View Full Context

Figure 8-4: Extract from the book.

Augustine Washington((3)) married, second, Mary Ball, March 6, 1730. She died August 25, 1789, aged eighty-two years. Mary Ball (Joseph, William), born "Epping Forest," Lancaster Co., Va., 1707 or '08; d. at Mount Vernon, Va., August 25, 1789, aged eighty-two. Will dated May 20, 1787, probated Fredericksburg, Va., October 23, 1789. Married probably at "Epping Forest," March 6, 1730, to Augustine Washington. They had issue:

I. George Washington, first president of the United States, b. Feb. 22, 1732, in Westmoreland Co., Va.; d. Dec. 14, 1799, s. p. aged sixty-seven. Married (Jan. 6, 1759)Martha, daughter of John Dandridge and widow of Daniel Parke Custis, of New Kent Co., Va., b. May, 1732; d. May 22, 1802, aged seventy years.

II. Elizabeth Washington, b. June 20, 1733. Married Col. Fielding Lewis.

III. Samuel Washington, b. Nov. 16, 1734; d. 1781, aged forty-seven years, in Berkeley Co., Va. Married, first, Jane Champe; second, Mildred Thornton; third, Lucy Chapman; fourth, Anne Steptoe.

IV. John Augustine Washington, of Westmoreland Co., Va., b. Jan. 13, 1735; d. 1787, aged fifty-two. Married Hannah, daughter of John Bushrod, Westmoreland Co.

V. Charles Washington, b. May 1, 1738. Married Mildred, daughter of Francis Thornton.

VI. Mildred Washington, b. June 22; d. Oct. 28, 1740.

Figure 8-5: A portion of the "Full Content" page.

and the filing of her will. Details of her six children are also listed. All of this information is pertinent to my research on that branch of the Ball family's descendants, and the clues here point me to search for original documents and other evidentiary sources.

A Local History

You can search or browse for histories of geographical areas. As an example, I browsed through the letter "F" in order to locate any histories that might exist for Floyd County, Georgia— another area where I had ancestors. There were several entries, but I chose George Magruder Battey's *A history of Rome and Floyd County, State of Georgia, United States of America*, published in 1922 (see figure 8-6 on page 148).

It would be interesting to know about the earlier days, so I clicked the section, "Part II. 'Ancient Rome' 1834–1861. Chapter I. Rome's establishment and early days." I can view the image of a page, save it to either my computer or my "Shoebox" on Ancestry.com, or e-mail the image, but it isn't possible to perform any of these tasks for an entire chapter, section, or book. Since I am interested in reading this chapter in Part II, I clicked on the link and the page was displayed in the Enhanced Image Viewer. I can enlarge the image or make it

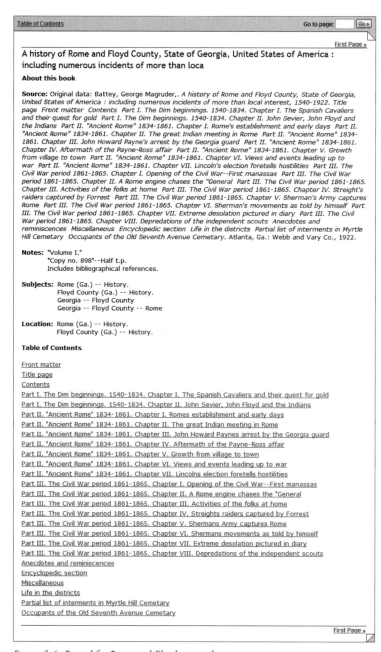

Figure 8-6: Record for Rome and Floyd county history.

smaller as I want. Figure 8-7 gives you a sense of the quality of an individual page.

Let's say I am interested in searching the book for any references to my Holder ancestors. I can use the "Exact matches only …" search to seek references to that surname. In the resulting search results page, I can click on each link to proceed to the page on which the name appears and read the references there.

As you can see, the value of using a published local history can not only help you learn about and better understand the environment in which your ancestors lived, it can also be searched for references to a specific surname or person.

Biography and Genealogy Master Index (BGMI)

CHAPTER I.

Rome's Establishment and Early Days

IN THE spring of 1834 two lawyers were traveling on horseback from Cassville, Cass County, to attend court at Livingston, the county seat of Floyd. They were Col. Daniel R. Mitchell, a lawyer of Canton, Cherokee County, and Col. Zachariah B. Hargrove, Cassville attorney, formerly of Covington, Newton County. The day was warm and the travelers hauled up at a small spring on the peninsula which separates the Etowah and the Oostanaula rivers at their junction. Here they slaked their thirst and sat down under a willow tree to rest before proceeding on their way.

Col. Hargrove gazed in admiration on the surrounding hills and remarked: "This would make a splendid site for a town."

"I was just thinking the same," returned his companion. "There seems to be plenty of water round about and extremely fertile soil and all the timber a man could want."

A stranger having come up to refresh himself at the spring, and having overheard the conversation, said: "Gentlemen, you will pardon me for intruding, but I have been convinced for some time that the location of this place offers exceptional opportunities for building a city that would become the largest and most prosperous in Cherokee Georgia. I live two miles south of here. My business takes me now and then to George M. Lavender's trading post up the Oostanaula there, and I never pass this spot but I think of what could be done."

The last speaker introduced himself as Maj. Philip Walker Hemp-

hill, planter. Learning the mission of the travelers, he added: "The court does not open until tomorrow afternoon. You gentlemen are no doubt fatigued by your journey, and it will give me great pleasure if you will accompany me home and spend the night. There we can discuss the matter of locating a town at this place."

Col. Mitchell and Col. Hargrove accepted with thanks. The three left the spring (which still runs under Broad street at the southeast corner of Third Avenue), crossed the Etowah River on John Ross' "Forks Ferry," and proceeded with Major Hemphill to his comfortable plantation home at what is now DeSoto Park. Here they went into the question more deeply. A cousin of Maj. Hemphill, Gen. James Hemphill, who lived about ten miles down Vann's Valley, had recently been elected to the Georgia legislature, and could no doubt bring about a removal of the county site from Livingston to Rome; he was also commanding officer of the Georgia Militia in the section.

After court was over, Col. Mitchell and Col. Hargrove spent another night with Maj. Hemphill, and the next morning Col. Wm. Smith was called in from Cave Spring, and became the fourth member of the company. It was there agreed that all available land would be acquired immediately, the ferry rights would be bought and the ground laid off in lots. Gen. Hemphill was requested to confer with his compatriots at Milledgeville and draw up a bill for removal. The projectors would give sufficient land for the public buildings and in time would make the ferries free and cause neces-

Figure 8-7: Page from local history book.

Millions of Americans have been profiled in collective biography volumes such as *Who's Who in America* and *Women of Science*. The *Biography and Genealogy Master Index* was created in the 1970s to index these names. The text has been updated periodically since the first edition appeared in 1980, most recently printed in March 2003. The index, compiled by Mirana C. Herbert and Barbara McNeil, concentrates heavily on the nineteenth and twentieth centuries. In addition to providing the individual's name, birth, and death dates (where available), the source document is also included. Sources for this index vary from *Who's Who of American Women* and *National Cyclopedia* to *American Biography*, *Directory of American Scholars*, and *American Black Writers*. This database is an essential tool for locating persons who appeared in a "Who's Who" publication in the nineteenth and early twentieth centuries.

To provide an example for you, I performed a search for my first cousin, once removed, named Alvis Weatherly. The search results I received are shown in figure 8-8.

Name: Weatherly, Alvis Morrison, Jr.
Birth - Death: 1925-
Source Citation:

- Who's Who in America(R) (Marquis(TM)). 56th edition, 2002. New Providence, NJ: Marquis Who's Who, 2001. (WhoAm 56)
- Who's Who in America(R) (Marquis(TM)). 57th edition, 2003. New Providence, NJ: Marquis Who's Who, 2002. (WhoAm 57)
- Who's Who in America(R) (Marquis(TM)). 58th edition, 2004. New Providence, NJ: Marquis Who's Who, 2003. (WhoAm 58)
- Who's Who in the World(R) (Marquis(TM)). 21st edition, 2004. New Providence, NJ: Marquis Who's Who, 2003. (WhoWor 21)

Figure 8-8: Portion of the search results for Biography and Genealogy Master Index.

Once you have located one or more entries, you can work with your library to locate a copy of the publication or request an Interlibrary Loan photocopy of the entry for the individual. This is a great way to obtain additional information on a person's life activities and can point you to other organizations and locations for additional evidence sources.

American Genealogical-Biographical Index (AGBI)

One of the most important genealogical collections, the "American Genealogical-Biographical Index," or AGBI, is the equivalent of more than 200 printed volumes. This database contains millions of records of people whose names have appeared in printed genealogical records and family histories. With data from sources largely from the last century, each entry contains the person's complete name, and birth date and place, as well as the year of the biography's publication, abbreviated biographical data, and the book and page number of the original reference. In addition to family histories, other genealogical collections are indexed. These include the *Boston Transcript* (a genealogical column widely circulated), the complete 1790 U.S. Federal Census, and published Revolutionary War records. The most recent update to this database reflects the inclusion of volumes 196–206. For researchers of American ancestors, this can be one of the most valuable databases available at Ancestry.com.

Most of the works referenced in the AGBI are housed at the Godfrey Memorial Library in Connecticut. A photocopy service is available. Contact Godfrey Memorial Library at 134 Newfield St, Middletown, CT 06457 or via e-mail to <referenceinfo@godfrey.org>.

For this example, I chose the name of John Davidson, who I know was born in Maryland and who was an officer in the Continental Army during the American Revolution. I performed a ranked search for him, and four search results displayed. I selected one, shown in figure 8-9.

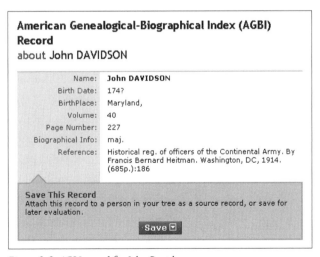

Figure 8-9: AGBI record for John Davidson.

The page displayed shows a record for a publication by Francis Bernard Heitman titled *Historical Register of Officers of the Continental Army*, published in Washington, DC, in 1914. The record shows that Davidson's information is in Volume 40 on page 227. With this information, I can work with my library to process an Interlibrary Loan request for a photocopy of the information. This should provide me with additional military service information, and then I would undoubtedly order copies of military service and pension records from the National Archives and Records Administration (NARA).

Slave Narratives

During the Great Depression of the 1930s in the United States, the Works Project Administration (WPA), an agency of the federal government, commissioned a project to record the experiences of Americans from many walks of life. Perhaps no other resource approaches the range of human experience found in the Slave Narratives at Ancestry.com. The collection contains over 20,000 pages of type-scripted interviews with more than 3,500 former slaves, which was collected over a ten-year period.

In 1929, an effort began at Fisk University in Tennessee and Southern University in Louisiana to document the life stories of these former slaves. Kentucky State College continued the work in 1934, and from 1936 to 1939, the Federal Writer's Project (a federal work project that was a part of the New Deal) launched a national effort to collect narratives from former slaves. This database provides a poignant picture of what it was like to live as a slave in the American South. This collection is the most complete available picture of the African-American experience with slavery.

You can search the database using ranked search and exact search, or you can browse it by category using the drop-down list, which includes the following options:

- Famous Personalities

- Folk Medicine, Herbs

- Ghost Stories

- Religious Experiences

- Runaway Slaves

- Songs and Hymns

- Voting

- War Stories

Figure 8-10 shows a representative sampling of extracts from the typewritten transcripts of the recorded interviews concerning voting. You can click on the "View Full Context" link to read more.

State: Alabama   **Interviewee:** Daniel, Matilda Pugh

"Durin' de war us warn't bothered much, but atter de surrender, some po' white trash tried to make us take some lan'. Some of 'em come to de slave quarters, an' talk to us. Dey say 'Niggers, you is jus' as good as de white folks. You is 'titled to vote in de 'lections an' to have money same as dey,' but most of us didn't pay no 'tention to 'em.

<u>View Full Context</u>

State: Alabama   **Interviewee:** Garry, Henry

"Git rid of de carpetbaggers? Oh, Yassah, dey vote 'em out. Well sah, tell you how dey done dat. De 'publicans done paid all de niggers' poll tax, an' gib 'em a receipt so dey could vote same as de whites. Dey made up to 'lect de officers at de co'te house all niggers an' den sen' yuther ones to Montgomery to make de laws. Same day de 'lection come off dar was a circus in Livingston an' de Demmycrats 'suaded de boss man of de circus to let all Sumter County niggers in de show by showin' dere poll tax receipts. Yessah, when de show was ober de 'lection was ober too, an' nobody was 'lected 'cepin' white Demmycrats.

<u>View Full Context</u>

Figure 8-10: Portion of the Slave Interview results list.

Dawes Commission Index

The Dawes Commission, commonly called the Commission to the Five Civilized Tribes, was appointed by U.S.

President Grover Cleveland in 1893. It was named after its chairman, Henry L. Dawes. In return for abolishing their tribal governments and recognizing state and federal laws, tribal members of the so-called Five Civilized Tribes—the Cherokee, Creek, Choctaw, Chickasaw, and Seminole—were given a share of common property. This database indexes the original applications for tribal enrollments under the act of 28 June 1898. It also indexes documents such as birth and death affidavits, marriage licenses, and decisions and orders of the Commission.

The rolls contain more than 101,000 names recorded between 1898 and 1914 (primarily from 1899 to 1906). They can be searched to discover the enrollee's name, gender, blood degree, and census card number. The census card may provide additional genealogical information and may also contain references to earlier rolls, such as the 1880 Cherokee census. A census card is generally accompanied by a file referred to as an "application jacket." These jackets sometimes contain valuable supporting documentation, such as birth and death affidavits, marriage licenses, and correspondence. The original documents are in the possession of the National Archives and Records Administration (NARA). Today these five tribes continue to use the Dawes rolls as the basis for determining tribal membership. Applicants are typically required to provide proof of descent from a person who is listed on these rolls.

My search example is for Billy Bowlegs, a Seminole chief who also was related to Chief Micanopy. When Billy Bowlegs finally relented and moved west to the reservation in Oklahoma, he was interviewed under oath and gave officials information about his enrollment in the Five Civilized Tribes. One of his records is shown in figure 8-11 on the next page.

```
Control Number: NRFF-75-53A-25372
Unit of Description: Item
Record Group Number: 75
Series ID: 53A
Item ID: 25372
Title: Enrollment for Billy Bowlegs
General Materials Designator Record Type: Textual Records
Reference Unit: National Archives--Southwest Region
Agency Name: National Archives and Records Administration
Facility Name: Building 1, Dock 1
Address: 501 West Felix Street
City: Fort Worth
State: TX
Zip Code: 76115
Telephone Number: 817-334-5525
Fax Number: 817-334-5621
Organizational Code: NRFF
Creating Organization: Commissioner to the Five Civilized Tribes, Bureau of Indian Affairs.
Scope and Content: Tribe: Seminole
Type: Parent
Sex: Male
Census Card Number: 384
City of Residence: SB
Personal Name Reference: Billy Bowlegs
Item Count/Item Type: item(s) |c 1
Source Project: Kiosk
View Full Context
```

Figure 8-11: Dawes Commission Index for Billy Bowlegs.

Billy Bowlegs went on to enlist as a captain in the Union Army in 1862 and was assigned command of Company A of the First Indian Home Guards. He died in 1864 of smallpox and was buried in the Officers' Circle of the Fort Gibson National Cemetery in Fort Gibson, Oklahoma, not far from Muskogee.

The index record at Ancestry.com provides details for ordering copies of the application file, or "jacket" from the NARA Branch in Ft. Worth, Texas. The information on the application, recorded narrative testimony, and copies of documentation can be essential for your Native American research.

Dictionary of National Biography

The *Dictionary of National Biography* began in 1882 as an ambitious project spearheaded by George Smith to produce a biographical dictionary of prominent British and Irish figures from the earliest of times up to 1900. The efforts of hundreds of contributors resulted in a 22 volume alphabetical series containing thousands of biographies. This database contains Volumes 1–20, and 22 of this series, which includes the biographies of those with surnames from Abbadie to Whewell. It also contains *The Concise Dictionary*, which is a summary guide and index to the rest of the series, and also the *Supplement*, which deals with people who died too late to be included in the earlier volumes. Queen Victoria, who died in 1901, is included in the *Supplement*.

Most people are familiar with the classics, *Alice's Adventures in Wonderland* and *Through the Looking Glass*, by English author Lewis Carroll. However, this was not his real name; it was a *nom de plume* for his writing.

I performed an Exact Search for Lewis Carroll in this database. There were four references listed in the search results list shown in figure 8-12.

View Record	Title	Chapter	Section	Page	View Image
Lewis Carroll	Index	Dictionary of National Biography	C	209	
Lewis Carroll	Index	Dictionary of National Biography	D	347	
Lewis Carroll	Supplement	Dictionary of National Biography Supplement	D	567	
Lewis Carroll	Supplement	Dictionary of National Biography Supplement	D	569	

Figure 8-12: Portion of the Search Results from the Dictionary of National Biography.

One entry listed Lewis Carroll's name, defined it as a pseudonym, and referred me to a record for Charles Lutwidge Dodgson (1832–1898). The second entry was a very brief biographical sketch of Dodgson. The third and fourth entries were both references to different parts of a detailed biographical work on Dodgson in which the pen name of Lewis Carroll is referenced.

If Charles L. Dodgson were an ancestor of mine, I could find many clues to the places of his birth, education, residence, appointments, and death, as well as people and institutions that played important roles in his life. All of these would provide many leads to other evidence sources.

Summary

We have explored a number of representative samples of the contents of the Family and Local Histories Collection at Ancestry.com. These materials are invaluable references that you might not be able to access without visiting a library or archive some distance away from you. My own experience has shown me that there are many older books and indexes in this collection of which I was unaware, and the contents have furthered my own research substantially. This is a tremendous online resource, and I encourage you to explore it in great depth for all your ancestral lines and locations.

Chapter 9

Directories and Member List Records

Placing your ancestors in a specific location at a specific point in time is essential to insure that you are searching in the right place for other records about them. Regular national census enumerations have been created in the United States since 1790; in the United Kingdom, Wales, the Channel Islands, and the Isle of Wight since 1801; and in most areas of Canada since 1871. In addition, colonial, state, provincial, and local censuses have been taken at other times. Genealogists use census records more often than any others to establish ancestors' location. But what about those intermediate years between enumerations, and those enumeration periods for which census records have been lost?

It is essential that you recognize that there are many types of alternative records that may be used to establish an ancestor's location at a specific point in time. For Americans, this is especially important because, with the loss of 99.99 percent of the 1890 U.S. Federal Census, substitutes must be used to locate ancestors during the twenty-year gap between the 1880 and 1901 censuses. The types of alternate records most frequently used in these cases include city directories, telephone directories, professional and trade directories, alumni directories and yearbooks, tax lists, religious membership rolls, and other types of annually created records. Using a sequence of local directories or other materials that are published annually may help you learn when your ancestor arrived in an area and when he or she moved away or died. Directories often include addresses, and even occupations, that can point your research in new directions to other sources of evidence.

Ancestry.com has long recognized the importance of directories in genealogical research and has amassed an impressive collection of various directories in their database collection. One recent addition to the collection for researchers in the British Isles is the British Telecom (BT) telephone directories archive, a growing collection of digitized telephone directories from 1880 to 1984 for BT and its predecessors. This collection debuted at Ancestry.co.uk in the fall of 2006 and will grow until the entire collection is digitized and online. What a tremendous resource this is and will continue to be for genealogists and other researchers!

While it would be impossible to compile a complete collection of city directories for every location, the existing collections at Ancestry.com can certainly be used to help you locate your ancestors and relatives, especially in between census records. And, if a location where your family lived at a particular time is not included in these electronic databases, you can certainly contact the libraries and archives in the local area and region to determine if there are printed copies of directories still in existence.

In addition to city directories, Ancestry.com has added such impressive collections as the UK and U.S. Directories, 1680–1830; the U.S. Public Records Index, 1994 to present; and U.S. School Yearbooks. The chronological span and the geographic coverage of these directory and membership records bring rare and difficult-to-access materials into your research options.

In this chapter, we will look at examples of a number of different record types that are available in the Directories and Member List Collection. These will give you a good idea of what to expect.

Searching a City Directory

You can access city directory databases from the **Search** tab by clicking "Directories and Member List Records" in the "Browse Records" section. On the "Directories and Member List Records" page, below the search template is a list of "Featured Directories & Member Lists Collections," along with the now-familiar scroll box, this one titled "Search Individual Directories & Member Lists Collections" (see figure 9-1).

You can scroll down the list of directories, which are arranged alphabetically by city name and include the location and time period covered in the specific directory. When you locate one of interest to you, double-click it. For example, I double-clicked the

Figure 9-1: Scroll box for searching individual databases.

Match Quality	View Record	Name	Location 1	City	State	Occupation
★★☆☆☆	View Record	J B Alexander		Charlotte	NC	drug clerk
★★☆☆☆	View Record	J B Alexander		Charlotte	NC	commission traveler
★★☆☆☆	View Record	Dr J B Alexander	5 w Trade	Charlotte	NC	physician
★★☆☆☆	View Record	J K Alexander		Charlotte	NC	

Figure 9-2: Partial search results for J. B. Alexander in the 1890 Charlotte, NC, Directory.

"Charlotte, North Carolina Directory, 1890." The page that is displayed shows the search template as well as a detailed description of the database's content and how it is used.

This database is a transcription of city directories originally published in 1890. In addition to providing the resident's name, it provides residential and occupational information. It includes over 16,000 names, mostly heads of households. For the researcher of ancestors from southern North Carolina, this can be a valuable collection.

I chose as my search subject a gentleman named J. B. Alexander, a first cousin, three times removed. I entered his name into the template and the search results list shown in figure 9-2 was displayed.

I already knew that Mr. Alexander had been a surgeon for the Confederate Army during the U.S. Civil War, so I surmised that the third entry, for Dr. J. B. Alexander, was the one I sought. I clicked the "View Record" link and the record shown in figure 9-3 was displayed.

As you can see, there are *two* addresses listed for him.

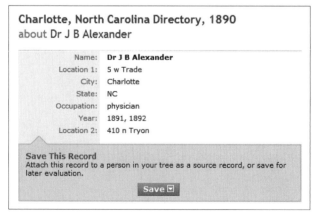

Charlotte, North Carolina Directory, 1890
about **Dr J B Alexander**

Name:	**Dr J B Alexander**
Location 1:	5 w Trade
City:	Charlotte
State:	NC
Occupation:	physician
Year:	1891, 1892
Location 2:	410 n Tryon

Save This Record
Attach this record to a person in your tree as a source record, or save for later evaluation.

Save ▾

Figure 9-3: City directory record for Dr. J. B. Alexander.

One is undoubtedly a residence and the other a business address. Using this information, there are several additional records and research directions I could pursue.

- I could contact the Charlotte-Mecklenburg County Public Library to obtain hard copies of these pages, both from the residential and business sections of the directory. I might also request that a search be conducted in other directories or using other library resources, and then order photocopies of those records.

- There may be land records of interest to me at the Mecklenburg County Courthouse, including deeds and tax rolls related to Dr. Alexander.

- I could contact the Probate Court and request copies of the contents of his will and probate files.

- I could return to the Family and Local Histories Collection at Ancestry.com and search for any matches on Dr. Alexander.

As always, I can save the record to a person in one of my Family Trees as a source or save it to my "Shoebox" for future reference. I can print a copy of the record or save it to my computer. The Source Information below the record provides the basis of a source citation for my personal genealogical database and for my family tree at Ancestry.com. I also can e-mail the record to a friend or relative who might be interested in it.

As you can see, there are many things I can do with just this one record.

U.S. Yearbook Collection

We all remember having photographs taken and published in a school or college yearbook. There often was a biographical profile included with the picture. The information there covered interests, school activities, aspirations, and perhaps even a nickname. The details gleaned from reading a yearbook entry can add another dimension to what you know about an individual and his or her personality.

Yearbooks are one of those home sources, usually found in an attic or basement, which many people don't think of as a family history source. While yearbooks may not provide information about the vital events that are usually associated with genealogical research, they do provide other information about individuals' lives. This information helps place people in a historical context and provides details that help turn individuals, sometimes only known by names and dates, into actual people.

The U.S. Yearbook database is a collection of middle school, junior high, and high school yearbooks from across the United States. If your school's yearbook isn't included in the collection, it *can* be added. If you would like to contribute yearbooks to this collection, you may send a CD with digital scans of the entire book to:

MyFamily Yearbook Submissions
4800 North 360 West
Provo, UT 84604

The page for this database includes a search template into which you can enter a person's name, estimated birth year (+/-), state, city, school name, yearbook year, and any keywords you would like. Since the collection is relatively small, however, you may want to use the browse function instead.

You can also click links in alphabetical order. Follow the sequence of links to city, school, and year, and you will at last arrive at a digitized image of the entire yearbook. I selected the state of Washington, the city of Spokane, Gonzaga High School, and had a choice of 1938 or 1939. I chose 1939 and was rewarded with images of all 199 pages of *The Luigian*. Figure 9-4 shows a page from the yearbook.

U.S. Public Records Index

The U.S. Public Records Index is a compilation of various public records spanning all 50 states in the United States from 1984 to the present. These records are accessible to the general public by contacting the appropriate agency. Ancestry.com has made the process of finding certain public records easier by making them available in an online searchable database. Each entry in this index may contain any or all of the following information:

Figure 9-4: Page from The Luigian, *1939, yearbook from Gonzaga High School in Spokane, Washington.*

- A person's first name, middle name or initial, and last name

- A street or mailing address

- A telephone number

- A birth date or birth year

The U.S. Public Records Index also can be a key resource to help do the following:

- Trace living relatives

- Find old friends and classmates

- Locate a long-lost love

- Track down military buddies

- Conduct an adoption search

- Trace the descendants of someone who has died since 1984

This database is only accessible by searching it; there is no browse function. You access this database as any other in the collection. Fill in the information that you know and press the **Search** button. Figure 9-5 shows an example of a record.

UK and U.S. Directories, 1680–1830

Let's look at another database, one of great international genealogical research significance. The UK and U.S. Directories, 1680–1830, were originally published under the name of *Biography Database, 1680–1830*, by Avero Publications, but Ancestry.com has renamed it online to help researchers better understand what it contains. The database is actually a massive collection of UK and U.S. biographical records, directories, and lists from the following sources:

- National, town, and trade directories of the UK and the U.S.

Figure 9-5: Individual record from the U.S. Public Records database.

- All known book subscription lists

- All birth, marriage, death, promotions, and bankruptcies from a number of regular journals, including the *Gentleman's Magazine* from its inception in 1731 to 1870

- All extant society membership lists from the period

- A number of miscellaneous additional biographical sources contributed by individual academics, who consulted for the project

You will find a complete description of the content sources for this database on the "U.K. and U.S. Directories, 1680–1830" page.

You access this database by selecting and double-clicking on its entry in the scroll box. You'll note on the resulting search template that the entries in the "Date Range" drop-down list extend from "1826–1850" and "1851–1875," which go beyond the scope of the database. At this time, I do not know why this is.

I performed an exact search for Samuel Boddy, who I believe might have lived in the vicinity of London in the late 1700s.

Viewing the first record in the list, which is in Lownde's London Directories in the 1780s, (see figure 9-6), I see that Samuel Boddy was, indeed, located in London

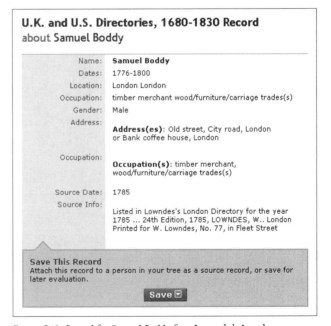

Figure 9-6: Record for Samuel Boddy from Lownde's London Directory.

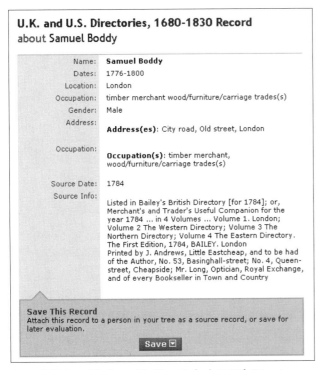

U.K. and U.S. Directories, 1680-1830 Record
about **Samuel Boddy**

Name:	**Samuel Boddy**
Dates:	1776-1800
Location:	London
Occupation:	timber merchant wood/furniture/carriage trades(s)
Gender:	Male
Address:	**Address(es)**: City road, Old street, London
Occupation:	**Occupation(s)**: timber merchant, wood/furniture/carriage trades(s)
Source Date:	1784
Source Info:	Listed in Bailey's British Directory [for 1784]; or, Merchant's and Trader's Useful Companion for the year 1784 ... in 4 Volumes ... Volume 1. London; Volume 2 The Western Directory; Volume 3 The Northern Directory; Volume 4 The Eastern Directory. The First Edition, 1784, BAILEY. London Printed by J. Andrews, Little Eastcheap, and to be had of the Author, No. 53, Basinghall-street; No. 4, Queen-street, Cheapside; Mr. Long, Optician, Royal Exchange, and of every Bookseller in Town and Country

Save This Record
Attach this record to a person in your tree as a source record, or save for later evaluation.

Save ☑

Figure 9-7: Record for Samuel Boddy in Bailey's British Directory.

and was involved in selling timber and was in the wood, furniture, and carriage trades. Between the years of 1776–1800, he apparently resided or did business at Old Street, City Road, or at the Bank Coffee House in London. All of these are clues to his personal location and business records. The Guildhall Library in London may be a repository that I want to contact regarding trade union records for the carriage trade and furniture makers. I may also want to try to trace property and tax records at The National Archives in Kew or at the London Metropolitan Archive.

Take a look at the last record, for Bailey's English Directory (see figure 9-7). The information is very similar to that of Lownde's London Directories.

British Phone Books 1880-1984 Release 1

I mentioned this collection at the beginning of the chapter. This image database is the last example to explore. You must have a World Deluxe subscription or be a UK Deluxe subscriber to use this resource. However, let's take a look at the facility.

There are three (3) required data elements which must be completed on the search template for this database:

- First Name

- Last Name

- County

This requires you to know something of the geography of the area you are searching. The "County" drop-down list includes the counties for which directories are available. "London," in this case, refers to the one-mile square area known as The City of London. The remainder of the metropolitan city spans the counties of Middlesex and, to the west, part of Surrey.

In this search, I want to perform an exact search for a specific person, Michael Sissons, who lived in London. The person I am seeking is the Michael Sissons on the search results page associated with the Tate Gallery, and you will see that there are directory listings for him in the 1978, 1980, 1982, and 1983 phone books. If I had specified a year in my search, I may have isolated the results to a single year. However, if I had specified the year 1981, I would have received no matches for the Michael Sissons I was seeking.

I clicked the "View Record" link for 1983 (see figure 9-8). The record provides the address, the telephone exchange, the directory title and year, the county, the year, and the page number in the directory where Michael's listing will be found. All of this, along with

British Phone Books 1880-1984 Release 1
about **Michael Sissons**

Name:	**Michael Sissons**
Address:	1024 Kings Ho,St. James Ct Sw1.
Exchange:	01-828
City/Town:	Tate Gallery, Victoria
Directory Title:	London Surnames S - Z
Publication Year:	1983
Directory County:	London
Page Number:	140

📄 View Original Image

Save This Record
Attach this record to a person in your tree as a source record, or save for later evaluation.

[Save ▾]

Figure 9-8: Record for Michael Sissons.

the Source Information below the box, can be used to produce a high-quality source citation.

I have all of the usual "View Records" options here, and when I click the graphic or the link labeled "View Original Image," the digitized image of the directory page is presented for viewing. Figure 9-9 shows a magnified image taken from

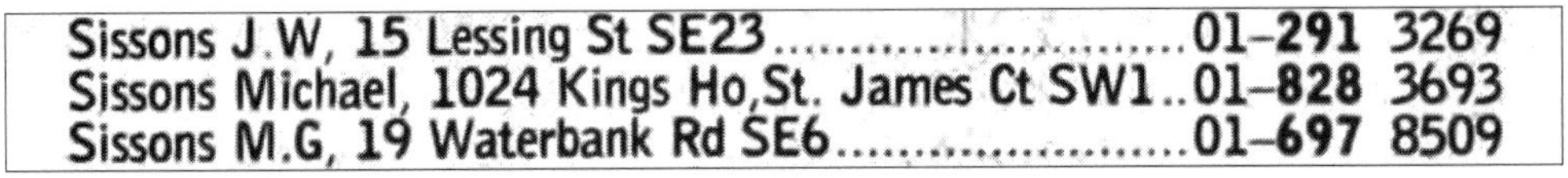

Sissons J.W, 15 Lessing St SE23.........................01–291 3269
Sissons Michael, 1024 Kings Ho,St. James Ct SW1..01–828 3693
Sissons M.G, 19 Waterbank Rd SE6....................01–697 8509

Figure 9-9: Michael Sissons in the "British Phone Books 1850–1984 Release 1."

the actual page in the directory. Michael Sissons' name, address, and telephone number are listed for my reference. By comparing his multiple listings throughout the years, I might determine that he did or did not relocate to a new address or change his telephone number. Verifying his presence at a specific address for any years helps me trace him, especially between censuses. It also allows me to investigate the possibility that other record types might exist in that area, such as parish records, land and property records, voter records, and others.

Summary

The Directories and Member Lists collection, as you have seen, provides you with access to a wide range of materials that ordinarily would be difficult if not impossible to track down for yourself. These records, most of which are secondary sources derived from transcriptions, provide you with excellent evidence of an ancestor's location in a specific location at a specific point in time. As an alternative source to census records and other non-annual records, the information found in this collection can point you to other primary and secondary records and evidence to establish your ancestor's arrival or departure dates at a location or help narrow the time of his or her death.

Ancestry.com continues to add resources to this collection, so it is prudent to check it through both searches and browsing on a regular basis. You may be surprised at what treasures you find here!

Chapter 10

Newspaper and Periodical Records

Newspapers and periodicals are the chronicles of everyday life. In the past, in order to locate information about our ancestors and family members in newspapers, it was necessary to either wade through stacks of old and fragile copies or pore endlessly, frame by frame, through microfilmed images. Quick searches and rapid access were not among our options.

Ancestry.com has brought together a wealth of newspaper resources in its Newspaper & Periodical Records Collection. These consist of digitized images of pages that have been scanned using optical character recognition (OCR) to produce every-word indexes to help you quickly locate all references to a name or subject. New newspapers are added frequently.

In this chapter, we will discuss two ways to access the Newspaper & Periodicals Records. We will also discuss three of the featured databases within the Newspaper & Periodicals Records: the Historical Newspaper Collection, the Obituary Collection, and the *Periodical Source Index (PERSI)*.

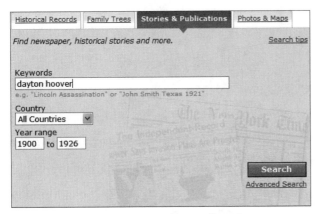

Figure 10-1: The **Stories & Publications** search template.

Searching the Newspaper & Periodical Records

There are two primary ways to search the Newspaper & Periodical Records. The first is on the **Stories & Publications** tab located on the main Home and Search pages. The second is under the "Browse Records" section on the Search page.

Select the **Home** tab on the main navigation bar at the top of the page to go to the Ancestry.com homepage. Select the **Stories & Publications** tab. This displays the Stories & Publications search template. Enter "dayton hoover" in the "Keywords" field, as shown in figure 10-1. In the "Year range" fields enter "1900" and "1926."

The results, shown in figure 10-2, are divided into "Periodicals & Newspapers" and "Family and Local Histories."

Historical Records	Family Trees	Stories & Publications	Photos & Maps

Find newspapers, books, and family and local histories.

Periodicals & Newspapers — 9,089

📄	1,107	The Newark Advocate (Newark, Ohio)
📄	768	Mansfield News (Mansfield, Ohio)
📄	674	Lima News (Lima, Ohio)
📄	476	Lima Daily News (Lima, Ohio)
📄	424	The Indianapolis Star (Indianapolis, Indiana)
	» View all 9,089 results	

Family & Local Histories — 326

📄	24	City directory, Phoenix and vicinity, 1947-1948

Figure 10-2: Portion of a search results list for a search on the **Stories & Publications** tab.

That's because the Stories & Publications search template is linked to both the Newspaper & Periodicals Records (indicated as "Periodicals & Newspapers" on this page) and the Family and Local Histories Records. Click a link to an individual newspaper under the "Periodicals & Newspapers" section to see a list of times that "dayton hoover" is mentioned in that newspaper, along with the date when it was mentioned.

The Stories & Publications search template, which searches the Newspaper & Periodicals Records, is also located under the **Search** tab. Select the **Search** tab on the main navigation bar at the top of the page and you will see the same Stories and Publications search template.

The second primary way to search the Newspaper & Periodical Records is also under the **Search** tab. Select the **Search** tab on the main navigation bar at the top of the page and go to the "Browse Records" section on the right-hand side. Find the "Stories & Publications" heading and click the "Newspapers & Periodicals" link underneath it. This will take you to a search template for the Newspaper & Periodical Records (see figure 10-3).

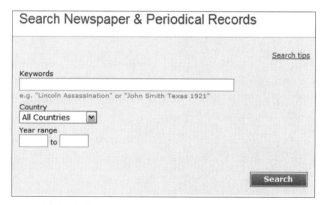

Figure 10-3: The "Search Newspaper & Periodical Records" search template.

You can search all of the Newspaper & Periodical Records collection by using the main search template at the top of the page. Or, you can search by individual newspaper collections within this larger collection. Some of the most popular newspaper and periodical collections are listed underneath the main search template in the "Featured Newspaper &

Searching on Ancestry.com

It is important to realize that the search engine on Ancestry.com is unlike Internet search engines. The search engine on Ancestry.com does not employ Boolean searches; it simply looks for a single word or multiple keywords as they are encountered in the search template. Searching for phrases (as opposed to single keywords) requires you to "fool" the Ancestry.com search engine.

Finding a series of keywords in close proximity to one other, for instance, can often be accomplished by using the "First Name" and "Last Name" fields of the template.

Let's say that you are searching for the Declaration of Independence. You can put the word "Declaration" in the "First Name" field and the word "Independence" in the "Last Name" field. The system will then search for all instances where the words "Declaration" and "Independence" are found relatively close to each other. Also remember that it makes no difference whether you type the words in upper, lower, or mixed case.

Periodical Collections" section. All of the individual newspaper collections are listed under the "Search Individual Newspaper & Periodical Collections."

In the rest of the chapter we will discuss how to search three of the collections in the "Featured Newspaper & Periodical Collections": the Historical Newspaper Collection, the Obituary Collection, and the *Periodical Source Index* (*PERSI*).

Historical Newspaper Collection

The Historical Newspaper Collection contains the records of over 1000 important newspapers from the U.S., the UK, and Canada, dating back to the 1700s. These include such newspapers as the *New York Times* (from 1857 to 1906), the *Washington Post* (from 1904 to 1924), and major newspapers from many other cities.

The Historical Newspaper Collection search template has fields for first and last name, the newspaper title, date, and location. It also has a field for keyword(s).

The large map box beneath the main search template allows you to search the Historical Newspaper Collection by location. Click on a geographical region and then browse through the available newspapers in the collection for that vicinity (see figure 10-4).

An important thing to keep in mind about the Historical Newspaper Collection is that it is sometimes more effective to browse the collection than to search for a particular name or term. Since the index for the collection was built using Optical Character Recognition (OCR) technology, it is sometimes less accurate than other collections that have been indexed manually. The OCR technology scans each image in the collection and indexes every word. While the technology is advanced and has a high level of accuracy, it is still less accurate than human eyes. If it does not recognize a word it "guesses." Sometimes the "guesses" are inaccurate.

Figure 10-4: Browse the Historical Newspaper Collection.

To browse through the collection, think of a newspaper or region you are interested in. For example, let's say your ancestor died in Washington, D.C. in April of 1920. You want to find an obituary for him. Select the "Washington, D.C." link in the large map box at the bottom of the Historical Newspaper Collection page (see figure 10-4). A list of all the available newspaper collections for the Washington, D.C. area appears. In this case, only two newspaper collections are featured: "The Daily Globe (Washington, D.C.)," from 1854–1855, and "Washington Post, The (Washington, D.C.)," from 1904–1924 (see figure 10-5).

Figure 10-5: Results when browsing for Washington, D.C. in the Historical Newspaper Collection.

Click the "Washington Post, The (Washington, D.C.)" link. A new template appears, allowing you to search only this particular newspaper collection. Go to the "Browse By Date" section. Select the month and year to search—in this case "April" and "1920." A template with all of the dates of the month reveals the dates for which Ancestry.com has images. In this case, only the days from the 16th to the 30th are available to search (see figure 10-6 on the next page).

Select the number "16." An image of the *Washington Post* for 16 April 1920 appears. Click the "Prev" and "Next" icons at the top of the page to browse the entire collection for that

day. Browsing through a
newspaper collection is more
time consuming than using the
search template, but in a case
where a collection has been
indexed using OCR it can also
be more effective.

The Obituary Collection

The Obituary Collection
contains primarily recent obituaries from hundreds of
newspapers in the U.S. The collection, however, is growing
and some older obituaries from as far back as the early
twentieth century are being added. Ancestry.com scours the
Internet daily to find new obituaries and extract the facts into
this database. They also provide source information and links
to the full obituary text. If you're searching for a recently
deceased ancestor, a living relative who might be mentioned
in an obituary, or former classmates or neighbors, this is an
excellent place to start.

The wealth of genealogical and biographical information to
be found in an informative obituary certainly makes the effort
of searching for one worthwhile. For many of our ancestors
and relatives, an obituary may be the only "biographical sketch"
that was ever devoted to that individual. In addition to names,
dates, and places of birth, marriage, and death, the obituary
often identifies relationships of the deceased as child, sibling,
parent, grandparent, and so on, to numerous other individuals.

Obituaries may even suggest other documentation of
an individual's death: a death certificate in another county
because the hospital was located there; church or cemetery

Browse By Date

			April ▾	1920 ▾		
Sun	Mon	Tue	Wed	Thu	Fri	Sat
				1	2	3
4	5	6	7	8	9	10
11	12	13	14	15	16	17
18	19	20	21	22	23	24
25	26	27	28	29	30	

Figure 10-6: "Browse By Date" section.

records (by identifying the place of burial or the officiating minister); or records of a coroner's inquest because the death was sudden or unexpected. You may learn about immigration and naturalization, military service, employment, membership in clubs and societies, church affiliations, and much more. The wealth of details in an obituary may open up many research avenues. You just need to learn to read between the lines for potential clues.

In an obituary search, remember that it is wise to investigate the files of *all* likely newspapers. It is impossible to know beforehand which, if any, paper is going to have the best or fullest obituary. Many cities have more than one paper and an obituary for a specific individual could appear in more than one place. Many people in their later years go to live with children and die far from where they spent most of their adult lives. But, if they still had connections with the home community, there is a good chance that an obituary will appear there—perhaps a more detailed one than will be found in the community of death, where that person was just a new or temporary resident. However, the opposite may also be true.

To search thoroughly for obituaries, the best approach is to use a variety of tools, including the Ancestry.com Obituary Collection, the Ancestry.com Historical Newspapers Collection, and local libraries, archives, and newspapers' archives.

The Obituary Collection provides a number of criteria fields on the template to allow you to expand or narrow your search. As an example, I performed a search for actress Jane Wyatt, who died in October 2006. You will remember her in the role of Margaret Anderson, the wife and mother on the 1950s television program, *Father Knows Best*. See the results of this search in figure 10-7 on the next page.

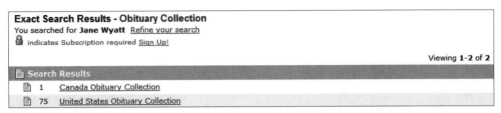

Figure 10-7: "Exact Search Results" in the Obituary Collection for actress Jane Wyatt.

Since Ms. Wyatt was such a well-known actress, there were many obituaries that appeared in newspapers around the world.

Clicking on the link to the "United States Obituary Collection" brings us to a somewhat unusual set of search results in that the term "Actress" appears in the "Name of Deceased" field in some of the entries (see figure 10-8). Many of the entries include Ms. Wyatt's age but some do not. Remember that not all obituaries include a year of birth or an age at the time of death. Therefore, this is a field you might consider omitting in your initial query. While the

View Record	Name of Deceased	Age at Death	Birth Date	Death Date	Other Name Mentioned	Newspaper Location	View Obit
View Record	Jane Wyatt	96			Actress Jane Wyatt	Denton, Texas, United States	
View Record	Jane Wyatt	96			Actress Jane Wyatt	Denton, Texas, United States	
View Record	Jane Wyatt	96			Actress Jane Wyatt	Denton, Texas, United States	
View Record	Actress Jane Wyatt	96			Best	Cincinnati, Ohio, United States	📄
View Record	Actress Jane Wyatt	96			Knows Best	Barstow, California, United States	📄
View Record	Actress Jane Wyatt	96			Broadway	Nashville, Tennessee, United States	📄
View Record	Actress Jane Wyatt	96			Broadway	Franklin, Tennessee, United States	
View Record	Actress Jane Wyatt	96			Bernard Johnson	Denton, Texas, United States	
View Record	Actress Jane Wyatt	96			Broadway	Hilton Head Island, South Carolina, United States	📄
View Record	Actress Jane Wyatt				Knows Best	Pittsford, New York, United States	📄

Figure 10-8: Search results for actress Jane Wyatt in the "United States Obituary Collection."

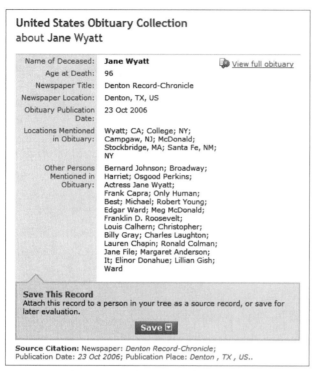

United States Obituary Collection
about **Jane Wyatt**

Name of Deceased:	**Jane Wyatt** 📄 View full obituary
Age at Death:	96
Newspaper Title:	Denton Record-Chronicle
Newspaper Location:	Denton, TX, US
Obituary Publication Date:	23 Oct 2006
Locations Mentioned in Obituary:	Wyatt; CA; College; NY; Campgaw, NJ; McDonald; Stockbridge, MA; Santa Fe, NM; NY
Other Persons Mentioned in Obituary:	Bernard Johnson; Broadway; Harriet; Osgood Perkins; Actress Jane Wyatt; Frank Capra; Only Human; Best; Michael; Robert Young; Edgar Ward; Meg McDonald; Franklin D. Roosevelt; Louis Calhern; Christopher; Billy Gray; Charles Laughton; Lauren Chapin; Ronald Colman; Jane File; Margaret Anderson; It; Elinor Donahue; Lillian Gish; Ward

Save This Record
Attach this record to a person in your tree as a source record, or save for later evaluation.

Save ☑

Source Citation: Newspaper: *Denton Record-Chronicle*; Publication Date: *23 Oct 2006*; Publication Place: *Denton , TX , US..*

Figure 10-9: Obituary record for Jane Wyatt from the Denton Record-Chronicle.

search template includes a "Keyword(s)" field, it also includes the option to narrow your search by inputting the name of someone else who might have been listed in the obituary. This may seem like an excellent way to narrow your search. However, when you examine figure 10-8, you will see that the words "Best," "Knows Best," "Broadway," and "Actress Jane Wyatt," have been picked up as contents of these fields. Take a look at figure 10-9, the record from the *Denton Record-Chronicle*. In the area titled "Other Persons Mentioned in Obituary" are both actors and character names (Margaret Anderson). You would definitely be interested in obtaining a copy of the original obituary notice.

When you click the link labeled "View full obituary," you are often rewarded with the text of the obituary itself. However, in some cases the obituary has been captured from online editions of newspapers and periodicals on the Internet. Those obituaries usually do not stay online forever. It is therefore important to refer to the source citation at the bottom of the record so that you can isolate the name of the publication, its publication location, and its date of publication. Armed with this information, you can usually request a copy of the obituary from the newspaper publisher or via Interlibrary Loan through your local library.

As you have seen with other records at Ancestry.com, you can save this record to your Family Tree or to your "Shoebox" for later evaluation. You can also make comments and corrections or display a printer-friendly version of this record for printing. Further, you can make connections with other researchers who may be researching Jane Wyatt. We will discuss more about that process in chapter 16.

The *PERiodical Source Index (PERSI)*

The *PERiodical Source Index (PERSI)* is the largest and most widely used subject index covering genealogy and local history periodicals written in English and French (Canada). The collection dates from approximately 1800. There are currently over 1.7 million searchable records and nearly 6,000 different periodicals, which library staff at the Allen County Public Library (ACPL) in Ft. Wayne, Indiana, has been compiling for a number of years. *PERSI* is widely recognized as essential for high-quality indexing to genealogical and historical periodical publications.

You can access *PERSI* in the Newspaper and Periodical Records Collection, but it is also available in the Reference and Finding Aids Collection, which we will discuss in chapter 14. For a more thorough discussion of *PERSI*, see page 232.

Summary

The use of the Historical Newspapers Collection, the Obituary Collection, and *PERSI* in tandem with other materials can certainly provide you with a great deal of secondary evidence whose leads you can pursue. As an example, I used the SSDI to identify the location and date of death for a "lost" great-aunt in 1966. Based on that information, I used the last residence shown in the SSDI and located a newspaper in Syracuse, New York in the newspaper database, and found an obituary for her. A periodical indexed by *PERSI* included a canvass of the cemetery in which she was buried and a transcription of her tombstone inscription.

Subsequently, I ordered a death certificate for her, a copy of her probate packet, copies of the deed for her home, and a copy of her marriage record. I also made contact with two surviving children and a grandchild. As a result, not only have I expanded my genealogical information, I have renewed contact with otherwise disconnected family members. You can do this type of extended research as well!

Chapter 11

Immigration Records

Immigration is generally defined as the process of entering one country from another, often to take up permanent residence. The migration of a person from one place to another is a fascinating study. It involves the study of geography, history, social and physical conditions, and any number of other factors.

Immigration Records at Ancestry.com

The collection of immigration records databases at Ancestry.com is unequalled anywhere in the world. It includes indexed and digitized images of all readily available U.S immigration passenger lists from 1820 to 1964; pre-1820 immigration references; available crew lists from post-1900; emigrant lists from parts of Germany; Canadian immigration records; denizations, naturalizations, and oaths of allegiance; naturalization stub books; and a variety of important reference books and other indexes.

In 1819, the U.S. Congress passed legislation requiring that the ship's master of each incoming ship carrying passengers provide a complete manifest of these passengers. Beginning in 1820, the law was implemented and these documents were presented to the customs officer at the port of arrival before any passenger disembarked. On a monthly basis, the customs officer was required to prepare a summary of all ships' arrivals and a list of passenger arrivals. This report was sent to Washington, D.C. Ultimately, when the National Archives and Records Administration (NARA) acquired the massive collection of passenger lists, it also received the customs officers' reports.

NARA has microfilmed all available passenger lists. Where any of the original manifests had not survived, the customs' officers' reports were used as substitute documents for microfilming. Consequently, the collection of passenger list records is incredibly close to complete for the 140 years it spans.

Passenger lists provide invaluable details such as names, gender, occupation, accompanying travelers, origin/port of departure, date and place of arrival, and others, all in the original handwriting. Later lists included much more detail, such as intended destination, place of birth, financial assets, and even the name of the nearest living relative in the country of origin.

An estimated 85 percent of Americans have an immigrant ancestor included in the Ancestry.com passenger list collection, which covers the height of American immigration, making Ancestry.com the source for the largest compilation of passenger list records available and fully searchable online. The passenger list collection records the arrivals of more than 100 million passengers. The compilation features printable images of 7 million original passenger list documents. The collection also contains approximately 1,000 images of the actual ships.

Until the completion of this project, U.S. passenger list records could only be found on microfilm or in limited selections online at various dispersed locations, such as libraries and museums across the nation. For the first time, people can look to a single centralized source online to find all readily available passenger list records. More than a hundred American ports of arrival are represented in the compilation, including the entire collection of passenger list records from Ellis Island (1892–1957), a historic landmark and icon of immigration. The collection also accounts for popular ports in Boston, Baltimore, New Orleans, and the Angel Island receiving station in San Francisco.

As you can see, there is a massive amount of information available in these online databases that previously would only have been accessible on microfilm at NARA and in other archives, or in books and indexes located in the special genealogical collections of libraries and other repositories. All of this content makes "jumping the pond" significantly more feasible.

Searching the Collections

There are such varied materials in the Immigration Records Collection that it makes sense for us to explore a number of different databases. First, here are some tips that you should consider when tracing your immigrant ancestors.

- **Search for your family members in U.S. records before looking in foreign records**—You are more likely to find an immigrant's birthplace or last foreign residence in American records. U.S. federal census records, beginning in 1850, include the names of everyone in a household and list each person's place of birth. Census records from 1880 and later indicate the birthplace of the individual and his or her parents. Census records from 1900 to 1930 include all this information, plus the year of arrival of a person who immigrated, plus whether they are an alien or a naturalized citizen, or whether their naturalization paperwork process is in progress. Native language spoken is also a key clue in your research. Exhaust all American resources before searching in sources for other countries because the American records can contain invaluable leads to point you to the country of origin. Remember, however, that boundaries changed and that you should consider the geopolitical and governmental jurisdictions at the time a person was born, married, and immigrated. The presence of different country names on two U.S. federal censuses may be indicative of a boundary change between the censuses, and may not represent the actual country from whence the person immigrated at the time of his or her relocation.

- **Consider immigration patterns**—Your ancestors may not have boarded a ship in their home country. For example, the famous Von Trapp family was Austrian but, to escape the Nazis, they traveled to Italy before boarding a ship to America. Your ancestors may also have stopped in other countries on the way to America. These "layovers" may have been a day, month, year, or even generations. It is important to consider the different aspects of your ancestors' journey and take into account any less common circumstances they may have experienced. Therefore, historical research into migration patterns and any recruitment programs or schemes to induce people to emigrate elsewhere may be invaluable to your research.

- **Look beyond Ellis Island**—Although the Ellis Island era is certainly the most famous time of immigration to the U.S., immigrants have been making their way to America for hundreds of years. The main wave of immigrants that came through Ellis Island arrived in New York between 1892 and 1924. You can narrow your search if you determine not only when your ancestors arrived, but also if they came in through New York or some other port of entry. Again, historical research into migration patterns and trends can greatly benefit your quest.

- **Consider other record types**—Other types of records may provide clues to your immigrant ancestors' origin and date and place of arrival. Voter registration records and military service and pension records may contain information about the national origin of your ancestor and his or her naturalization. Don't overlook the Family & Local Histories Collection at Ancestry.com or at libraries and archives. These may include references to your ancestors, their families, and even some personal details about their immigration and where they settled. If your ancestors hailed from England, Ireland, Scotland, Wales, Isle of Man, and the Channel Islands from the nineteenth and twentieth centuries, the United Kingdom and Ireland Records Collection, which includes censuses, parish records, and civil registration indexes, may provide significant help in your research. Keep an open mind about the different types of records that just may contain references to your ancestors' immigration details.

Some excellent books can help you research your ancestors' immigration and naturalization. Here are the bibliographic citations for the five that are considered authoritative standards:

Colletta, John Philip, Ph.D. *They Came in Ships: A Guide to Finding Your Immigrant Ancestor's Arrival Record*. 3rd ed. Orem, UT: Ancestry, 2002.

Morgan, George G. *How to Do Everything with Your Genealogy*. Emeryville, CA: McGraw-Hill/Osborne, 2004.

Schaefer, Christina K. *Guide to Naturalization Records of the United States*. Baltimore, MD: Genealogical Publishing Co., 1997.

Szucs, Loretto Dennis. *They Became Americans: Finding Naturalization Records and Ethnic Origins*. Orem, UT: Ancestry, 1998.

Tepper, Michael. *American Passenger Arrival Records: A Guide to the Records of Immigrants*. Baltimore, MD: Genealogical Publishing Co., 1999.

You have already learned that the search templates vary for different databases and collections, depending on their content. To begin your search of the Immigration Records Collection, click the **Search** tab and then the "Immigration" link in the "Browse Records" section. You should be on the "Search Immigration Records" page.

Let's say that we want to search for physicist Enrico Fermi, who visited the United States on several occasions to attend conferences and deliver lectures. I performed an "exact matches only" search for Fermi and specified that I wanted to see passenger arrival records between 1920 and 1940. The "Exact Search Results" page indicates that there are five New York Passenger Lists that match the name and the years shown.

When I click on the "New York Passenger Lists, 1820–1957" link, the detailed list is displayed as shown in figure 11-1 on the next page. Fermi made trips to the U.S., arriving in New York in 1930, 1933, 1935, 1936, and 1937.

View Record	Name	Arrival Date	Estimated birth year	Gender	Port of Departure	Place of Origin	Ship Name	View Ship Image	View Passenger List
View Record	**Enrico Fermi**	16 Jun 1930	abt 1901	Female	Naples	Italian	Roma		
View Record	**Enrico Fermi**	13 Jun 1933	abt 1901	Male	Genoa	Italian	Conte Di Savoia		
View Record	**Enrico Fermi**	20 Jun 1935	abt 1901	Male	Naples	Italy	Roma		
View Record	**Enrico Fermi**	2 Jul 1936	abt 1901	Male	Naples	Italy	Conte Di Savoia		
View Record	**Enrico Fermi**	22 Jun 1937	abt 1901	Male	Naples	Italy	Roma		

Figure 11-1: Detail of "Exact Search Results" for Enrico Fermi.

The detailed list allows me to view a record of the information. I can also view the original passenger list (or manifest) by clicking "View Passenger List." Figure 11-2 shows a portion of this digitized passenger list for his arrival on 16 June 1930. Note that the gender for Enrico Fermi in figure 11-1 is listed as "Female" on the first entry. When you examine the actual passenger list, notice that the preparer of the list made a typographical error and typed an "f" instead of an "m" under

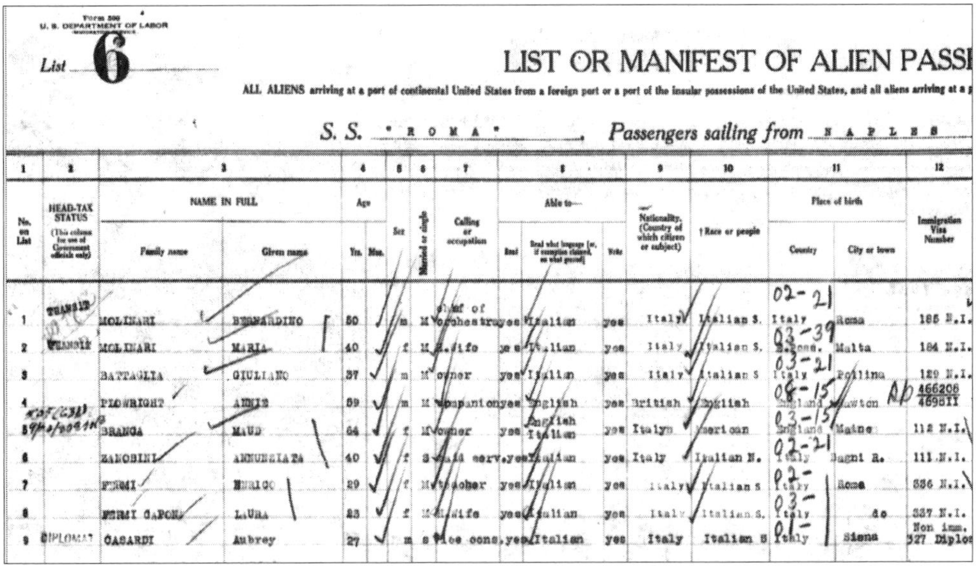
U. S. DEPARTMENT OF LABOR

List 6

LIST OR MANIFEST OF ALIEN PASS

ALL ALIENS arriving at a port of continental United States from a foreign port or a port of the insular possessions of the United States, and all aliens arriving at a p

S. S. ROMA Passengers sailing from NAPLES

Figure 11-2: Detail of a passenger list showing Enrico Fermi and his wife in 1930.

the "Sex" column. Enrico is traveling with his wife, Laura Fermi Capon. He is listed as a 29-year-old teacher from Italy who was born in Rome.

Where Ancestry.com has been able to acquire a photograph or other image of the ship, the option to "View Ship Image" is displayed on the detailed search result list (see figure 11-1). In this case, the Fermis traveled aboard the *Roma*, and an image was available (see figure 11-3). If you were related to Enrico Fermi, the images of both the ship's manifest *and* the ship itself would be great to save to your own computer and to add to your collection of information about his life.

Figure 11-3: Image of the ship, Roma

Note the date range in the Quick Links at the top of the page (see figure 11-4).

You are here: <u>Search</u> > <u>Immigration</u> > <u>Passenger Ships and Images</u> > <u>R</u> > <u>Roma</u> > **1926–1943**

Figure 11-4: Quick Links to the image of the Roma.

Sometimes Ancestry.com has been able to acquire multiple images of the same ship from different time periods. If you click on the link titled "Roma," the page shown in figure 11-5 on the next page is displayed. There are two links to images: one for the years 1902 to 1929 and another for the years 1926 to 1943. These are the years for which these images were typically used for advertising, press releases, newspaper stories, postcards, and other print media. If you click on each link, you will see different images of the ship. Ancestry.com has matched the image from the appropriate time period, in

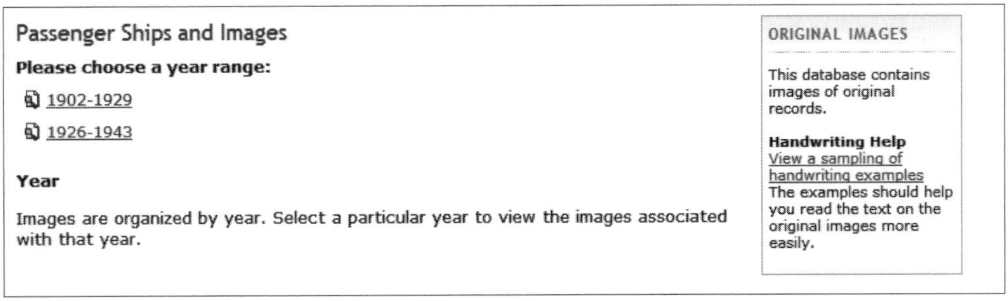

Passenger Ships and Images
Please choose a year range:

📖 1902-1929

📖 1926-1943

Year

Images are organized by year. Select a particular year to view the images associated with that year.

ORIGINAL IMAGES

This database contains images of original records.

Handwriting Help
View a sampling of handwriting examples
The examples should help you read the text on the original images more easily.

Figure 11-5: Page showing multiple ship image links.

this case 1930, with the entry on the detailed search results list of my search.

Featured Immigration Records

As you should expect, on the "Search Immigration Records" page, you will find a list of "Featured Immigration Records" (see figure 11-6). These are the most frequently used of all the databases in this category, or the ones that have been recently updated.

📁 **Featured Immigration Records:**
- New York Passenger Lists, 1820-1957 - **Updated!**
- Baltimore Passenger Lists, 1820-1948
- Boston Passenger Lists, 1820-1943
- California Passenger and Crew Lists, 1893-1957 - **Updated!**
- New Orleans Passenger Lists, 1820-1945
- Philadelphia Passenger Lists, 1800-1945
- Passenger & Immigration Lists Index, 1500s - 1900s - **Updated!**

Figure 11-6: "Featured Immigration Records" list. These lists change frequently, so what you see might have new additions.

One of the most comprehensive immigration resources is the *Passenger and Immigration Lists Index, 1590s–1900s*. First published by P. William Filby in 1985, the index has been compiled for many published sources, manuscripts, and other resources and a new supplement has been published annually. Gale Research has created a database of this landmark series and Ancestry.com has made it available online. The 2005 data set contains approximately 4,461,000 individuals who arrived in United States and Canadian ports from the 1500s through the 1900s. Each entry has been indexed by name and is searchable by keyword. For each individual listed, you may find the following information:

- Name and age

- Year and place of arrival

- Naturalization or other record of immigration

- Source of record

- Names of all accompanying family members together with their age and relationship to the primary individual

As an example of a search in this database, I will perform a general search for my ancestor Joseph Alexander, who was born approximately 1660 and immigrated to America.

There are ten matches shown in the "Ranked Search Results" page (see figure 11-7). However, since I have already proved through land records that he purchased and settled land in Virginia, an arrival in Maryland (probably Baltimore Harbor) seems most likely. Therefore, I checked each of the five listings concerning Maryland.

Match Quality	View Record	Name	Year	Age	Estimated birth year	Place of Arrival
★★★★☆	View Record	Joseph Alexander	1714			Maryland
★★★★☆	View Record	Joseph Alexander	1719			Maryland
★★★★☆	View Record	Joseph Alexander	1720			Maryland
★★★★☆	View Record	Joseph Alexander	1720			Maryland
★★★★☆	View Record	Joseph Alexander	1681			New Hampshire
★★★★☆	View Record	Joseph Alexander	1811			Baltimore, MD
★★★★☆	View Record	Joseph Alexander	1799			New York, NY
★★★★☆	View Record	Joseph Alexander	1799			New York, NY
★★★★☆	View Record	Joseph Alexander	1840			New York, NY
★★★★☆	View Record	Joseph Alexander	1840			New York, NY

Figure 11-7: "Ranked Search Results" for Joseph Alexander.

I clicked on the first entry, the arrival in 1714, and the full record shown in figure 11-8 was displayed. This gives me a full bibliographic entry for a primary immigrant named James Alexander who was accompanied by his father, Joseph Alexander. This is consistent with the pedigree I have traced. I can use the "Source Bibliography" to locate the book through *PERSI*. I can also use *PERSI* to locate and obtain copies of pertinent pages from *The Magazine of American Genealogy* mentioned in the "Annotation" section. Either or both of these may point me to the original records from which the information was derived.

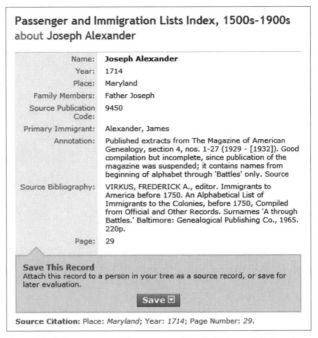

Passenger and Immigration Lists Index, 1500s-1900s
about Joseph Alexander

Name:	**Joseph Alexander**
Year:	1714
Place:	Maryland
Family Members:	Father Joseph
Source Publication Code:	9450
Primary Immigrant:	Alexander, James
Annotation:	Published extracts from The Magazine of American Genealogy, section 4, nos. 1-27 (1929 - [1932]). Good compilation but incomplete, since publication of the magazine was suspended; it contains names from beginning of alphabet through 'Battles' only. Source
Source Bibliography:	VIRKUS, FREDERICK A., editor. Immigrants to America before 1750. An Alphabetical List of Immigrants to the Colonies, before 1750, Compiled from Official and Other Records. Surnames 'A through Battles.' Baltimore: Genealogical Publishing Co., 1965. 220p.
Page:	29

Save This Record
Attach this record to a person in your tree as a source record, or save for later evaluation.

Save ▾

Source Citation: Place: *Maryland*; Year: *1714*; Page Number: *29*.

Figure 11-8: "Passenger and Immigration Lists Index" record for Joseph Alexander.

Individual Immigration Records

On the "Search Immigration Records" page, the "Search Individual Immigration Records" scroll box contains the names of all the other immigration and immigration-related databases at Ancestry.com (see figure 11-9 on page 196). Some of these are records, while others are indexes or digitized book images. An example of the latter is the *Emigrants from Fellbach (Baden-Wuerttemberg, Germany), 1735–1930*. Books will generally be searchable using a template and browsable by table of contents, section, chapter, index, or other organizational schemes.

Search Individual Immigration Records:

Immigration of Irish Quakers to Pennsylvania, 1682-1750
Index to Declaration of Intent for Naturalization: New York County, 1907-1924
Iosco County, Michigan Naturalization Index, 1885-1910 - Free
Irish Emigrants in North America [1670-1830], Part Six
Irish Emigrants in North America [1775-1825]
Irish Emigrants in North America, Part Four and Part Five
Irish Immigrants: New York Port Arrival Records, 1846-1851
Italian Passengers to Louisiana, 1905-10
Italians in Poland
Juab County, Utah Citizenship Certificate Stubs, 1908-1928
Laramie County, Wyoming Naturalization Records, 1867-1920
Later Scots-Irish Links, 11575-1725 Part Four - New!
Later Scots-Irish Links, 1575-1725 Part Three - New!
Later Scots-Irish Links, 1725-1825 - New!
Massachusetts Crew Lists, 1917-1943 - New!
Michigan Eastern District Naturalizations
Minnesota Crew Lists, 1929-1952
Minnesota Naturalization Records Index, 1854-1957
More Emigrants in Bondage, 1614-1775 - New!
More English Adventurers and Emigrants, 1625-1777 - New!
Naturalizations in America and the West Indies, 1740-1782

Figure 11-9: "Search Individual Immigration Records" scroll box.

Among the databases in this collection are some that deal with naturalization. Many of these are simple indexes to the original declarations of intention, petitions for naturalization, or naturalization certificate stub books. However, there are some digitized images of actual application files, and the overall collection continues to grow. Let's look at three examples of these naturalization-related resources.

The "Juab County, Utah Citizenship Certificate Stubs, 1908–1928" is an example of an index to actual naturalization certificates. At the time that the court grants the petition for naturalization, after having verified that all requirements have been met and that an oath of allegiance has been administered, a certificate is issued. The uniquely numbered certificate comes from a book that contains an informational stub and the certificate, perforated on one edge. The stub book acts as something like a checkbook register and lists the name of the naturalized citizen, the date, the court, and the certificate number.

Most often these stub books have remained in the courthouse in which the naturalization took place. Once you have the name of the individual and his or her certificate number, it becomes simpler to locate the person's naturalization file(s) and obtain copies of application forms

and correspondence. Those documents may provide the most
direct link back to the country of origin, a birthplace, a date
and port of arrival, and other clues.

After searching for "Mortensen" in the "Juab County, Utah
Citizenship Certificate Stubs, 1908–1928" template, I find only
one match: a gentleman named Gotlieb Edward Mortensen
(see figure 11-10). The information on the search results entry

Match Quality	View Record	Name	Date	Certificate	Volume	Page
☆☆☆☆☆	View Record	**Gotlieb Edward Mortensen**	9 Sep 1919	778254	22101	4

Figure 11-10: Search results for Gotlieb Edward Mortensen.

tells me that he was naturalized on 9 September 1919. He was
issued naturalization certificate #778254, and the certificate
was attached to the stub that resides in "Volume 22101"
on "Page 4."

Normally this information would be sufficient for me to
continue my research. However, if I want to save the record
to a tree in one of my Family Trees or to my "Shoebox," make
comments, or print a copy for my files, I would click the "View
Record" link and take action from there.

A second example is the "Index to Declaration of Intention
for Naturalization: New York County, 1907–1924." The "Exact
Search Results" page for a search for "mary johnson" shows one
match (see in figure 11-11). Mary Johnson's Declaration of
Intention is recorded in "Declaration Volume 474," "Page 381."

In some cases, such as that of Bernard Jones, shown in
figure 11-12 on page 198, when both the Declaration of Intent

View Record	Name	Declaration Volume	Declaration Page	Petition Volume	Petition Page
View Record	**Mary Johnson**	474	381		

Figure 11-11: "Exact Search Results" for Mary Johnson's Declaration of Intention.

Match Quality	View Record	Name	Declaration Volume	Declaration Page	Petition Volume	Petition Page
★★★★☆	View Record	Mary Jane Jones	525	451		
★★★★☆	View Record	Mary Jane Jones	637	169		
★☆☆☆☆	View Record	William Jones			297	56
★☆☆☆☆	View Record	Bernard Jones	1	345	12	54

Figure 11-12: "Ranked Search Results" for Bernard Jones's Declaration of Intention and Petition for Naturalization.

to become a citizen and the Petition for Naturalization are filed and processed by the same court, this database shows both index entries. Using the index entries, you should be able to locate and obtain copies of the applications and any other pertinent documents. These documents are typically stored in the NARA branch that holds the records for that court district. Loretto D. Szucs's book, *They Became Americans*, and Christina K. Schaefer's reference, *Guide to the Naturalization Records of the United States*, will help you locate the correct NARA branch to contact for document copies.

The third example I want to share with you is the "New York Petitions for Naturalization" database. What differentiates this from the previous two examples is that it presents images of the actual index cards to the petitions for naturalization. Using the search template for this database, I looked for "Abraham Jones."

The "Exact Search Results" page yields six entries for people with the name Abraham Jones. As always, you can click on the "View Record" link and save information to one of your trees or your "Shoebox," make comments, and print the record.

The index cards vary in content. The simplest list only the name of the petitioner, the date of the petition, and the petition number. However, let me show you two sample index cards with more detailed information.

The first example is located under he fourth entry for Abraham Jones, who was naturalized on 18 October 1879 (see figure 11-13). This card shows that he was formerly a subject of the Emperor of Russia. His address and occupation are also listed. However, the entry of Superior Court, New York County under "Title and Location of Court" is a great clue as to where to find his naturalization file. The card even tells you to seek it in Bundle 300 and record number 32.

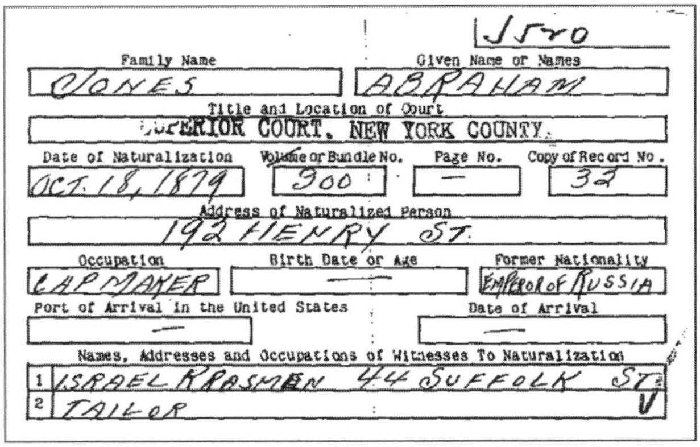

J570

Family Name: JONES
Given Name or Names: ABRAHAM
Title and Location of Court: SUPERIOR COURT, NEW YORK COUNTY.
Date of Naturalization: OCT. 18, 1879
Volume or Bundle No.: 300
Page No.: —
Copy of Record No.: 32
Address of Naturalized Person: 192 HENRY ST.
Occupation: CAP MAKER
Birth Date or Age: —
Former Nationality: EMPEROR OF RUSSIA
Port of Arrival in the United States: —
Date of Arrival: —
Names, Addresses and Occupations of Witnesses To Naturalization
1 ISRAEL KRASMAN 44 SUFFOLK ST.
2 TAILOR

Figure 11-13: Abraham Jones's index card—18 October 1879.

The second example is located under the fifth entry in the "Exact Search Results " page, this one for an Abraham Leopold Jones, who was naturalized on 18 February 1929 (see figure 11-14). This card shows his petition number, 136882, and his Declaration of Intention number, 159510. Both of these reference numbers can be used to help locate the original documents. The card also lists additional useful information, such as his address, the names of his two children, and a few physical characteristics.

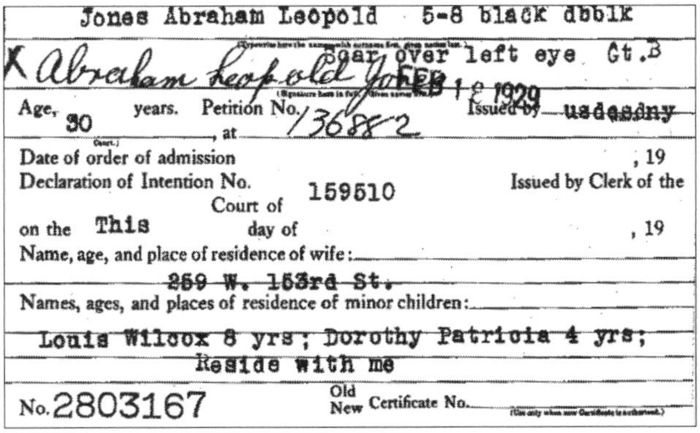

Jones Abraham Leopold 5-8 black dbblk
X Abraham Leopold Jones Scar over left eye Ct.3
FEB 18 1929
Age, 30 years. Petition No. 136882, at Issued by usdcsdny
Date of order of admission , 19
Declaration of Intention No. 159510 Issued by Clerk of the Court of
on the This day of , 19
Name, age, and place of residence of wife:
259 W. 153rd St.
Names, ages, and places of residence of minor children:
Louis Wilcox 8 yrs; Dorothy Patricia 4 yrs;
Reside with me
No. 2803167 Old/New Certificate No.

Figure 11-14: Abraham Leopold Jones's index card—18 February 1929.

The disparity of information in the formats of the index cards should make you even more curious as to what is on the actual application forms and other documents in the files. As you can see, too, there are many different types of immigration-related databases in the Ancestry.com collection. You will find much to explore and you will learn a great deal about immigration and naturalization across the centuries.

Chapter 12

Court, Land, and Probate Records

The Ancestry.com collection of Court, Land, and Probate Records is an extensive compilation of reference materials that can further your genealogical research and expand your knowledge of your ancestors' lives and deaths. You will find many different types of records in this collection that perhaps you have not considered before. Some examples include the following databases:

- Bute County, North Carolina: Minutes of the Court of Pleas and Quarter Sessions, 1767–1779

- Caswell County, NC Will Books, 1777–1843; 1784 Tax List; and Guardians' Accounts, 1794–1819

- Darke County, Ohio Common Pleas Court Records, 1817–1860

- Davis County, Utah Divorce Case Files, 1875–1886

- Denver Land Office Records, 1862–1908

- Florida Land Records

- Frederick County, Virginia, Wills & Administrations, 1795–1816

- French And British Land Grants In The Post Vincennes (Indiana) District, 1750–1784

- Georgia Cherokee Land Lottery, 1832

- Hartford, Connecticut Probate Records, 1635–50; 1700–29; 1729–50

- Henry Mining District, Sevier County, Utah, 1883–1896

- Kansas Settlers, 1854–1879

- Kentucky Land Grants

- Leavenworth, Kansas Voter Registration, 1859

- Massachusetts Applications of Freemen, 1630–91

- Nevada Car Registration Records, 1913–18

- Nevada Orphan's Home Records, 1870–1920

- New York City Wills, 1665–1782 (multiple databases)

- Providence Early Town Records

- Salem Witches

- Salt Lake County, Utah Civil and Criminal Case Files, 1852–1887

You will probably find the sheer diversity of record types referenced in the list above intriguing. Many of the databases consist of transcriptions of indexes, which can provide the necessary information for you to request original copies of the records from the source repository. Remember that the source is listed under the search template on the page where you enter your search criteria for the specific database.

Others of the databases included consist of digitized books from the Family and Local Histories Collection. As an example, a book by Katharine Kerr Kendall, *Person County, North Carolina Compilations: Land Grants; 1794, 1805 & 1823 Tax Lists; Record Books Abstracts, 1792–1820; Letters of Attorney*, is an assemblage of indexes and abstracts to some unique period documents for Person County, North Carolina. Having used the database, I have requested copies of the original records for several of my ancestors from the courthouse in Roxboro, North Carolina.

In the upper right-hand corner of the "Search Court, Land, & Probate Records" page (which I accessed on the **Search** tab, and the "Court, Land, & Probate Records" link in the "Browse Records" section) is a link labeled "Welcome to the Court, Land, & Probate Records Center." I urge you to visit this introductory page for tips about effectively searching for different records. At the bottom of that page are some informative articles written by Donn Devine, Michael John Neill, and myself about using these types of records. These and other articles are in the Learning Center at Ancestry.com, which we will discuss in chapter 15.

Searching the Databases

As I mentioned earlier, this collection of databases is very diverse indeed. However, let's examine a few of them by performing searches. This will allow you, as you follow along and input these searches on your own computer, to see and work with the search results. If you see additional areas or links as you work through the examples, I urge you to explore further to see what you find.

Let's perform two searches from the template on the "Search Court, Land, & Probate Records" page. In both cases,

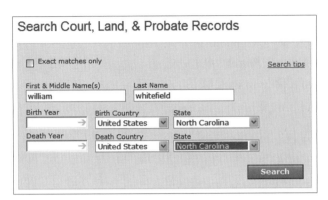

Figure 12-1: General search template on the "Search Court, Land, & Probate Records" page, including information for William Whitefield.

I want to locate my great-great-grandfather, William Whitefield, who was born and died in North Carolina. In the first search, I have entered his name and have specified that he both was born and died in the United States and in North Carolina (see figure 12-1).

The "Ranked Search Results" page is shown in figure 12-2a. I expected to see the William Whitefield matches for North Carolinians at the top of the list. What I have learned is that, with a ranked search, matches in databases with individual records are displayed first. These are then followed with matches from digitized materials from the databases in the Family and Local Histories Collection. Looking at the results in figure 12-2a (on the next page), I knew that my great-grandfather was probably the person matched in the seventh, eighth, and tenth matches. I would check each of these, which are from Katherine Kendall Kerr's books, and then proceed to the next page to see if there are additional matches. Remember you can click on the links in the "Narrow Your Search" section to the left of the search results to refine your results to that specific database.

I decided to click the match for the "Person County, North Carolina Deed Books 1792–1825" database. A new "Ranked Search Results" page is shown with a single entry (see figure 12-2b on the next page). It tells me that there is a reference in "Deed Book E" on page "174."

I want to see the image from this book, so I click the link at left labeled "william whitefield." The image displayed contains

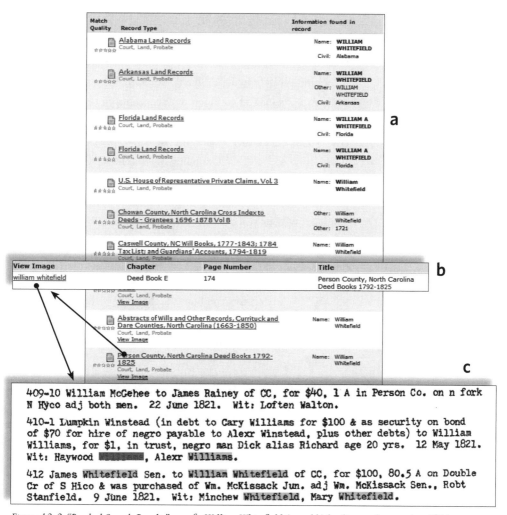

Figure 12-2: "Ranked Search Results" page for William Whitefield (a and b) leading to the record itself (c).

a page of typed deed abstracts (see figure 12-2c). In the one
labeled 410-1, Lumpkin Winstead has conducted a business
transaction and there are two witnesses to it with the surname
of Williams. You will note that their surnames are highlighted.
These appeared as part of the general search. However, in the

next entry, James Whitefield, Senior, sold a parcel of 80.5 acres to William Whitefield. This was my great-great-grandfather's land, on which he built a new home. The witnesses are Minchew Whitefield and Mary Whitefield, a brother and sister.

Now, let's look at conducting a search using the "Exact matches only" option and see what results we get. In this case, when I click that "Exact matches only" box, I can specify whether to use an "Exact" spelling or "Soundex." I can also indicate the country, and even the state, where William Whitefield lived, as well as the date range. All of these criteria can narrow your search. However, remember it is often best to start simple and *then* narrow your search by adding other qualifiers. In this case, I chose to "Exact" spelling, and I included North Carolina and a year range of 1800–1850 in my criteria.

My first search returned no matches. I therefore revised my search by removing the years from the template. This time I had more success, as you can see with the "Exact Search Results" page shown in figure 12-3.

🗎 Search Results	
Court, Land, Probate Records	12
🗎 1 Abstracts of Wills and Other Records, Currituck and Dare Counties, North Carolina (1663-1850)	
🗎 1 Alabama Land Records	
🗎 1 Arkansas Land Records	
🗎 1 Caswell County, NC Will Books, 1777-1843; 1784 Tax List; and Guardians' Accounts, 1794-1819	
🗎 1 Chowan County, North Carolina Cross Index to Deeds - Grantees 1696-1878 Vol B	
🗎 2 Florida Land Records	
🗎 4 Person County, North Carolina Deed Books 1792-1825	
🗎 1 Texas Land Title Abstracts	

Figure 12-3: "Exact Search Results" page for William Whitefield.

What is interesting is that, even though I specified that he lived in North Carolina, matches with other databases covering Alabama, Florida, and Texas were included. The search engine still searched for exact matches for the first and last names I entered, but it also returned other alternatives.

Please note that the "Person County, North Carolina Deed Books 1792–1825" is still listed, and that it shows that there are 4 matches to William Whitefield. When I click on the link to that database, the "Exact Search Results" page shown in figure 12-4 presents me with all four matches. Do

View Image	Chapter	Page Number	Title
william whitefield	Deed Book D	134	Person County, North Carolina Deed Books 1792-1825
william whitefield	Deed Book E	151	Person County, North Carolina Deed Books 1792-1825
william whitefield	Deed Book E	165	Person County, North Carolina Deed Books 1792-1825
william whitefield	Deed Book E	174	Person County, North Carolina Deed Books 1792-1825

Figure 12-4: "Exact Search Results" page for William Whitefield.

you remember when I used the ranked search and found results within the first ten matches displayed on the page? I commented that I would check the matches on that page and then continue to the next page and look for additional matches. Well, here you can see that I would have found a total of four matches in that way in this same database.

Of the four matches shown here, the first match retrieved and displayed in the general search was the one for "Deed Book E," page "174," which we already looked at. The reason for that is the search engine is programmed for general searches to search for and return matches where the person is, in the case of land records, either the seller (grantor) or buyer (grantee) first, followed by other, less perfect matches or cases where the person is perhaps a witness. In each case, William Whitefield is a witness to a transaction. Look at a portion of the record from "Deed Book D," page "134," in figure 12-5 on page 208.

You will notice that the names highlighted show Wm. Whitefield; the search engine has located an abbreviation of the name William. This illustrates the power and flexibility of the search.

497–8 Div of land (292 A) of Daniel Sergent decd on both sides S Hico into 7 parts & each to have 41½ A: 1. Samuel Winstead, 2. Thos Lipscomb, 3. Stephen Sergent, 4. Delpha Sergent, 5. Daniel Sergent, 6. John Sergent, 7. Henry Sergent. Total value $1099.95. Commrs: Moses Fuller, Benjamin Lea, Abner Lea, James Dollarhide, John Rice. 9 Aug 1816.

498–9 Stephen Pleasant to Elijah Jacobs, for $736.25, 147¼ A both sides Neds Cr adj James McMurry, Joseph Carney, John Russell; also 18 A adj first tract. 23 Sept 1816. Wit: Lawrence Vanhook, ▓▓. Whitefield.

499–500 Stephen Smith of Rockingham Co., NC, to Lawrence V. Hargis of Person Co., for $15, ¼ undivided part of his father Conrad Messer Smith Jun's undivided one-fifth part of 306 A adj Duncan Cameron, Thomas Sneed, James Williamson. 4 Oct 1816. Wit: Thos Hargis, James Gooch.

134

Figure 12-5: Portion of Deed Book D showing "Wm.Whitefield" as a witness.

Let's look at another type of record. Back on the "Search Court, Land, & Probate Records" page, scroll down to and click "Alabama Land Records" under "Search Individual Court, Land, & Probate Collections." I entered the surname of "Swords" into the "Last Name" field and clicked "Exact matches only," and then clicked **Search**.

Each of the individuals shown on the "Exact Search Results" page is related to my family: John N. Swords is another of my great-great-grandfathers. If you click on the "View Record" link for John N. Swords's purchase of 80.11 acres from the Lebanon Land Office on 1 August 1849, the record shown in figure 12-6 is displayed.

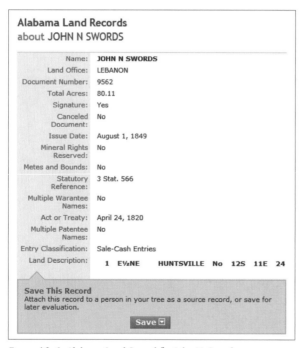

Alabama Land Records
about JOHN N SWORDS

Name:	**JOHN N SWORDS**
Land Office:	LEBANON
Document Number:	9562
Total Acres:	80.11
Signature:	Yes
Canceled Document:	No
Issue Date:	August 1, 1849
Mineral Rights Reserved:	No
Metes and Bounds:	No
Statutory Reference:	3 Stat. 566
Multiple Warantee Names:	No
Act or Treaty:	April 24, 1820
Multiple Patentee Names:	No
Entry Classification:	Sale-Cash Entries
Land Description:	1 E½NE HUNTSVILLE No 12S 11E 24

Save This Record
Attach this record to a person in your tree as a source record, or save for later evaluation.

Save ▾

Figure 12-6: Alabama Land Record for John N. Swords.

Here you see even more information, including the land description. This can be used to locate the exact piece of property he purchased. In addition, you can also visit the NARA website at <www.archives.gov> and their Order Online facility at <https://eservices.archives.gov/orderonline>. You will be asked to register and establish a user ID and password, and then you can order many record types, including the land record case files.

Finally, let's look at an example of a database containing will information. On the "Search Court, Land, & Probate Records" page, scroll down to the database titled "New York City Wills, 1730–1744" and click on it. On the search template, click the "Exact matches only" box, enter the name Henry Gillam, and click **Search**. The "Exact Search Results" page shown in figure 12-7 has two records: one in which Henry Gillam is a witness and one in which he was the testator.

Witnesses, **Henry Gillam**, Nathaniel Allcock, William Forster. Proved, December 15, 1732.
View Full Context

Page 404.--In the name of God, Amen, December 12, 1730. I, **HENRY GILLAM**, of the Borrough town of Westchester, joyner, being very sick. All of my debts are to be paid out of my personal estate, and the proceeds of the sale of my lands in Bedford and Eastchester and Westchester. I leave to my wife Hannah, ▢100, "and one blue bed, with all belonging to it;" Also a silver Tankard, and four silver spoons, a large looking glass, two oval tables, and one large Copper Porridge Pot. I leave to my son Henry, ▢60 and my wearing apparel. I leave to Thomas Griggs and his wife, ▢50. To my son-in-law James Baxter, and his wife and his two children, George and Charles Baxter, each 5 shillings. I leave to Thomas and John, the two sons of Thomas Griggs, ▢50, and to Thomas Griggs' three daughters, Elizabeth, Hannah, and Mary, ▢50. To my grand-daughter, Mary Wilson, ▢50 when of age. My executors are to sell all lands and buildings in Bedford, Eastchester, and Westchester, and the proceeds are to go to my wife and my son Henry, and to Thomas Griggs and his wife and children. I appoint my wife Hannah, and my son-in-law, Thomas Griggs, and John Bell and Nathaniel Underhill, executors. The last two are to have ▢10 each.
View Full Context

Figure 12-7: "Exact Search Results" page for Henry Gillam in "New York City Wills, 1730–1744."

When you click "View Full Context" on the first entry where Henry was a witness, the full database text is displayed. There his name appears, along with the names of other witnesses. If you click the link to the previous page, you will see that he was witnessing the will of Cicely Eddos.

In the second entry, the actual transcript of Henry Gillam's will, you learn a great deal about him. He was a "joyner" [*sic*, joiner] who lived in the Borough of Westchester, New York. He was a man of some means, owning land in Bedford, Eastchester, and Westchester. His wife, Hannah, survived him, along with what appear to be one son and two married daughters. We know the daughters' husbands' names and the names of grandchildren mentioned as beneficiaries of the estate. We also know that one son-in-law and another man were to be executors of the estate.

You may note in this record a square character preceding numbers. This actually should read as the British currency symbol for pounds sterling, £. However, not all browsers are equipped or set up with the character set to display special characters. You may be able to remedy this by going to the menu bar in your browser, choosing **Encoding** from the **View** menu, and then selecting another character set. However, in this case, I didn't bother because I know that British currency was in use at the time in question and that the correct symbol should be pounds sterling, £.

Summary

It would be impossible to demonstrate all the different types of records in the Court, Land, and Probate Records in this chapter. There simply are too many. However, as you can see, there are many possibilities to explore. By now, however, you should feel very comfortable with using the different search templates, the ranked and exact search facilities, the search results pages, and the records that are displayed. You can explore any of the other databases here to discover what clues they may hold for your research.

Chapter 13

Military Records

Armies, navies, and other martial forces have been part of human history since ancient times, and military history is the focus of immense publication and research. Huge bodies of military records have been preserved in archives and government repositories around the world. The National Archives (TNA) in England, for example, maintains documentary military records of the British Army from 1760 forward as part of its War Office (WO) record group, Royal Navy records from 1667 forward in the Admiralty (ADM) record group, and massive quantities of other military records dating from the Civil War in England in the 1640s and backwards into the twelfth century. Many of these have been indexed at various levels and can be searched on-site at TNA in Kew, Richmond, Surrey. Other records are in the possession of the respective branches of the military and in collections of manorial documents across the United Kingdom.

North American military records at all levels are maintained by the National Archives and Records Administration (NARA) in the U.S. and at the Library and Archives Canada, not to mention in the state and provincial archives and libraries.

As genealogists, we should be intensely interested in military history and the related records produced over time. Military records are many and varied, including indexes to unit and service records, draft registration and enlistment records, military service records, death and casualty lists, pension files, and other associated documentary records.

Since this book concentrates on Ancestry.com rather than all the other Ancestry database collections in the UK and Ireland, Canada, Australia, and Germany, we will primarily examine different types of military records databases that exist for the United States and its colonial predecessors. However, we will also list some of the other geographies' military records that are available to World Deluxe subscribers.

Ancestry.com hosts searchable indexes to actual records and, in some cases, to digitized images of actual documents. As with all the databases at Ancestry.com, source information and descriptions of the contents of each collection are available for your reference. If you are searching for an actual record or a folder for an individual, you will want to contact the repository cited in the source to determine the availability of copies of documents. The source information will also provide you with the details you need to write a source citation to document the evidence you have located.

To follow along with the examples in this chapter, access the "Search Military Records" page by clicking "Military" in the "Browse Records" section on the **Search** tab. (For more information about searching and browsing records, see chapter 2.) In the upper right-hand corner of the page is a link labeled

"Welcome to the Military Records Center." I urge you to visit this introductory page for tips about effectively searching for military records here.

Another interesting link on the page is the "Use census records" link in the "Next Steps" section on the right-hand side of the page. It links to information found on U.S. federal census records that may point you to military records and expedite your search:

- 1840—Included the names and ages of military pensioners.

- 1850—Listed the occupations (including military service) of all males over the age of fifteen.

- 1890—Collected a special census of Union veterans and widows.

- 1900—Detailed separate military schedules and indexes for all military personnel.

- 1910—Recorded survivors of Civil War service, including Confederate and Union forces.

- 1920—Separately enumerated all overseas military and naval forces, and many domestic bases. Some bases are listed under state and county records.

Links to the search pages for each of the censuses are provided to expedite your navigation to those databases.

Early American Military Databases

It is important to recognize that the earliest colonial documents for the American colonies may no longer exist. Some of the only reference material available may have been compiled and published in the form of family, local, and military histories. The information may have been culled from rare documents, journals, and colonial government records located in the U.S. and overseas. With that in mind, let's look at two databases for Revolutionary War era military information.

In the "Search Individual Military Collections" scroll box, locate the database titled "Muster and Pay Rolls of the War of the Revolution, 1775–1783: Miscellaneous Records." The description of this database tells us that the books from which this database was created were originally published as Volumes XLVII and XLVIII of *Collections of the New-York Historical Society* for the years 1914 and 1915 (New York: 1916).

I performed an exact search for John Alexander, with no keyword information entered. The "Exact Search Results" page contained the three entries shown in figure 13-1.

Muster and Pay Rolls of the War of the Revolution, 1775-1783.
  6th Pennsylvania Battalion 1776
    A Muster Roll of Capt Abraham Smiths Company in Colonel [William] Irvine's Battalion of Forces raised in the State of Pennsylvania and now in the Service of the United States of America, Dated in Camp on Mount Independance, November 28th, 1776.

    <b>**Name:** John Alexander
    Rank: 1st Lt
    Enlistment Date: 23 Mar
    Comments: Recruiting in Penna G. Gates Orders
    View Full Context

Muster and Pay Rolls of the War of the Revolution, 1775-1783.
  6th Pennsylvania Battalion 1776
    A Muster Roll of Capt Abraham Smiths Company in Colonel [William] Irvine's Battalion of Forces raised in the State of Pennsylvania and now in the Service of the United States of America, Dated in Camp on Mount Independance, November 28th, 1776.

    <b>**Name:** John Alexander
    Rank: 2nd Lt
    Enlistment Date: 09
    Comments: Promoted
    View Full Context

Muster and Pay Rolls of the War of the Revolution, 1775-1783.
  Virginia Line--6th Regiment
    Lieutenant Samuel Selden's Company, December 12th, 1780 A Description & Size roll of Lieut Samuel Seldens Company of Colo [John] Green's Detachmt taken at Petersberg, Dec. 12, 1780

    <b>**Name:** Jno Alexander
    Rank: Corpl
    Age: 23
    Comments: Size 5 11 1/2; Trade Cordmaker
    View Full Context

Figure 13-1: "Exact Search Results" page for the "Muster and Pay Rolls Records" for John Alexander.

The information in this database was transcribed exactly as it was published. You will note that the first two entries apply to one John Alexander who served in the 6th Pennsylvania Battalion 1776. One of these records refers to his recruitment and the other refers to his promotion. When you click the link labeled "View Full Context" in this and other databases, this particular record and all other records from the database will be displayed in the contextual sequence in the entire database. You can then browse forward and backward to see other records in the database. This may help you locate other personnel in the same military unit, or activities relating to a particular time period.

Let's look at another Revolutionary War—related database. In the "Search Individual Military Collections" scroll box, click "American Revolutionary War Rejected Pensions."

This time I searched strictly for the surname of Patterson. I was rewarded with thirteen results, the first ten of which are shown in figure 13-2.

The information in the "View Record" pages provides me with names, states, and locations, along with the reason for

View Record	Name	State	Location	Reason
View Record	**Mary Patterson, widow of William**	Maine	Edgecomb, Lincoln	No satisfactory proof that the vessels were public ones on board of which service was performed.
View Record	**Robert Patterson (deceased)**	New York	Erwin, Steuben	He did not establish six months' service before he died.
View Record	**Peter Patterson (deceased)**	New Jersey	Freehold, Monmouth	For further proof--claim withdrawn May 19, 1838, by J. T. Randolph.
View Record	**James Patterson**	Pennsylvania	Upper Chaunceford, York	He did not perform six months military service.
View Record	**Peter Patterson**	Pennsylvania	--, Fayette	Name not on the rolls of service. If he served every alternate month in the New Jersey militia, and cannot, from old age, specify each tour, he can only be allowed at the lowest rate provided for by the act, viz: six months.
View Record	**Ann Patterson, widow of John**	North Carolina	--, Iredell	For further evidence.
View Record	**Elizabeth Patterson**	North Carolina		For further proof.
View Record	**Honor Haze, formerly widow of Matthew Patterson**	Ohio	--, Clermont	A soldier of the regular army.
View Record	**Nancy Childress, widow of Patterson**	Tennessee	Dandridge, Jefferson	No proof of service.
View Record	**John Patterson (deceased)**	Indiana	Brownstown, Jackson	Claim for alleged service in this case already allowed.

Figure 13-2: "Exact Search Results" page for "Patterson" in "American Revolutionary War Rejected Pensions."

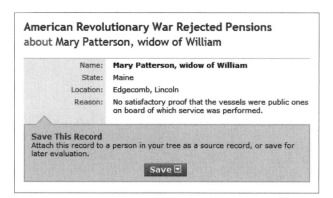

Figure 13-3: Record for Mary Patterson in "Rejected Pensions."

the rejection of the pension application (see figure 13-3). The original pension applications are held at the National Archives and Records Administration if you decide you want to order copies to examine for yourself.

American Civil War Records

The American Civil War, or the War Between the States, stands as the bloodiest period in United States history. More has been written about this period and the participants than about any other topic in American history. Military regimental histories and personal memoirs were published by the hundreds between 1865 and 1900, and along with magazine articles and dedicated periodicals such as the monthly *Confederate Veteran*, they recounted the campaigns, battles, and individual stories of men and women during this tumultuous period. In addition, there are literally millions of documents associated with military service; muster and pay rolls; casualties and deaths; hospitalization; pensions to veterans, widows, and orphans (including the surviving 1890 Federal Census special Veterans Schedules); military unit records; and many others.

Ancestry.com has compiled an excellent collection of databases and finding aids for American Civil War research. You can certainly browse through the databases listed in the "Search Individual Military Collections" scroll box and choose to work with specific Civil War—related databases. You might also choose to simply go to the "Featured Military Collections" section and click the entry titled "Civil War Collection" (see figure 13-4). If you do so, you will be brought to a page that includes a search template that allows you to search *all* of the Civil War databases or to click on an individual Civil War database and work exclusively with that and its records. It is important to check the scroll box periodically to insure that you don't miss the addition of any new military-related databases associated with the Civil War.

Let's start with a search of my great-great-grandfather, Jesse Holder, from Georgia. The "Ranked Search Results" page started with all persons named Jesse Holder and whose record included the keyword "Georgia" anywhere.

The first record that I know must be my ancestor's is from the "American Civil War Soldiers" database for the man whose residence was listed as Gwinnett County, Georgia. When I click the link to that record for him, the record shown in figure 13-5 is displayed.

Civil War Collection

☐ Exact matches only
First Name   Last Name
Keyword(s)
[Search]

📁 **Civil War Databases @ Ancestry**
American Civil War Battle Summaries
American Civil War General Officers
American Civil War Regiments
American Civil War Soldiers
Civil War Pension Index: General Index to Pension Files, 1861-1934
Civil War Service Records
Confederate Research Sources
Confederate States Field Officers
Kansas Civil War Soldiers

Figure 13-4: A portion of the "Civil War Collection" search page.

American Civil War Soldiers
about **Jesse Holder**

Name:	**Jesse Holder ,**
Residence:	Gwinnett County, Georgia
Enlistment Date:	24 August 1861
Distinguished Service:	DISTINGUISHED SERVICE
Side Served:	Confederacy
State Served:	Georgia
Unit Numbers:	368
Service Record:	Enlisted as a Private on 24 August 1861 Enlisted in Company F, 24th Infantry Regiment Georgia on 24 August 1861.

Save This Record
Attach this record to a person in your tree as a source record, or save for later evaluation.
[Save ▾]

Source Citation: Side served: *Confederacy*; State served: *Georgia*; Enlistment date: *24 August 1861*..

Figure 13-5: Record for Jesse Holder in the "American Civil War Soldiers" database.

This database is one that is growing, with more than 2 million soldiers' records entered of the more than 4 million soldiers who served in the war. This record tells me that Jesse Holder enlisted as a Private in "Company F, 24th Infantry Regiment Georgia" on 24 August 1861. The link to the unit in which he enlisted can be clicked and takes me to an "Exact Search Results" page for the "American Civil War Regiments" database (see figure 13-6).

View Record	Name of Regiment	Date of Organization	Muster Date	Regiment Type
View Record	24th Infantry Regiment GA		09 April 1865	Infantry

Figure 13-6: "Exact Search Results" page for the "American Civil War Regiments" database.

When I click the "View Record" link, there is a "Regimental History" in some cases and a list of battles and armed conflicts in which it was involved. A portion of the history record for the "24th Infantry Regiment GA" is shown in figure 13-7.

You will notice that some of the names of battles are links. They will present you with a descriptive record of the engagement and the name of the source from which the account was taken. You can also click "View Full Context" to see this account in context with the entire military history for that date.

American Civil War Regiments

Regiment:	24th Infantry Regiment GA
Date Mustered:	09 April 1865
Regiment Type:	Infantry
Regimental Soldiers and History:	List of Soldiers

Regimental History

Battles Fought

Fought on 06 May 1862 at Williamsburg, VA.
Fought on 31 May 1862 at Near Seven Pines, VA.
Fought on 31 May 1862 at Seven Pines, VA.
Fought on 18 June 1862 at Richmond, VA.
Fought on 29 June 1862 at Savage's Station, VA.
Fought on 01 July 1862 at Malvern Hill, VA.
Fought on 02 July 1862 at Malvern Hill, VA.
Fought on 30 August 1862 at 2nd Manassas, VA.
Fought on 14 September 1862 at Crampton's Gap, MD.
Fought on 16 September 1862 at Sharpsburg, MD.
Fought on 17 September 1862 at Sharpsburg, MD.
Fought on 18 September 1862 at Near Sharpsburg, MD.
Fought on 01 October 1862 at Sharpsburg, MD.
Fought on 14 October 1862.
Fought on 16 October 1862 at Charles Town, WV.
Fought on 15 November 1862.
Fought on 13 December 1862 at Fredericksburg, VA.

Figure 13-7: A portion of the regiment history for the 24th Infantry Regiment GA.

Look at figure 13-7 again. At the top is another link labeled "List of Soldiers." When you click this link, you are presented with an "Exact

Search Results" page for the entire military unit, starting with the highest ranking officer and working down to the privates. The "24th Infantry Regiment GA" had a total of 1,304 personnel. Instead of scrolling through to locate my Jesse Holder, it is possible to scroll to the template at the bottom of the page and simply enter his name with the information I have already determined into the template.

What you have seen is an example of the interrelationship between these databases. You can see that you could begin with a name or a regiment, if you know one or both, and locate detailed information about an individual. The details about enlistment date, regiment, regimental history, battle and engagements, and rosters of all the unit personnel can help add a tremendous amount of context to your understanding of your ancestor's military life. Based on the knowledge of the regiment and the battles in which it participated, you can study the engagement, the conditions, and other factors and really bring your ancestor back to life. Perhaps you will then want to check the "Civil War Pension Index: General Index to Pension Files, 1861–1934" database for a pension application file at NARA, and then order copies to add to your research. The "National Home for Disabled Volunteer Soldiers" database is another resource you might want to check. This is an exciting part of your family history research!

World War I Draft Registration Cards, 1917–1918

One of the most exciting collections on Ancestry.com is the "World War I Draft Registration Cards, 1917–1918" database. This database contains an index and images of World War I draft registration cards completed by approximately 24 million men living in the U.S. in 1917 and 1918. Information that may be found for an individual includes name, place of residence, date and place of birth, race, country of citizenship, occupation, and employer. Also included is the name and address of the registrant's nearest relative, which can be either a clue to connect an individual to the rest of his family *or* a confirmation that you have located a long-lost relative.

One of my most exciting genealogical finds came when Ancestry.com completed its digitization and scanning of these records. I had been desperately searching for a missing great-uncle, Brisco Washington Holder, who left home in Rome, Georgia, in about 1906. I entered his name in the search template as an exact search. Sure enough, an "Exact Search Results" page yielded only one exact match.

This listing and the "View Record" page provided me with a middle name and a date of birth, neither of which I had known before. However, when I clicked the "View Image" link, even more information was revealed, as shown in figure 13-8.

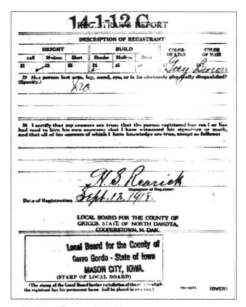

Figure 13-8: WWI Draft Registration Card for Brisco Washington Holder (front and back).

The draft registration card was obviously completed by Brisco, based on a comparison of his signature and other handwriting on the card. From Georgia he had found his way to live in Mason City, Cerro Gordo County, Iowa, and worked as a separator tender for Max Wild of Griggs, North Dakota. (Research for Max Wild in Griggs County, ND, in the 1910 Federal Census showed that he was in the grain business.) Brisco stated his age as 41 and listed his oldest brother, E. E. Holder of Rome, Georgia, as his nearest relative. (This verified that I had the exact match I wanted.)

The back of the card was almost as exciting as the front. The physical description of Brisco told me he was tall, slender, and that he had grey eyes and brown hair. I have only seen one photograph of Brisco and these details help bring his appearance to life for me. The remaining information was completed by the registrar, H. S. Rearick, on 12 September 1918, which was the date of the third draft call in the U.S. for World War I. The stamps of both the local draft boards of counties in North Dakota and Iowa seems contradictory, but it is possible that the Griggs County, North Dakota, draft board pre-stamped cards and sent a supply to the Cerro Gordo County, Iowa, board for use in the third draft call. I may never resolve that discrepancy, but I did find Brisco on 12 September 1918.

U.S. World War II Army Enlistment Records, 1938–1946

A database of more recent military records is the "U.S. World War II Army Enlistment Records, 1938–1946." Figure 13-9 on page 222 shows an example from this database, found using the search methods outlined in chapter 2.

As you can see from the example of Joe B. Mason, his year of birth and location are listed and his nationality is noted.

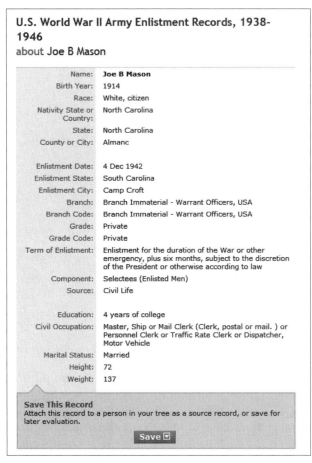

U.S. World War II Army Enlistment Records, 1938-1946

about **Joe B Mason**

Name:	**Joe B Mason**
Birth Year:	1914
Race:	White, citizen
Nativity State or Country:	North Carolina
State:	North Carolina
County or City:	Almanc
Enlistment Date:	4 Dec 1942
Enlistment State:	South Carolina
Enlistment City:	Camp Croft
Branch:	Branch Immaterial - Warrant Officers, USA
Branch Code:	Branch Immaterial - Warrant Officers, USA
Grade:	Private
Grade Code:	Private
Term of Enlistment:	Enlistment for the duration of the War or other emergency, plus six months, subject to the discretion of the President or otherwise according to law
Component:	Selectees (Enlisted Men)
Source:	Civil Life
Education:	4 years of college
Civil Occupation:	Master, Ship or Mail Clerk (Clerk, postal or mail.) or Personnel Clerk or Traffic Rate Clerk or Dispatcher, Motor Vehicle
Marital Status:	Married
Height:	72
Weight:	137

Save This Record
Attach this record to a person in your tree as a source record, or save for later evaluation.

Save ☑

Figure 13-9: U.S. World War II Army Enlistment Record.

His enlistment date of 4 December 1942 at Camp Croft, South Carolina, as a private is also noted. He was six feet tall, weighed 137 pounds, had four years of college, and was married.

The fact that we have an enlistment record would point to ordering a copy of any military service records from NARA. You might also want to check the Ancestry.com "World War II Prisoners of War, 1941–1946," the "WWI, WWII, and Korean War Casualty Listings," and the "World War II and Korean Conflict Veterans Interred Overseas" databases for any listing. These may confirm or refute any hypotheses that the person was taken prisoner, killed, or buried overseas.

Summary

If you've followed along and traveled through the Ancestry.com databases in this chapter, you've got a good sampling of the wealth of databases in the Military Records Collection and how to work with them. We've focused on the American-related military records. However, there are military records in the other geographical areas of the Ancestry family:

- **Ancestry.co.uk**—The "Indian Army Quarterly List for 1 January 1912," "The Royal Irish Constabulary 1816–1921," "British Army Pensioners Abroad, 1772–1899," and others. The list continues to grow.

- **Ancestry.ca**—The "United Empire Loyalists," "War of 1812: Miscellaneous Canadian Records," and the "Rebellion of 1837, Upper Canada" databases are included and there are more to come.

- **Ancestry.au and Ancestry.de**—Military records databases are being evaluated for addition to these two geographies.

Ancestry.com continues to be committed to expanding the military databases *and* the historical military reference materials to help you with your research. As you continue to hone your database search skills, you will be prepared to effectively use each new resource as it is added. In the meantime, continue to use Internet search engines and the libraries' and archives' collections on the Internet to expand your knowledge, and study political history, social history, and geography to place your ancestors in context and bring their military experiences to life.

Chapter 14

Reference and Finding Aids

Reference materials are a hallmark of genealogical research. Ancestry.com has the largest collection of searchable databases, many of which, as you already know, consist of indexed, digitized document images. It should therefore be no surprise that Ancestry.com would also provide the largest collection of online reference works and finding aids.

We explored the impressive Family and Local Histories Collection in chapter 8, and that collection continues to grow to support your research. In addition, the Reference and Finding Aids Collection contains a diverse amount of printed resources including dictionaries, maps, and gazetteers that will help family historians find and understand genealogical records. Among the resources here are *The Source: A Guidebook to American Genealogy*, the *Genealogical Library Master Catalog*, *PERSI*, *Genealogical Publications: A List of 50,000 Sources from the Library of Congress*, the *U.S. Cemetery Address Book*, and other core reference works, all in full text and every-word searchable.

In addition to general family history resources, the collection includes country studies for numerous countries outside of the United States and the United Kingdom. These studies can provide invaluable information about the native lands of your non-Anglican ancestors. Some of the more unique countries included in these studies are Egypt, Belarus, Cyprus, Hungary, Italy, Japan, Mongolia, Poland, and Russia, as well as many others. The *World Fact Book* is an excellent supplement to the country studies.

You will find that the Reference and Finding Aids Collection, along with materials on the **Learning Center** tab, will provide you with an excellent online genealogical reference library at your fingertips twenty-four hours a day, seven days a week. (We will explore and discuss the **Learning Center** tab in chapter 15.)

For the examples in this chapter, go to the "Search Reference & Finding Aids Records" page by clicking "Reference & Finding Aids" in the "Browse Records" section of the **Search** tab. For more information about searching, see chapter 2.

In the upper right-hand corner of the "Search Reference & Finding Aids Records" page is a link labeled "Welcome to the Reference & Finding Aids Center." I urge you to visit this introductory page for tips about effectively searching for different records here. At the bottom of that page are some informative articles written by Donn Devine, Dick Eastman, Juliana Smith, and myself about using these types of records.

Searching the Reference and Finding Aids Records

The databases that comprise the Reference and Finding Aids Collection are many and diverse. It is important for you to realize that some deal with geographical locations and some with "how-to" topics. Some contain individuals' names—maybe including one of your ancestors—and others are strictly indexes that can direct you to other materials.

Look at the search template on the "Search Reference & Finding Aids Records" page. You will be using this and other search templates in the Reference and Finding Aids Collection differently than you have used them before. Let me explain.

Since the databases here are so diverse, you may or may not be searching for a name, and you probably won't be using dates to narrow your searches. Instead, you may find yourself wanting to locate information on a geographical location, in which case you may use only the exact search facility and then only a country or the keyword field. Let me show you some examples.

Let's say that I want to search for the name Stephen Danko. The "Ranked Search Results" page (which I get by deselecting the "Exact matches only" box) begins with several three-star matches from the Biography & Genealogy Master Index (BGMI) (see figure 14-1). I clicked on the link for Kevin Stephen Danko born in 1959.

Match Quality	Record Type	Information found in record
★★★☆☆	Biography & Genealogy Master Index (BGMI) Reference & Finding Aids	Name: **Kevin Stephen Danko** Birth: 1959
★★★☆☆	Biography & Genealogy Master Index (BGMI) Reference & Finding Aids	Name: **Stephen Gaspar Danko** Birth: 1942
	💬 To get better results, **add Birth or Death Information**. Take a guess if you're not sure. Add this information now | Learn more	
★★★☆☆	Biography & Genealogy Master Index (BGMI) Reference & Finding Aids	Name: **Stephen John Danko** Birth: 1955

Figure 14-1: Top three results for "Stephen Danko" in a ranked search of the Reference & Finding Aids Collection.

The search result consists of a single record for *Who's Who of Emerging Leaders in America. Third edition, 1991–1992.* With this information, I can check with my local public or academic library to determine if they have a copy of this book. If not, I can ask for their assistance in initiating an Interlibrary Loan to obtain a photocopy of the entry for this individual.

In this case, if I had checked "Exact matches only" on the search template, I would have had a similar result. Figure 14-2 does, indeed, show three Stephen Dankos—the same three that appeared in the "Ranked Search Results" page.

Let's now go back to the "Search Reference & Finding Aids Records" page and search for a specific geographical

---

Name: Danko, Kevin Stephen
Birth – Death: 1959-
Source Citation:

- Who's Who of Emerging Leaders in America. Third edition, 1991-1992. Wilmette, IL: Marquis Who's Who, 1991. (WhoEmL 3)

Name: Danko, Stephen Gaspar
Birth – Death: 1942-
Source Citation:

- Who's Who in American Law. Fourth edition, 1985-1986. Wilmette, IL: Marquis Who's Who, 1985. (WhoAmL 4)
- Who's Who in American Law. Fifth edition, 1987-1988. Wilmette, IL: Marquis Who's Who, 1987. (WhoAmL 5)
- Who's Who of Emerging Leaders in America. First edition, 1987-1988. Wilmette, IL: Marquis Who's Who, 1987. (WhoEmL 1)

Name: Danko, Stephen John
Birth – Death: 1955-
Source Citation:

- American Men & Women of Science(TM) (Bowker(R)). A biographical directory of today's leaders in physical, biological and related sciences. 19th edition. Eight volumes. New Providence, NJ: R.R. Bowker, 1994. (AmMWSc 19)
- American Men & Women of Science(TM) (Bowker(R)). A biographical directory of today's leaders in physical, biological and related sciences. 20th edition. Eight volumes. New Providence, NJ: R.R. Bowker, 1998. (AmMWSc 20)
- American Men & Women of Science. A biographical directory of today's leaders in physical, biological and related sciences. 21st edition. Eight volumes. Detroit: Gale Group, 2003. (AmMWSc 21)

Figure 14-2: The three records in the BGMI with an "Exact matches only" search.

location: Poland. With the "Exact matches only" option deselected, my first impulse is to simply use the "Birth Country" drop-down list to select Poland, as shown in figure 14-3. However, when I click **Search**, there are no matches found! What do I do now?

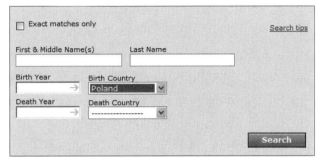

Figure 14-3: Search Reference & Finding Aids Records template with "Exact matches only" deselected and "Poland" entered in the "Birth Country" field.

Instead, let's click the "Exact matches only" option. The template changes, and now I can use the" Lived in" drop-down list to select Poland (see figure 14-4).

This time, when I click **Search**, I am rewarded with an "Exact Search Results" page. There are six databases listed with a total of 1,178 matches!

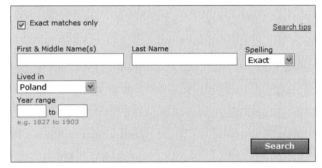

Figure 14-4: Exact search template used to search for databases about Poland.

Here is what I found in those six databases:

- **Canadian Genealogy Index, 1600s–1900s**—One entry is displayed for an individual born in Vilna, Poland.

- **Geographic Reference Library**—There are fifty-six records about places, natural features, and buildings containing the name "Poland" in the United States.

- **Origin of Certain Place Names in the United States**— Two records describe that two towns in Poland have namesake place names in the United States.

- **Poland Country Study**—There are 1,097 separate records (in this case, mentions) of Poland. The first record represents the first mention of Poland, which is in the title of the country study. You can click on the link labeled "View Full Context" and read the entire study. It contains information you would find in an almanac and an encyclopedia, and also contains social and political demographics and evaluations. If, within that country study for Poland, you wish to narrow your search to a topic, such as the army, go to the bottom of the "Poland Country Study" page and enter "army" in the "Keyword(s)" field of the "Refine Your Search of the Poland Country Study" box (see figure 14-5).

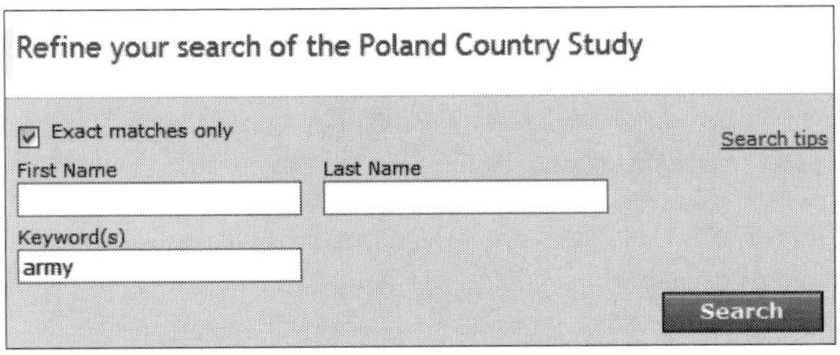

Figure 14-5: "Refine your search" search template for the Poland Country Study.

Keywords

The "Keyword(s)" field only allows you to search for records that have the single or multiple keywords you enter. You cannot use quotation marks around multiple words to make it into an "exact phrase" search as you would in an Internet search engine. However, all words entered in the "Keyword(s)" field will be displayed in bold in the records in the search results.

- **U.S. Gazetteer, 1854**—There are eight records describing places in the United States with the name of Poland as of 1854.

- **World Foreign Gazetteer, Vol. 1**—There are fourteen records for populated places, lakes, islands, waterways, and so on, named Poland.

As the examples above have illustrated, you have to concentrate on using the search templates in the Reference and Finding Aids Collection a little differently than you have in other databases at Ancestry.com. The "Keyword(s)" field will be more useful to you in locating records and narrowing your searches than ever before. I would encourage you not to make an assumption to use just the exact search function. That may omit important results that a ranked search may yield.

Searching Books

Many reference books have been made into every-word searchable as databases and are included in the Reference and Finding Aids Records Collection. Two of the most important are published by Ancestry Publishing: *The Source: A Guidebook to American Genealogy*, rev. ed. and *Ancestry's Red Book: American State, County, and Town Sources,* rev. ed. *The Source* covers all the important aspects of genealogical research, including censuses, land records, military records, church records, and many more. It describes the records in detail, what they contain, where they can be located, and how they can be used in your research. *Ancestry's Red Book* is the definitive work about United States research. Organized by U.S. state, this reference easily directs you to information-rich resources including vital records, census, land, probate, church, and military records, and much more.

I want to search *The Source* for references to the word "obituaries" and read more about them (see figure 14-6).

The "Exact Search Results" page indicates there are seventy-three matches for the word "obituaries." Figure 14-7 on page 232 shows the

Figure 14-7 on page 232

Searching *The Source*

To find the search template for *The Source*, follow these steps:

1. Click the **Search** tab.
2. Click "Reference & Finding Aids" in the "Browse Records" section.
3. In the "Featured Reference & Finding Aids Collections" section, click "The Source: A Guidebook of American Genealogy."

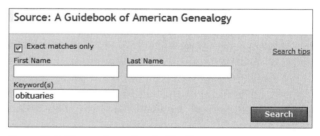

Figure 14-6: The search template for The Source.

first two of the records. The records are displayed in the search results list in the order that they appear in the reference work. In this case, the first record is taken from the "Introduction" (page 3); the second record is from "Chapter 1" (page 11). In this way, you can easily progress through the book's contents on the subject. If one of these text records seems to contain the information most pertinent to what you want to know, you

---

The Source: A Guidebook of American Genealogy
Introduction
*Arrangement of **The Source***
Record Types

Szucs and Luebking, The Source: A Guidebook of American Genealogy, p.3
James L. Hansen surveys newspapers from all aspects, first discussing the **various** types of information to be found in them and how to evaluate this evidence. In describing obituaries, for example, he points out that this information was sometimes provided directly by close relatives of the deceased, and in other instances was filtered through a professional obituary writer. Hansen then describes the techniques necessary to find newspapers appropriate to the researcher□s problem, and how to carry out the search once the newspaper has been found. He concludes with an extensive bibliography of inventories of newspapers, indexes and abstracts of their contents, and other related items.
View Full Context

The Source: A Guidebook of American Genealogy
Chapter 1: The Foundations of Family History Research
The First Steps
Family Bibles

Szucs and Luebking, The Source: A Guidebook of American Genealogy, p.11
Check each page of a Bible or inherited book for notations or enclosures. Some owners recorded the dates of events, such as memorial services, weddings, and christenings, in the margin **adjacent** to the Bible text used for the occasion. Others used favorite books to hold prayer cards, obituaries from newspapers, significant scraps of church bulletins, and handwritten notes. Such a note enclosed in one book contained, in German script, the full name and birth date of each child born to the finder□s great-grandparents.
View Full Context

Figure 14-7: A portion of the "Exact Search Results" page for the word "obituaries" in The Source.

can click on the "View Full Context" link and see the record in its place in the book. You can then read text before or after that text, or even read the entire chapter or the whole book. If you want to revise your search or enter a new search, simply go to the "Refine your search of the Source: A Guidebook of American Genealogy" search template at the bottom of the page and enter the new search word(s).

The *PERiodical Source Index* (PERSI)

The *PERiodical Source Index*, also known as *PERSI*, is a subject index to genealogical and local history periodicals. Periodicals are simply publications produced regularly as part of a series—magazines, newsletters, journals, and so on. There is an amazing amount of genealogical information published in these periodicals every year.

PERSI is an index to this material. *PERSI* began as an ambitious project of the Allen County Public Library (ACPL) in Ft. Wayne, Indiana. Their lofty goal was to gather all genealogical periodicals, both past and present, and index their contents. This growing database has become the largest dataset of its kind, containing over 1 million references to helpful articles.

The information *PERSI* indexes may be the only record ever published of materials such as cemetery interment canvasses, courthouse records, and rare historical materials that have been otherwise filed and forgotten. *PERSI* provides access through its indexes to the issue, the title of the article, and identifying details that allow you to order copies of the article, either directly from the ACPL, via Interlibrary Loan from any of the other repositories listed in the *PERSI* record, or directly from the publishing society.

You can find *PERSI* in the scroll box on the "Search Reference & Finding Aids Records" page (see figure 14-8). You can search its indexes using the following categories:

- Surname

- Locality (United States, Canada, and Foreign)

- Methodology ("How-to" articles)

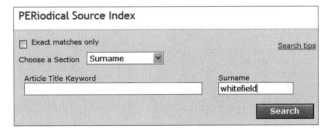

Figure 14-8: PERSI *search template.*

Depending on which category you select, the template will change to facilitate your search. You can change the type of search performed by selecting from the "Choose a Section" drop-down list. Remember that using the exact match search facility allows you to also use wildcards. Let's look at samples of the different search options for *PERSI* database queries. During the first example, the "Surname" template, I'll explain the process for locating periodical articles, identifying the repository(ies) where copies are held, and obtaining copies.

Surname Template

A search by surname or keyword will find all matching articles, regardless of where these families resided. To do so, select "Surname" from the "Choose a Section" drop-down list (this option is selected in the example shown in figure 14-8). You can add keywords to help narrow your search. However, I suggest that you always start with a broad search, view the results to see what kind of matches you get the first time, and then narrow your search accordingly.

A portion of the search results list for the search for the surname "Whitefield" is shown in figure 14-9. The first two

---

Article Title: Ben. Franklin-Geo. Whitefield friends.
Surname: WHITEFIELD
Volume: 35
Number: 4 (July 1997)
Periodical Title: Methodist History

Article Title: Benjamin Franklin & George Whitefield
Surname: WHITEFIELD
Volume: 50
Number: 3 (July 1993)
Periodical Title: William And Mary Quarterly

Figure 14-9: Part of a PERSI *"Exact Search Results" page.*

results drew similarly titled articles, one from a periodical titled *Methodist History* and another from the *William and Mary Quarterly*.

Note that the periodical titles are links. We'll visit one of those in a moment. However, first of all, you will need to record some identifying information before you can obtain a copy of an article. Here is what you do.

Let's say you want to order the second record on the list. Record the following information:

- Article Title: Benjamin Franklin & George Whitefield.

- Periodical Title: William and Mary Quarterly

- Volume: 50

- Number: 3 (July 1993)

Next, click on the link to the periodical, the *William and Mary Quarterly*. The next page provides detailed information about the publication, including the publisher and the address, and its ISSN (see figure 14-10).

Periodical Title: WILLIAM AND MARY QUARTERLY
Persi Code: WMMY
Topics: VA
Issues Per Year: 4x
ISSN Number: 0043-5597
ACPLHoldings: 1-2ser. 1892-1943, 3rd ser. v.1- 1944-
Repositories: Allen County Public Library
Los Angeles Public Library
Dallas Public Library
Atlanta-Fulton Public Library
Family History Library
Library of Congress
New York Public Library
Newberry Library
New England Historic Genealogical Society Library
State Historical Society of Wisconsin Library
Public Library of Cincinnati & Hamilton Co. (partial holdings)
Publisher: Institute, Early Amer Hist & Cultur
Address: POB 220 : Williamsburg , VA 23187

Figure 14-10: PERSI periodical detail record.

In addition to the items listed before, there is one more piece of information you'll need to obtain a copy of the article:

- *Persi* Code: WMMY

Every periodical is assigned a unique code to differentiate it from another publication that may also have the same or a very similar name.

Figure 14-11: Pop-up window with repository's address.

Look at figure 14-10 again. You will see a list of links to a number of repositories (libraries or archives) that hold copies of the periodical in their collections. (Some may be marked as partial holdings.) If you click on any of these links, a small window will pop up with the address of the repository (see figure 14-11). Please note that not all periodicals will be held in so many facilities. In fact, since ACPL is the initiator and coordinator of *PERSI*, that library may be the only repository listed. In other words, if it is listed in *PERSI*, you can be confident that the ACPL has the periodical issue you have found cited.

Now that you know that the ACPL has the article you found, and now that you have the five pieces of information you need to uniquely identify the article, you can request the copies. As I said earlier, you can order the copies directly from the ACPL, via Interlibrary Loan, or directly from the publisher.

If you want to order copies through the ACPL, it's a simple process. Go to the search results page and scroll to the bottom. At the end of the "Description" section is a link labeled "Learn more …" Click the link, near the bottom of the resulting page is the address of the ACPL and a link called, "Click here for order form." Click that link and a blank "Periodical Source Index (*PERSI*) Order Form" will be displayed. Print the form and you can then add the five pieces of identifying information you collected earlier. You can request up to six articles at a time. Mail the completed form with a check for $7.50. The ACPL will locate and copy the article(s) requested and send the copies to you within six to eight weeks. They will send you an invoice for the copies, charging $0.20 per page copied for you. You are on the honor system to pay the invoice. It's as easy as that!

Now that you know how the search, locate, identify, and order process works, let's continue looking at the other *PERSI* search templates.

U.S. Locality Template

When you select "U.S. Locality" from the "Choose a Section" drop-down list, the template changes to the format you see in figure 14-12. The surname field is removed. Another drop-down

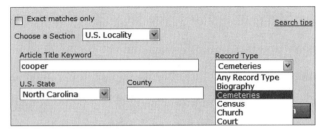

Figure 14-12: PERSI *"U.S. Locality" search template.*

list for "Record Type" is added and you can see the different types from which you can select (including the default, "Any Record Type"). Another drop-down list allows you to select the "U.S. State" and another field is added into which you can type a county name, if you like. This is optional.

In the example shown, I was searching for anything published about a cemetery in North Carolina known as the Cooper Cemetery. I completed the search template as you see and clicked **Search**. I was rewarded with eight matches. The Virginia-North Carolina Genealogical Society published the results of their canvass of the Cooper Cemetery in three successive issues of its *Piedmont Lineages* quarterly in 1997 and 1998. I ordered these from the ACPL and found a wealth of tombstone inscription information transcribed there.

Canada Locality Template

When you select "Canada Locality" from the "Choose a Section" drop-down list, the template changes to the format

Figure 14-13: PERSI *"Canada Locality" search template.*

you see in figure 14-13. Again, the surname field is removed and a drop-down "Record Type" list is available. Instead of "U.S. State," there is another drop-down list for the selection of a "Canadian Province," if you like. (You can also leave it at the default of "All Canadian Provinces.") In this case, I was searching for anything relating to Lutheran churches in Ontario. My search was rewarded with fifteen matches.

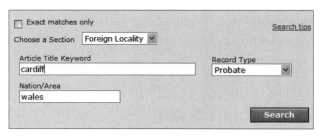

Figure 14-14: PERSI *"Foreign Locality" search template.*

Foreign Locality Template

When you select "Foreign Locality" from the "Choose a Section" drop-down list, the template changes again (see figure 14-14). The surname field is removed and a drop-down "Record Type" list is available. Instead of a drop-down list for "U.S. State" or "Canadian Province," a field for "Nation/Area" is available into which can type a place. My search for an article about probate records in Wales and with the word "Cardiff" in the title was unsuccessful. However, when I removed Cardiff, I obtained six matches.

Methodology Template

When you select "Methodology" from the "Choose a Section" drop-down list, the only search criteria choices are the drop-down "Record Type" list and the "Article Title Keyword." In the example, I wanted to search for articles about research methodology for working with land records, and specifically

about bounty lands (see figure
14-15). I was rewarded with
nine search results with the
word "bounty" in the article
title.

Figure 14-15: PERSI *"Methodology" search template.*

There are many ways to
use *PERSI.* Three generations
of one of my family lines and two of another lived in Rome,
Floyd County, Georgia. I am always looking for more historical
and genealogical information about the area during the years
in which my forebears lived there. Therefore, I have used the
"U.S. Locality template" to locate many periodical articles
about that city, its history, people, and culture during the more
than 106 years my family members lived there.

Ancestry Map Center

Maps are indispensable reference materials *and* finding aids.
Visualizing the places your ancestors lived and where their life
events occurred in geographical relation to one another helps
you better understand them and their movements. It also helps
you place them into context with the historical events and
social patterns of their time.

Ancestry.com has compiled a most impressive collection
of digitized map resources over the years, many of which are
not easily located elsewhere. You will definitely want to use
the gazetteers and map resources in the Map Collection to
help locate the places where your ancestors were born, lived,
migrated, worked, died, and buried.

You can find the Map Collection in the Ancestry Map
Center, which is one of the featured databases on the "Search
Reference & Finding Aids Records" page. Note that when
you search using the **Photos & Maps** tab on the main search
template, you are also searching the Map Collection.

There are literally hundreds of different types of maps today. And while Ancestry.com does not have maps representing all of these types, their collection continues to grow on a regular basis.

There are eleven broad categories of maps that you will find in the Map Collection and it is important that you know the differences between them. This knowledge will make you a more astute researcher and will allow you to seek appropriate types of maps in other venues by their descriptive names.

On the search template, you can filter your search using these eleven map categories with the "Map Topic" drop-down list. These categories are as follows:

- **Cadastral Map**—A cadastral map is used to show boundaries and ownership. Some also show such details as survey district names, block numbers, certificate of title numbers, positions of existing older structures, government-described runhold section and lot numbers and their respective areas, adjoining and adjacent street names, selected boundary dimensions, and references to prior founding maps. In the United States, the Cadastral Survey in the Bureau of Land Management is responsible for maintaining records of all public lands. These surveys often required detailed investigation of the history of land use, legal accounts, and other documents. Examples of some cadastral maps include country maps showing state boundaries, state maps showing county boundaries, plat maps, as well as demographic maps that illustrate population growth or density, income levels, slave ownership, and other characteristics. Cadastral maps often use color, shading, or other methods of identifying specific areas and characteristics.

- **Cartographic Map**—In the Ancestry.com collection, a cartographic map is defined as a simple map showing political boundaries.

- **Civil War**—This is a map specifically devoted to the United States Civil War, 1861–1865.

- **Discovery & Exploration**—This is a map that usually illustrates the discovery of an area, the shape and features of an area, and notations regarding flora, fauna, waterways, peoples, and other interesting discoveries.

- **Geo-political**—A geo-political map represents the boundaries of a political entity, such as a country, empire, country, province, canton, or other political entity.

- **Land Ownership Map**—A land ownership map is typically a representation of a large tract of land and the subdivisions into townships, plats, lots, and other measurement divisions. This type of map will vary depending on the period and geographical location.

- **Panoramic Map**—Panoramic maps were exceedingly popular in the eighteenth to early twentieth centuries as a way of representing a town, city, or other area in a "bird's eye" view. They provide an interesting visualization of how a place appeared at that time. In the late nineteenth and early twentieth centuries, panoramic photography replaced the cartographic, panoramic representations of places. Photography was much less laborious, cheaper, and more accurate.

- **Parks**—A park map is used to represent the boundaries and features, both natural and manmade, of a piece of property set aside for the purpose of preservation or recreation. President Theodore Roosevelt established wildlife preservation areas in the United States, the first being Pelican Island in the Indian River Lagoon in Florida. This led to additional U.S. Congressional legislation that established wildlife and natural area preservation areas, ultimately resulting in a massive National Park Service.

- **Railroad Map**—A railroad map shows rail transportation lines in relationship to the geographical area a railroad traverses and, if created in granular enough detail, usually shows all stations, depots, freight offices, and other locations serviced for mail, freight, and passengers.

- **Relief Map**—A relief map is similar to a topographic map. However, a true relief map refers to the portrayal of three-dimensional geography. Raised relief maps must be experienced in person. However, a visual representation of the physical characteristics of the geography, elevation, and features of an area can be represented on paper or digitally. A panoramic map seeks to achieve a similar visual effect.

- **Transportation Map**—A transportation map illustrates transportation routes, usually of overland roads and trails.

When searching for maps, unless you know the exact name of the map, you may want to simply enter the name of the area for which you wish to search, such as "pennsylvania." You may, alternatively, put the name of the area in the "Keyword(s)" field. Also, the advanced search features of "Map Topic" and "Year range" are best left blank for your first search. Refer to figure 14-16 on the next page for an example of a search results page in the Map Collection.

Summary

The Reference and Finding Aids Collection at Ancestry.com is filled with information to help you learn and improve your skills, and to help you work with all types of genealogically

Map	Map Title	Map Topic	Area	Year	View Image
	A Map of the western parts of the province of Pennsylvania, Virginia, &c.	Topographical Map	Ohio	1753	
	A Map of the western parts of the province of Pennsylvania, Virginia, &c.	Topographical Map	Indiana	1753	
	A map of the Federal Territory from the western boundary of Pennsylvania to the Scioto River laid down from the latest informations and divided into townships and fractional parts of townships agreeab	Topographical Map	Pennsylvania	1788	
	Map of the seat of war. Maryland & Delaware with parts of Pennsylvania. Showing the railroads. 1861-65	Military Map	Delaware	1865	

Figure 14-16: Search results list for the Map Collection.

important records and materials. New materials are added often, so you should make this area a regular stop in your online research visits.

Chapter 15 will present the **Learning Center** tab, another collection of important reference materials that can help you with your research. Let's proceed there and explore the wealth of that collection too.

Chapter 15

The Learning Center

Chapter 14 explored the tremendous wealth of materials in the Reference and Finding Aids Collection at Ancestry. com. I want to continue the discussion of the informational and reference materials by jumping to the Leaning Center. Here you will find even more materials to help you learn about record types and methodologies that can further your personal research.

At the top of the **Learning Center** tab is the search template used to search the Library. What is the Library? Well, the Library at Ancestry.com is the core of the Learning Center. It is comprised of the following:

- Magazine articles from *Ancestry* Magazine and the former *Genealogical Computing* quarterly

- Online columns that have been written by the leading genealogical experts and published on the Ancestry.com publications over the years, including the *Ancestry Monthly*,

Ancestry Daily News, the *Ancestry Weekly Journal*, and the Ancestry *24/7 Family History Circle* blog

- Tips and suggestions made by genealogists just like yourself that have been published in the Ancestry publications, both print and electronic

The Library can be searched in a variety of ways or browsed by category. Let's explore the different sections of the **Learning Center** tab a bit and then we will focus on searching and browsing.

Family Facts

You will remember that we discussed Family Facts in chapter 7. The reason we introduced the collection there is because it is so helpful in placing your ancestors into geographical and historical context. Learning more about the demographic patterns of your ancestral surname could help you to better focus on a time period or place. Let me suggest that you look again at the Family Facts materials here in the Learning Center and refer back to chapter 7.

Today @ Ancestry.com

Skipping down a bit on the **Learning Center** tab, you will see a list of links in the "Today@Ancestry.com" section to a variety of materials, the most important of which is the *Ancestry Weekly Journal*. This is a weekly newsletter that you can receive via e-mail or that you can read here in the Learning Center. I personally enjoy receiving it as an e-mail so that I can always catch the latest news and read the excellent articles published there. Edited by Juliana Smith, this high-quality electronic newsletter features columns, photographs, tips, and more.

Move to the top of the next column on the page to the section labeled "Weekly Journal." This is where you can

subscribe to the *Ancestry Weekly Journal*. It's absolutely free and you will enjoy the great information you get there. Figure 15-1 shows the table of contents of what was in a typical issue on 4 December 2006.

Another excellent electronic resource is the blog, *24/7 Family History Circle*, which is also edited by Juliana Smith <http://blogs. ancestry.com/circle/>. Figure 15-2 shows the top of the blog from 30 November 2006. You will find news, columns, tips, and a variety of information included here. You may also add your comments and suggestions to each article. The blog is updated regularly.

In the right-hand column of the blog, you will see links to the *Ancestry Weekly Journal*, News, Blog Extras (some great additional genealogical links), and links to the archives of the blog's articles, back to its beginning in March of 2006.

Figure 15-1: Ancestry Weekly Journal

Figure 15-2: 24/7 Family History Circle *blog*

You will definitely want to bookmark this site so you can return week after week. Note that the easiest way to access the blog is by typing the URL shown previously into your browser.

Learn More About

In the "Learn More About" section of the **Learning Center** tab is a collection of links about different record types. You will recognize, when you click to visit them, that they will take you to the same pages as the "Welcome to the Census Center," for example, that you found when you were using the main category links in the "Browse Records" on other pages. One important addition, however, is the African American Records link, which leads to a special census search template for searching for African Americans, describes important collections of materials in the Ancestry.com databases, and links to articles and other website links to help with your research.

Each of the collections in this group will help you get started and advance your research in the respective area.

Searching the Library Collection

I mentioned earlier that you can either search the Library or you can browse its contents. Let's first explore using the search template, and then we will look at the browse capabilities.

The search template shown at the top of the **Learning Center** tab allows you to search the library's contents in several ways. The "Search Type" drop-down list shows six options from which you can select in order to search the Library's contents.

- **Search Any Word**—You may enter a word in the input field to the right of the "Search Type" drop-down list. The search engine will search the contents of the Library to find anything that has ever been published in an *Ancestry* Magazine, *Genealogical Computing*, or any of the electronic, online newsletters and blogs. As an example, I searched for the word "rome" and was rewarded with the page shown in figure 15-3.

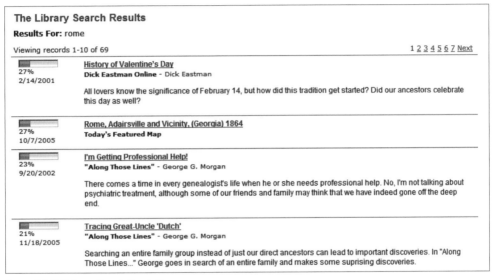

The Library Search Results

Results For: rome

Viewing records 1-10 of 69   1 2 3 4 5 6 7 Next

27% 2/14/2001	**History of Valentine's Day** **Dick Eastman Online** - Dick Eastman All lovers know the significance of February 14, but how did this tradition get started? Did our ancestors celebrate this day as well?	
27% 10/7/2005	**Rome, Adairsville and Vicinity, (Georgia) 1864** **Today's Featured Map**	
23% 9/20/2002	**I'm Getting Professional Help!** **"Along Those Lines"** - George G. Morgan There comes a time in every genealogist's life when he or she needs professional help. No, I'm not talking about psychiatric treatment, although some of our friends and family may think that we have indeed gone off the deep end.	
21% 11/18/2005	**Tracing Great-Uncle 'Dutch'** **"Along Those Lines"** - George G. Morgan Searching an entire family group instead of just our direct ancestors can lead to important discoveries. In "Along Those Lines..." George goes in search of an entire family and makes some suprising discoveries.	

Figure 15-3:"Library Search Results" page.

The "Library Search Results" page shown here indicates that there were sixty-nine matches found in the Library. They are arranged and displayed in a relevancy ranking order determined by the Ancestry.com search engine. Relevancy is determined by the position of the word in the article or title, the frequency of the word's occurrence, and other factors. You will note that the first link is to an article by Dick Eastman about Valentine's Day. The second link is to a map titled "Rome, Adairsville, and Vicinity, Georgia (1864)" that was one of the maps featured in the *Ancestry Daily News* on 7 October 2005. Other articles listed in this example include my "Along Those Lines" column that I wrote that included mention of or references to Rome, Georgia, a prominent location in my maternal line's family history.

- **Keyword Search**—The "Keyword Search" is similar to "Search Any Word." The difference, however, is that the words "and," "or," "but," "the," "those," "a," and other grammatical articles are not indexed and will therefore never be searched.

- **Exact Phrase**—When you enter a series of two or more words in the input field, they are treated as an exact phrase. The search engine will seek to find that series of words, in the exact sequence and continuous to one another, anywhere in an article in the Library. You do not have to enclose the phrase in quotation marks. By doing so, the search engine may or may not be able to locate the phrase you are seeking.

- **Search by Author**—You may search by author's name for articles written by an individual.

- **Title**—You may use this selection to search for a word in the title of an article or you may enter the exact title in full, if you know it, to narrow your search.

- **Free Text**—A Free Text search allows you to enter multiple words, in no particular order, and the search engine will seek to locate any and all articles that have those words included. Note that a Free Text search is similar to a Keyword search, but searches on a wider scope.

As you can see, there is some search flexibility in using the "Search the Library" template. However, most people like to simply browse the Library. Let's see why.

Browse the Library

The contents of the Library at Ancestry.com have been categorized into topical groups. This makes them easier to browse by actual subject. There are two ways to browse the Library.

- Between the "Family Facts" section and the "Today @ Ancestry.com" section on the Learning Center tab, there is an area titled "Learn How to Do Your Family History." When you click the link there labeled "Ancestry Library," a page is displayed that shows twelve categories. Figure 15-4 shows these categories. Each category link is followed by a number, indicating the number of articles in that category, and a description of the type of information included in those articles.

- **How-to** (2559)
  Discover the basics of family history research, and learn how to organize and document your work effectively.

- **Record Sources** (1765)
  Learn how to use various records to trace your family history, including vital, census, and a plethora of others available from government and private sources.

- **Family Origins** (576)
  Finding family origins is both interesting and challenging. Tap into general immigration records and instructions to trace ethnic groups.

- **Technology** (1338)
  Follow the changing role of technology and stay current with the latest trends in software, databases, Web sites, distance research, and more.

- **Organizations** (847)
  Genealogical societies, historical organizations, museums, libraries, and archives can lead researchers to rich sources of information.

- **Geography** (251)
  Learn useful tools and techniques, as well as how to use maps, atlases, and gazetteers for discovering the place your ancestors called home.

- **Preserving Family History** (1182)
  Preserve precious heirlooms and learn how to record and write about your family history and traditions for future generations.

- **Home Sources** (383)
  Your home is the source of a number of clues to your family's past. Learn how to identify unique, fascinating, and often overlooked details from ordinary objects.

- **Religion** (90)
  Discover step-by-step instructions to find and effectively use the records and information of various denominations.

- **Genealogy Products** (667)
  With literally thousands of books, periodicals, software and other genealogical supplies available, it is important to know which ones are most useful for your research.

- **Current Events** (1030)
  Stay current with the latest news and learn what records are available, which ones are at risk, and how you can influence decisions regarding access and preservation.

- **Historical Context** (785)
  Discover the rest of the story with biographical details and historical facts to add life and inspiration to your family history.

Figure 15-4: The categories of the "Browse the Library" page.

If you click a category link, you will be presented with a list in reverse chronological order (most recent to oldest) of articles relating to that category. You can then browse, page by page, until you find an article of interest. Then, simply click on the title and the article will be retrieved for you to read, print, or send as an e-mail. (Look for the "Printer Friendly" icon to obtain a simple and clean copy of the article to print. Look for the "E-mail to a Friend" icon and you can e-mail a copy of the article to yourself or to a friend).

- On both the bottom right of the Learning Center tab and the top right of the "Browse the Library" page are boxes listing links to categories in the Library which, when you click them, take you to the respective category. This gives you immediate access to a list of links to the articles in which you may be interested.

Summary

Between the Reference and Finding Aids Collection discussed in chapter 14 and the Learning Center resources, you have plenty of material at your fingertips to help extend your knowledge of genealogy and further your research. Don't forget you regular dose of genealogy available through a free subscription to the *Ancestry Weekly Journal* newsletter and to the *24/7 Family History Circle* blog. These will make your continuing education fun and exciting, and your research expertise will keep expanding.

Chapter 16

Ancestry Community

We have focused in this book so far on the essential concepts of genealogy, how to navigate the Ancestry.com site, and how to search, access, and use the databases at Ancestry.com. We have also discussed Family Trees, including searching existing trees and building and growing your own Family Trees. This is all very exciting for the modern genealogical researcher. However, it can be truly exhilarating to make connections with other researchers who are researching the same people or lines that you are studying.

Ancestry.com makes this process easier than any other online service through the Ancestry Community. Here you can post queries to message boards and share information with other researchers. You can also make connections with people who share common interests concerning a particular surname, location, or other criteria.

It has not been too many years since the only way to make these connections was through submitting queries to printed publications. That method of networking with other people was slow, tedious, and haphazard at best. With the explosive growth and proliferation of the Internet in the past twenty years, more people have become interested in genealogy and family history and are actively searching every resource they can find on the Web. It truly *is* a wonderful time to be a genealogical researcher!

The Components of the Ancestry Community

The primary component of the Ancestry Community is people like you—researchers seeking information, clues, leads, and connections with other researchers. It is important to remember, as we've discussed before, that not every person is as conscientious in his or her research work, source citations, and attention to accuracy as perhaps you want to be. I always urge researchers to treat their genealogical research work as a scholarly pursuit, and to assess the evidence and document the findings in a way that other researchers will find the most reliable and accurate possible.

The Ancestry Community is primarily accessible from the **Ancestry Community** tab (see figure 16-1 on the next page). Of course, as you read through this chapter and as you return to other areas of Ancestry.com, you will notice many other areas where you will see references to connecting with others researching the same names. Once you have read this chapter, you will have a better idea regarding making contacts from other areas.

We will discuss each of the following areas in this chapter:

- **My Public Profile**—This link, in the upper right-hand corner of the page, allows you to share information about yourself and your research interests. This helps other

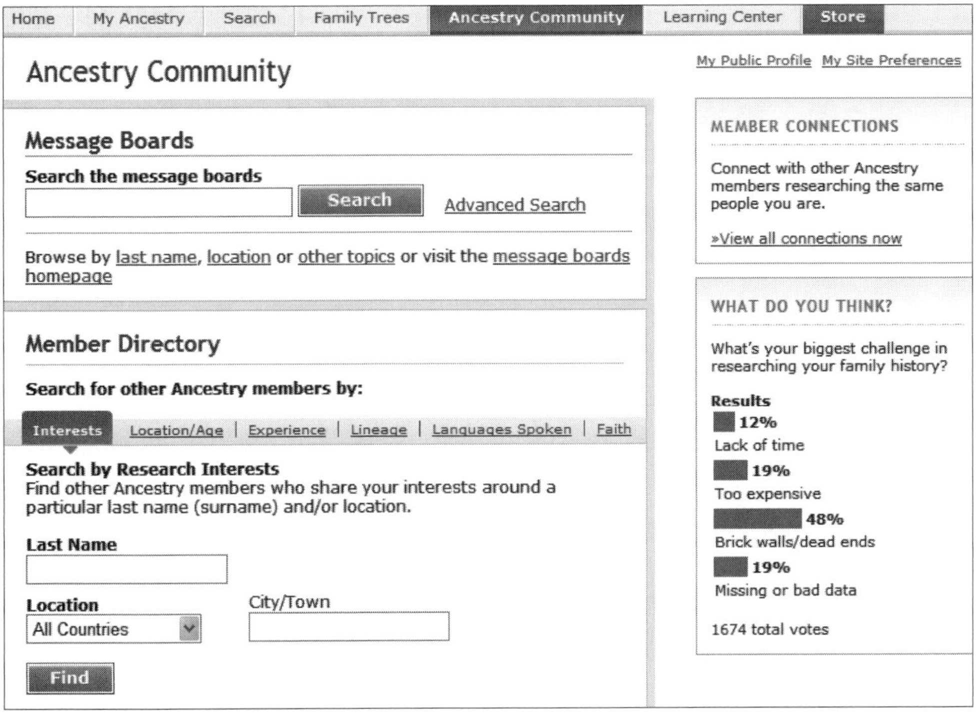

*Figure 16-1: The **Ancestry Community** tab.*

people seeking to connect with you to know that you share interests with them. You will remember that this was one of the areas we discussed in the **My Ancestry** tab. It now becomes more important when we discuss community.

- **My Site Preferences**—This link is also located in the upper right-hand corner of the page. It was part of the information you set up in the **My Ancestry** tab. You may specify an e-mail address to which messages and alerts from Ancestry.com, as well as other members' inquiries are sent.

- **Message Boards**—The Message Boards at Ancestry.com are the largest collection of their type anywhere on the

Internet. A message board is devoted to a topic, and a topic may be a surname, geographical location, record type, ethnic group, religious group, research methodology, event, genealogy software, heraldry, and an abundance of other subjects. You may read messages there and respond. You may post messages there and read other researchers' responses. You can make contacts off the message boards to discuss common research and to perhaps begin collaboration on your research.

- **Member Directory**—The Member Directory utilizes information that members enter in their public profile and allows you to search for others who

  - share your research interests;

  - are located in the same area, are the same gender, or who are of a particular age;

  - have certain experience, longevity, and frequency in genealogical research;

  - are of a specific nationality, ethnic group, or geographical heritage or lineage;

  - speak or read specific a language; or

  - share a common faith.

- **Member Connections**—The Member Connections section is an important tool that allows you to search for other Ancestry members who are performing similar research as you.

- **What Do You Think?**—This is a poll section in which you may choose to participate. The questions relate to research and allow you and other members of the Ancestry Community to share your opinions with one another.

These component areas all work together to help form
a solid networking facility at Ancestry.com. In addition,
RootsWeb.com hosts e-mail mailing lists on topics similar to
the Message Boards at Ancestry.com. You can learn more about
them and subscribe to one or more at <http://lists.rootsweb.com>.

Let's now explore each of the component areas of the
Ancestry Community so that you understand how to use them
to your best research advantage.

My Public Profile

Your public profile can contain as much or as little information
as you would like to share with other Ancestry.com members.
Figure 16-2 shows the "My Public Profile" page that I set
up when writing this book. It shows my username which,
in this case, is AncestryUserID. It also displays where I am
from, the date
when I became
a member (with
this username),
and the last time
I updated the
profile.

Beneath that
section is an area
with two tabs:
Profile Details
and **Research
Interests**. You
will notice the
blue **Edit** arrows
at the right of
each section. By

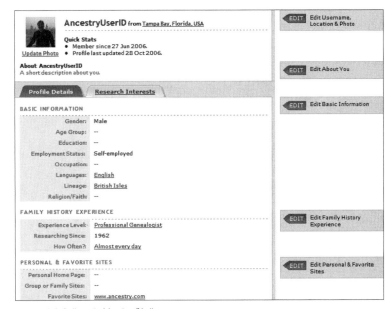

Figure 16-2: "My Public Profile."

clicking on one of these, you can change the contents of your Public Profile. Let's explore these areas.

The top **Edit** arrow allows you to edit your username, location, and photo. You can do any of the following:

- **Change Your Username**—Your username identifies you to other Ancestry members. If you want additional privacy, choose a username that does not include any personally identifiable information. You will notice that there are rules listed for creating a new username. It has to be unique from that of any other Ancestry.com member. Some suggested usernames are shown as links below the input field. You may certainly try establishing a new one of your choice but, if that username is already in use by someone else, you will be given an error message that tells you, "The Username you entered is unavailable."

- **Change Your Location**—The next area is Location, and it is here that you can define where you are geographically located. There is a drop-down list of countries from which you can select. Depending on the country you choose, there may be additional sub-areas in another drop-down list from which you may choose, such as state, province, and county. You may then enter the name of the city or town where you live.

- **Change Your User Photo**—You may choose to upload a photograph of yourself for your profile. You will see the rules listed here as well. You can upload a photo or, if you already have one there and want to remove it, you can do that as well. The photo you upload will be resized to a 60 x 60 pixel image so be sure to choose a photo that is detailed enough to show your face. If you have any questions about what types of photos are or are not acceptable, click on the link labeled "guidelines" and another page with all the Community Guidelines will be displayed. This link to the Community Guidelines is also shown at the bottom of the My Public Profile page and you should take a few moments to read them.

Once you have made the changes in this area that you want to make, click the orange **Save** arrow or the link labeled "Save your edits" and your profile will be updated. If you choose not to save what you have done, simply click on the link labeled "Cancel."

The second **Edit** arrow on the right side of the "My Public Profile" page is labeled "Edit About You." Here you may type up to 200 words to describe a little more about yourself. There are Community Guidelines that apply to what you enter here.

Again, you can click the orange **Save** arrow or the link labeled "Save your edits" and your profile will be updated. If you choose not to save what you have done, simply click on the link labeled "Cancel." The information you enter will be displayed, in my case, in the area labeled "About AncestryUserID."

We now come to the two tabs on the "My Profile Page" mentioned before. Each tab has unique information and therefore also has editable areas as we have seen before. Figure 16-2 on page 257 shows this area of the "My Public Profile" page with the **Profile Details** tab selected.

Click on the first **Edit** arrow to the right, labeled "Edit Basic Information," and the page shown in figure 16-3 on page 260 is displayed.

You may choose to provide or not provide a response in any of the fields. Remember, however, that the information you provide will help other Ancestry.com members make connections with you. Click the orange **Save** arrow or the link

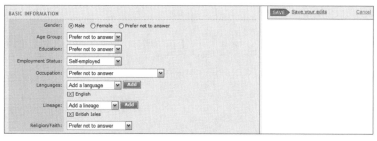

Figure 16-3: The "Basic Information" section of the **Profile Details** tab.

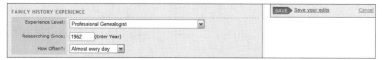

Figure 16-4: The "Family History Experience" section of the **Profile Details** tab.

labeled "Save your edits" and your profile will be updated. If you choose not to save what you have done, simply click on the link labeled "Cancel."

The next area of the **Profile Details** tab is "Family History Experience." When you click the **Edit** button labeled "Edit Family History Experience," the box shown in figure 16-4 is shown. Here you can use the drop-down list to indicate how much experience you've had with your research, the year in which you started, and select from another drop-down list to indicate how frequently you work on your research. You have the same save and cancel options in this box as you have in all others we have seen.

The last section on the **Profile Details** tab is labeled "Personal & Favorite Sites" (see figure 16-5). You can list your personal homepage, enter one or more group or family websites, and enter one or more favorite websites. Simply enter the name of the site and its Web address (URL). Then save or cancel your changes, as you prefer.

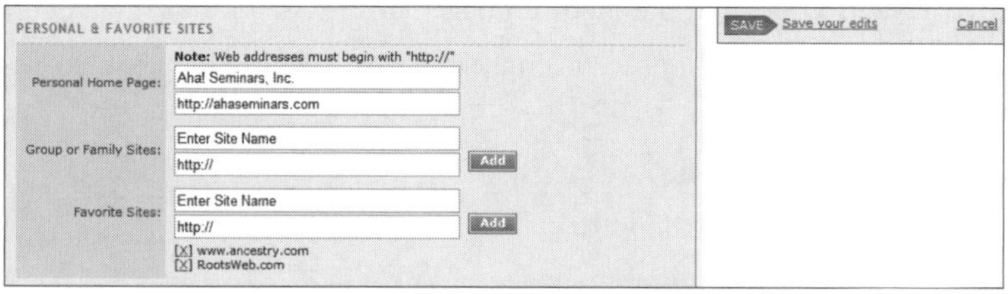

Figure 16-5: The "Personal & Favorite Sites" section of the **Profile Details** tab.

Let's click the **Research Interests** tab, a sample of which is shown in figure 16-6. There are two sections on

*Figure 16-6: The **Research Interests** tab on the "My Public Profile" page.*

this tab: "People I'm Looking For" and "Names and Locations I'm Researching."

If you have a Family Tree that is marked as personal (non-public) and have persons in that tree whom you are researching, they will not appear in this list. However, you can still click the **Edit** button to the right and you will be taken to the **My Ancestry** tab and the "People I'm Looking For" section (see chapter 4).

The last section here is labeled "Names & Locations I'm Researching." You can add new people to the list at any time by clicking "Edit information in list by visiting My Ancestry" and then clicking the green plus (+) sign or the link labeled "Add New." Ancestry will search its databases for records with the names and locations you have indicated. If and when a match is found, you will receive an e-mail alert. Please note that this area is also in the **My Ancestry** tab.

You may also choose to click on the two-persons icon, which you see throughout the site, to make possible connections with other members researching one of the persons on your list. You will be presented with a list such as the one shown in figure 16-7 on the next page that shows possible connections.

You will note that there are links with a key icon and labeled "Contact." If you want to make a connection with the person whose tree and records may hold additional

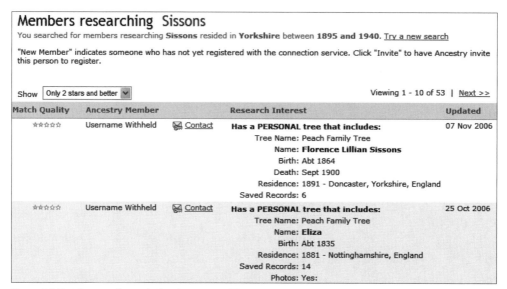

Figure 16-7: A Portion of a results list showing possible Ancestry members with similar research interests.

information, you can click here and another page, pre-formatted with a message to that person, will be presented. An example is shown in figure 16-8.

In this case, I simply added my name at the end of the message and clicked the option labeled "Send a copy of this message to me." I could have added more text to the message if I wanted to clarify my inquiry. I clicked the option for a copy of the message so that I could have a copy for follow-up purposes if necessary. I could now click the **Preview** button to review the message. I can also simply click the **Send** button to send the message to the other Ancestry.com member. Hopefully I will get a response.

At this point, you can see how important the information in "My Public Profile" can be to your research.

Let's continue to the next component of the **Ancestry Community** tab, the link in the upper right-hand corner labeled "My Site Preferences." Click this link.

It is on this page that you can define your preferences regarding communications with other Ancestry.com members. You can choose to only be contacted anonymously through the Ancestry Connection Service, or you can display your e-mail address to allow others to contact you directly. If you choose to be contacted through the Connection Service, members can contact you anonymously by clicking on a link in your public profile. They'll see the form shown in figure 16-8 to

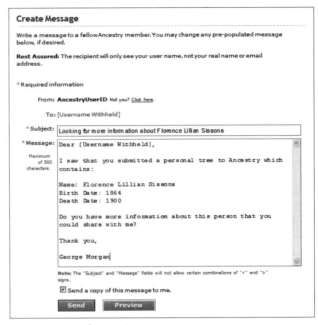

Figure 16-8: Pre-formatted contact message page.

compose and send a message to you through the Connection Service. Then you can begin communicating back and forth via your username only, without sharing your e-mail address and thus protecting your anonymity. If you choose to display your e-mail address in your public profile instead, users will see your e-mail address as you communicate back and forth. Members will also have the option to contact you anonymously through the Connection Service as described previously.

You can also allow or deny other Ancestry.com members the ability to contact you. You can be contacted about things you add or post to the site, as well as other personal research activities. Things you add or post to the site may include the following:

- Things in your tree(s)

- Comments and corrections you make in OneWorldTree, on records and images, etc.

- Your Public Profile

- Records you link to a person in OneWorldTree

Other personal research activities may include the following:

- Records you save in your "Shoebox"

- Favorites you add on the site

You can control all of these by the settings you choose on the "My Site Preferences" page. In addition, there are places where you can change your e-mail address, your username, and your location. In addition, you have the ability to block unwanted communications from another member at any time.

The combination of information and settings you specify in the "My Public Profile" and "My Site Preferences" areas are, as you can see, exceptionally helpful in controlling communications with other members in the Ancestry Community.

Message Boards

The Message Boards at Ancestry.com are among the most powerful tools for communicating, sharing, and collaborating with other researchers. A message board is defined as a place on the Internet where people may visit and exchange information. They do so by either posting a message and waiting for replies or by reading messages and sending replies. It's as simple as that. However, Ancestry.com has added some additional tools that make your use of message boards much simpler.

Format

Let's explore the starting points in message boards. First, let's talk about format. A message posted on a message board may be similar to an e-mail message. It consists of two important parts: the subject line and the body of the message.

Subject Line

A subject line should be meaningful and informative. It should communicate to the reader what is inside the message. If you use a subject line that reads "HELP!!!!!," don't expect a lot of people to read and respond. Likewise, if you are posting a message to the Wilson surname message board with a subject line that reads, "Looking for Wilsons," don't expect many responses there.

A good subject line will include a name, a location, a time period, and then perhaps what you are seeking. For example, if I were seeking information about my grandmother, I might write a subject line as follows:

> Laura A. "Minnie" Wilson (1873-1966)—Mecklenburg Co., NC

This tells the reader which person I am seeking and where. By including that much information in the subject line, it may be enough to attract the attention of a reader to open the message and read it, and then to respond if he or she has information to share.

Message board users sometimes use a form of shorthand to indicate certain information, particularly migration movement. The use of the ">" character indicates that someone moved from one place to another. Therefore, another good subject line for a message board posting might look like this.

> Brisco Holder (1877-?)—GA>IA>?—Seeking Death Location

In this case, I am indicating that I am seeking information about a man named Brisco Holder who was born in 1877 in Georgia. I know that he migrated to Iowa and then somewhere else. I do not know where he went from Iowa or when he died. The subject line of this message would indicate the who, when, where, and what is being sought inside the text of the message.

Body of the Message

Just as the subject line of a message should be informative, the body of the message should also contain enough detail to help the reader determine if he or she knows anything about the subject of your inquiry that could be helpful. There are a number of important points to keep in mind when writing the body of the message:

- Provide enough information to let the reader know what you are seeking.

- Do not go into excessive detail that may only confuse the reader.

- If seeking information about an individual, include the person's full name and any nickname(s) by which he or she may have been known. Be sure to provide a woman's maiden and married names.

- Include the dates and locations where you know the person to have been at key periods in his or her life.

- Include names of parents, siblings, spouse(s), and children.

- Describe *exactly* what you are seeking.

- Tell the reader what you already know *and* where you have already researched. Don't make the reader respond with information you already have or check sources you have already exhausted.

- Indicate if you want the reader to respond to you on the message board or privately by e-mail.

- Offer to share information you have about a person or family line if you have such information.

- Thank the readers for taking the time to read and respond to you.

An example of a well-written message posted at Ancestry.com is shown in figure 16-9. It has an informative subject line regarding surnames and a location, and the body of the message is informative but concise.

As a result of this good posting, there were four strong responses posted to it, as shown in figure 16-10.

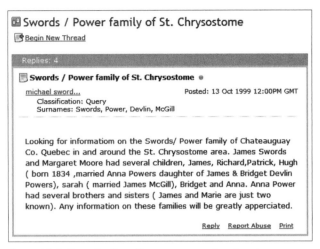

Figure 16-9: Example of a well-written message board posting.

Subject	Author	Date Posted
Swords / Power family of St. Chrysostome	michael sword...	13 Oct 1999 12:00PM GMT
● swords	Mario Lefebvr...	15 Oct 1999 12:00PM GMT
● Swords / Power family of St. Chrysostome	Michael Sword...	15 Oct 1999 12:00PM GMT
● Power	tedofocala	30 Dec 1999 12:00PM GMT
● McCollam McCollum McGill	@@christinale...	10 Feb 2002 6:29AM GMT

Figure 16-10: List of original posting and responses to message board posting.

You can read any message in the list shown in figure 16-10 by clicking the subject line. The orange dot to the left of a message indicates that you have not read it. Likewise, you can click on the name of the author of the e-mail. As a result, you might see a link to a member to whom you can send an e-mail. Also, because the message board postings go back a number of years before Ancestry.com made a number of Ancestry

Community enhancements, you might see a page with an image such as that in figure 16-11.

Figure 16-11: "Contact E-mail" information page for a member without a public profile.

Before Ancestry.com required that someone wishing to use the Message Boards complete a registration, only e-mail addresses were required for a posting. The person who in 1999 posted the message I used in the figure 16-9 is simply now identified by his e-mail address.

Searching the Message Boards

With the concepts of good subject line and message body content in mind, let's return to the "Message Boards" section of the **Ancestry Community** tab and begin discussing how to browse and search the Message Boards effectively.

In the "Search the message boards" field on the "Message Boards" section, you can enter anything: surname, location, topic, and so on. Note, however, that the Ancestry.com Message Boards search tool does not function like an Internet search engine. It does not use an exact phrase search, for example. If I enter "madison, nc" into the field, I will receive matches for postings in which both terms appear, such as "Madison County," "James Madison, NC," and on and on.

A more finite search may be performed by clicking the "Advanced Search" link and using the page shown in figure 16-12.

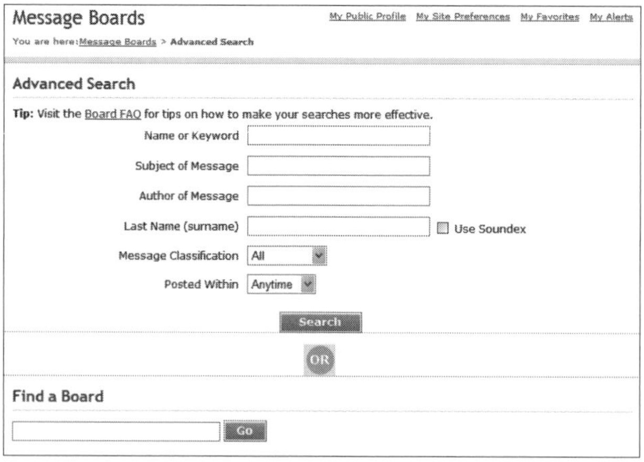

Figure 16-12: The "Advanced Search" template for the Message Boards.

The first thing I would recommend that you do is click the link labeled "Board FAQ." The page displayed contains all the information you will need to successfully understand and work with the Ancestry.com Message Boards.

In figure 16-12, there are two sections to this page: the "Advanced Search" template and the "Find a Board" search template. The "Advanced Search" template can be used to search for one or multiple things about a posting:

- **Name or Keyword**—You can enter a name, a location, or some keyword that you think is comparatively unique to help narrow a search.

- **Subject of a Message**—Here you can enter the entire subject, if you know it, or a word that you think would likely be included in a subject line.

- **Author of Message**—You may know the username of an Ancestry.com member whose research may parallel yours in some area. You can search for messages by him or her here.

- **Last Name (surname)**—You can use this field to search for every message on the boards containing a specific surname. This may be helpful when you have searched the specific surname board and not found anything new or helpful and want to literally search everywhere. You can also click the "Soundex" option in the event you also want to see alternate spellings (or misspellings) of the surname you are seeking.

- **Message Classification**—Message board users may (or may not) classify the topical content of their message, using a drop-down list. You can search by these topics, which include "Biography," "Birth," "Obituary," and more. I suggest that you search both with and without a classification.

- **Posted Within**—You can specify the time period within which messages you are seeking were posted. Check the drop-down list and you will find the choices of "1 Day," "3 Days," "1 Week," "1 month," "6 Months," and "1 Year." If you leave the option set at "Anytime," all messages will be checked.

The "Find a Board" template allows you to search directly for a message board. Simply enter a surname, location, or other topic and click the **Go** button. Sometimes your search will come up empty. At that time, it makes sense to return to the "Advanced Search" template shown in figure 16-12.

The Message Boards can be browsed using the links in the "Message Boards" section on the **Ancestry Community** tab. Let's look at each of the link options.

Browse by Last Name

Click the "last name" link and the page shown in figure 16-13 is displayed. The first field, "Names or Keywords," allows you to search for a surname or a keyword. The Advanced Search tool

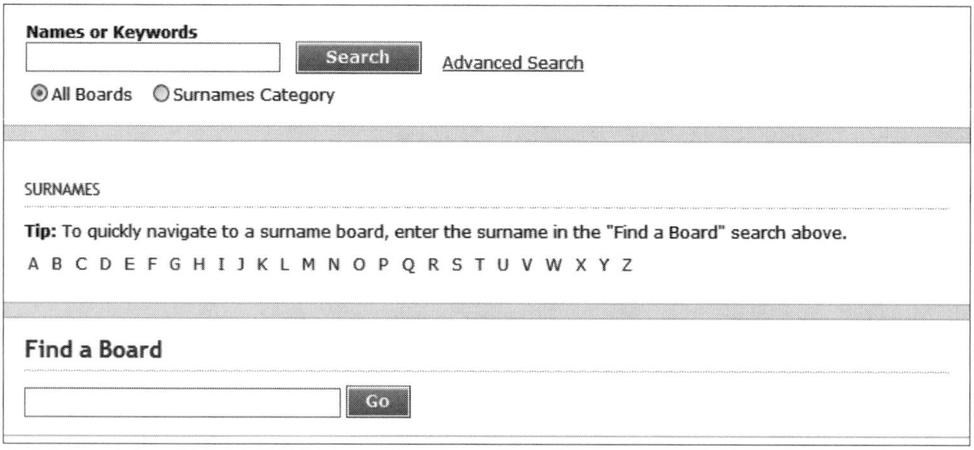

Names or Keywords

[ ] Search Advanced Search

◉ All Boards ○ Surnames Category

SURNAMES

Tip: To quickly navigate to a surname board, enter the surname in the "Find a Board" search above.

A B C D E F G H I J K L M N O P Q R S T U V W X Y Z

Find a Board

[ ] Go

Figure 16-13: Last name browse page.

you saw in figure 16-12 is also available here. Click the "All Boards" or "Surname Category" options to refine your search. You also can use the "Find a Board" field, as discussed above.

The other option available on this page is to refer to the "Surnames" section, where letters A through Z are shown. If I click the letter P, the list expands to show another line with two-letter codes.

Perhaps I am searching for the Patterson surname. I will then click the "Pa" combination and am given a new list of three-letter options.

Next I click on the three-letter combination for "Pat" and am rewarded with a list of the first ten surname listings within that group,

Board	Threads	Messages	Last Post
Pata75	1	1	19 Oct 2000
Patacomb	0	0	
Patai	0	0	
Patak	3	6	18 Aug 2004
Pataki	4	12	10 Oct 2006
Patakidis	1	1	4 Oct 2003
Patala	1	4	21 Jan 2004
Patalano	2	6	2 Apr 2004
Patane	14	37	4 Dec 2006
Patay	1	1	24 May 2001

Pat...

Viewing 1 - 10 of **179** | Next »

Results per page 10

Viewing 1 - 10 of **179** | Next »

Figure 16-14: First ten search results for "Pat."

shown in figure 16-14. Because there are 181 matches, I will need to scroll through the list until I locate the Patterson message board.

The other information displayed on the match shown in figure 16-14 bears a little explanation. Look at the "Patane" surname and you will see that there are fourteen threads and thirty-seven messages, and the last post was made on 4 December 2006. You may very well ask, "What is a thread?"

A thread is a series of messages posted on a specific subject. It consists of the original message and all responses to it. And so, in this case, the Patane surname has had fourteen original subjects posted to the message board and, in response to those fourteen messages, there have been a total of thirty-seven various responses posted there, the last one made on

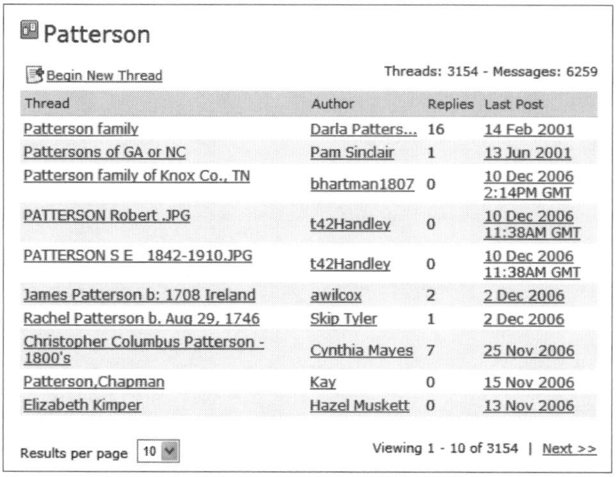

Patterson

Begin New Thread — Threads: 3154 - Messages: 6259

Thread	Author	Replies	Last Post
Patterson family	Darla Patters...	16	14 Feb 2001
Pattersons of GA or NC	Pam Sinclair	1	13 Jun 2001
Patterson family of Knox Co., TN	bhartman1807	0	10 Dec 2006 2:14PM GMT
PATTERSON Robert .JPG	t42Handley	0	10 Dec 2006 11:38AM GMT
PATTERSON S E 1842-1910.JPG	t42Handley	0	10 Dec 2006 11:38AM GMT
James Patterson b: 1708 Ireland	awilcox	2	2 Dec 2006
Rachel Patterson b. Aug 29, 1746	Skip Tyler	1	2 Dec 2006
Christopher Columbus Patterson - 1800's	Cynthia Mayes	7	25 Nov 2006
Patterson,Chapman	Kay	0	15 Nov 2006
Elizabeth Kimper	Hazel Muskett	0	13 Nov 2006

Results per page 10 — Viewing 1 - 10 of 3154 | Next >>

Figure 16-15: The Patterson message board.

4 December 2006. We will look at threads and how they are displayed a little later in this chapter.

When I reached the Patterson surname in the list, there were 3,154 threads and 6,259 messages—a whole lot of messages to work my way through! However, I clicked on the Patterson surname (see figure 16-15).

The "Names or Keywords" search field at the top of the page can come in very handy in a message board. If, as in the case of the Patterson board, there are hundreds or thousands of messages, you certainly may want to narrow the scope of what you have to search. I am looking for my great-grandmother, Lydia Lenora Patterson from North Carolina. I therefore enter "lydia" and "nc" in the "Names or Keywords" field and then click the "Patterson Board" option to indicate the Patterson Board. In this case, doing so narrows 6,259 messages to three. Now, be careful not to make any assumptions about what another researcher might enter in a message board posting. He or she may have entered "North Carolina" rather than "nc." You should therefore try "carolina" as another search keyword option rather than "nc."

Let's return to figure 16-15. Look at the message with the thread (subject) titled "Rachel Patterson b: August 29, 1746." The author posted this new subject on 2 December 2006 and had received 1 reply by the time of this writing. (You will notice that other postings include both a date *and* a time; they were written on the current day's date and are time stamped to assist you in following the thread of postings. Let's proceed to click the thread name/subject of this posting and examine the result in detail. The resulting page is shown, in part, in figure 16-16.

The author wrote a good subject line and has indicated in his message body what he was seeking. You will note that the message was originally posted on 10 April 1999 but that a response was not received until 2 December 2006. The answer he received looks like a great match too! (See figure 16-17.)

There are two different ways to view message board postings. Look at figure 16-16 again. What you see is the "Thread View." In this view, the initial message in the thread is displayed in its entirety. It is then followed by

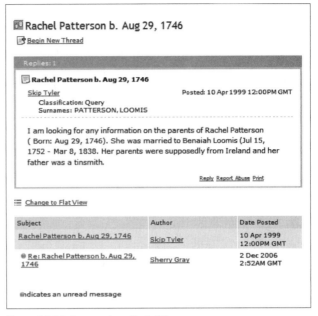

Figure 16-16: Posting about Rachel Patterson.

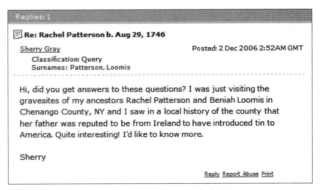

Figure 16-17: Response to posting about Rachel Patterson.

each of the responses, displayed only with its subject line. You must click on each response to read it and is great when you may only want to read certain replies.

Beneath the initial message is a link titled "Change to Flat View." If you click that link, the display changes so that the initial message in the thread and all responses, in chronological sequence, are displayed in full. This is an easy way to read *all* of the responses and print them. When you are in "Flat View," a link is present that is labeled "Change to Thread View."

Ancestry.com remembers from session to session which view you last selected and will use that for all message board displays until you change the view again.

You will note that at the bottom of every message there are three links. The first is "Reply." This allows you to respond to the message board posting with another posting. A new page is displayed into which I can type a reply to the message, shown at the bottom of the page.

The second of the three links at the bottom of each message is labeled "Report Abuse." If you read the Community Guidelines, you will clearly understand what is and is not acceptable behavior at Ancestry.com. The "Report Abuse" page, shown in figure 16-18, is displayed with an area for you to type text to describe an infraction you believe has occurred. See, also, that there is a drop-down list of different categories of objections from which you can choose.

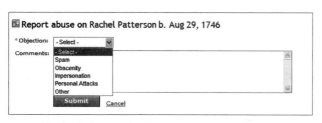

Figure 16-18: The "Report Abuse" page.

The third link at the bottom of each message is a "Print" link. This allows you to get a clean print image, without the boxes and shading. Simply display this page and press the "CTRL" and "P" keys simultaneously. This will send the page to your printer. Click "Return to Message" to return to where you were.

At the top of the Patterson message board and on every thread's page is a link that allows you to "Begin New Thread." In other words, you can begin a new thread on your own. Click that link and a new page, like the one shown in figure 16-19 will appear.

Figure 16-19: Example of a "Post new thread" page.

You will also note that I used a strong subject line and concise content. You will note a check box labeled, "Send me an alert when anyone replies to this thread." By checking this box, Ancestry.com will send me an e-mail whenever anyone responds to this message or any reply posted to it. I also posted the two surnames mentioned in the new message. This helps when someone is searching for either Patterson or Wilson to also make a connection with my new thread in the "Surnames" field. Since I am seeking information about a marriage record, I have used the Classification drop-down list to select an appropriate subject. Finally, if I wanted to attach a file, such as a GEDCOM or a photograph, I could do so.

Once you have finished writing your new message, you can click on the **Preview** button to see what it looks like. It's always good to proofread your messages for accuracy. You can also click on the **Post** button to place your new message on the message board. However, if you change your mind about posting it, you can always do so by clicking "Cancel."

In the upper right-hand corner of a Message Boards page is a "Page Tools" section containing three links.

- **Board Information**—The administrator of the message board will post guidelines for getting the most out of the message board. There will be a link to allow you to contact him or her as well. There may also be Web links to other sites of interest.

- **Add Thread to Favorites**—Rather than have to re-search for a message board, thread, topic, or location of interest to you each time you want to check it, you can add it to a list of Favorites. Whatever place you are in, click on "Add Thread to Favorites" and it is automatically added to your list. If you want to remove it from your Favorites, simply go to that place, look in the "Page Tools" section, and there will now be a link titled "Remove from Favorites." Click there and it will be removed.

- **Add Board to Alerts**—This third link allows you to add this message board to a list of your personal alerts. Whenever there is a new thread or reply posted, Ancestry.com will send you an e-mail with a link to the message board. You also can "Remove Board from Alerts" similar to the way you remove a thread from your favorites: visit the board and click on the link to remove it.

In addition to the "Page Tools," many of the Message Board pages contain links in the upper right-hand corner of the page that include "My Favorites" and "My Alerts." A click on "My Favorites" displays a page such as the one shown in figure 16-20. You can click on "Shared Trees" and on Message Board "Categories," "Boards," "Authors," and "Threads."

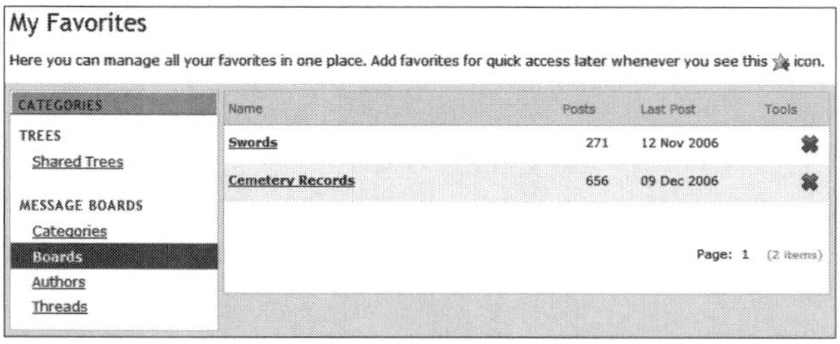

Figure 16-20: The "My Favorites" page.

The other link at the top of the page is "My Alerts" and a click of this link displays a page like the one shown in figure 16-21 with all of your Message Board alerts listed.

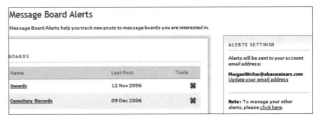

Figure 16-21: The "My Alerts" page.

The Ancestry.com Message Boards may seem complicated, but once you begin working with them, you will wonder what you ever did without them. Message boards really can extend your research reach exponentially. They can also introduce you to many wonderful people who are part of the Ancestry Community and happy to help you with your research.

Browse by Location and Other Topics

So far, we have concentrated on surnames. However, the "Message Boards" section on the **Ancestry Community** tab also includes a link to search by locations, and the world is grouped into geographical areas and then by localities within each area. You will want to explore by country or other locale for yourself. Remember, too, that you may post a message to a surname list *and* to a geographical location in order to maximize your exposure and opportunity to make connections with others. You can also explore message boards for every conceivable genealogical topic by clicking the "other topics." Topics range from "Adoption" to "Volunteer Projects." There is a wealth of information to be gleaned from other members of the Ancestry Community on the Ancestry.com Message Boards.

The Member Directory

Another component on the **Ancestry Community** tab is the Member Directory (see figure 16-22 on page 278).

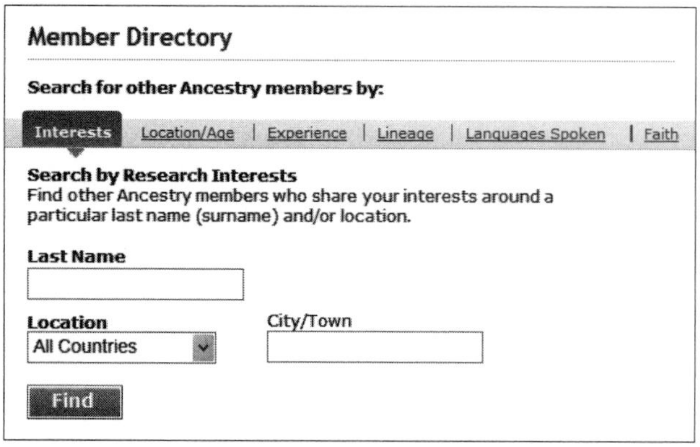

Figure 16-22: The "Member Directory" search template.

The first tab of the "Member Directory" section is **Interests**. I performed a simple search and selected England from the drop-down list of countries, and then chose the county of Essex. I clicked the **Find** button and the page shown in figure 16-23 was displayed. I might now make contact with any of the 441 users in this search results list. I could also revise my search or choose to search in another way.

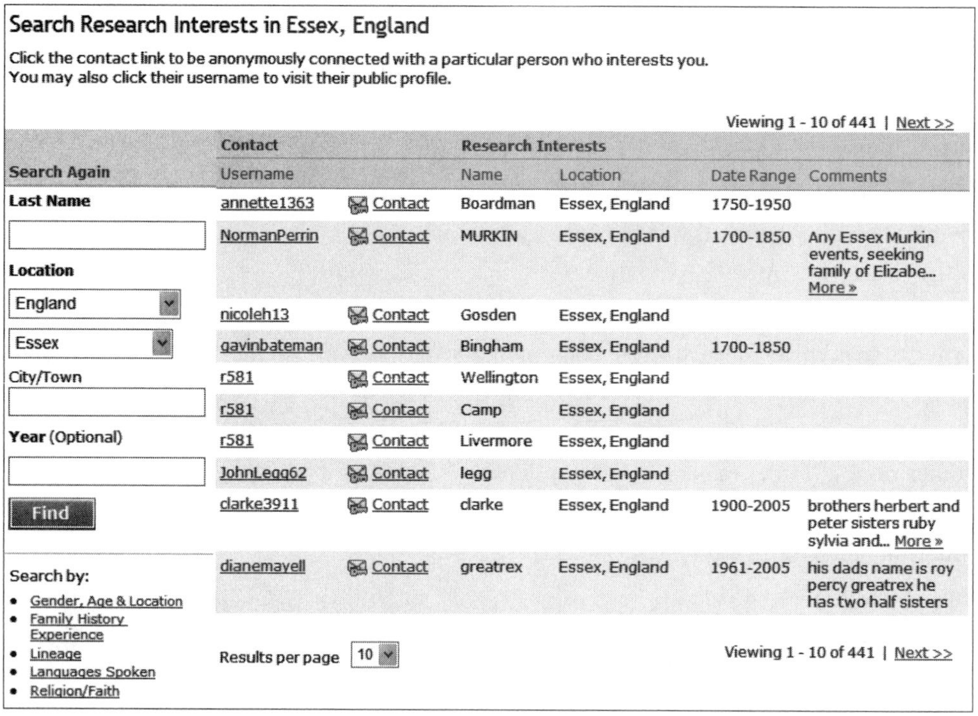

Figure 16-23: Search results for "Interest."

The second tab of the Member Directory is **Location/Age**. I may select to find other members who completed their profile for the fields of gender, age group, and location.

The third search tab shown represents **Experience**. The drop-down lists indicate experience in terms of "Beginner," "Intermediate," "Advanced," or "Professional." You may also specify the length of time the members you are seeking have been involved with their research, and also by how frequently they currently engage in research.

The **Lineage** tab is used to search for persons of specific geographical or ethnic heritage.

The **Language Spoken** tab has a drop-down list of languages, and you can search for persons who speak or are studying ancestry based on language.

Finally, the sixth tab, **Faith**, is used to locate other members who indicated their faith in their profile.

Member Connections

On the right side of the **Ancestry Community** tab is the section labeled "Member Connections." You will find the Member Connections icon throughout Ancestry.com. When you click it, a page similar to that shown in figure 16-24 is displayed.

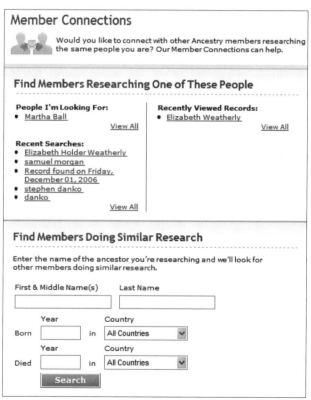

Member Connections

Would you like to connect with other Ancestry members researching the same people you are? Our Member Connections can help.

Find Members Researching One of These People

People I'm Looking For:
- Martha Ball
  View All

Recently Viewed Records:
- Elizabeth Weatherly
  View All

Recent Searches:
- Elizabeth Holder Weatherly
- samuel morgan
- Record found on Friday, December 01, 2006
- stephen danko
- danko
  View All

Find Members Doing Similar Research

Enter the name of the ancestor you're researching and we'll look for other members doing similar research.

First & Middle Name(s)   Last Name

Born   Year   in   Country All Countries

Died   Year   in   Country All Countries

Search

Figure 16-24: The "Member Connections" page.

The "People I'm Looking For," the list of "Recent Searches," and the "Recently Viewed Records" are shown. Click on "View All" to display your complete lists. When you click on any of these links you have been working with, a search results list similar to the one in figure 16-25 appears.

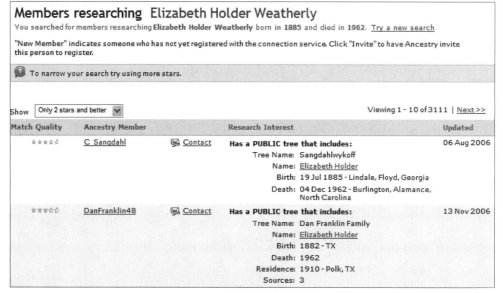

Figure 16-25: Search results from the "Member Connections" page.

Don't overlook using the specific template, "Find Members Doing Similar Research," which is on the main "Member Connections" page, which yields similar results.

Summary

The Ancestry Community is a vast group of highly active genealogical researchers. They are a friendly and helpful group overall who want to share and collaborate on their genealogical research.

The Ancestry.com Message Boards are a tremendous tool for expanding your research possibilities and making new contacts. It is not unusual to make a "cousin connection" on a frequent basis.

The Member Directory can bring you together with other people with similar interests in common with yours. And the Member Connections facility can definitely help you find others conducting research on your lines and other collateral lines.

When you combine the content of the Ancestry.com databases, the search facilities, the indexes, the images, the message boards, and the communications facilities, you can certainly understand why this really *is* the right online genealogy service to be using.

Chapter 17

The Ancestry Store

Just as Ancestry.com provides access to the world's largest online repository of genealogical records, the Ancestry Store offers the most extensive collection of retail products relating to genealogy and family history. The store, located at <www.theancestrystore.com>, was re-launched in November 2006 with a new design and a selection of more than 10,000 products. They are constantly adding new products and features, so be sure to check back often to see what's new.

You can access the Ancestry Store from the **Store** tab at the top of the Ancestry.com pages. The main landing page changes frequently to showcase featured offers, but will look similar to figure 17-1. Notice the search template in the upper right-hand corner of the page, which allows you to search the entire store or use the pull-down list to search within a specific category.

In the six categories of merchandise available, you will find a wide variety of products that are appropriate for the casual

The Ancestry Store

Figure 17-1: The Ancestry Store homepage.

family historian as well as the experienced genealogist. Let's briefly discuss each category.

Books

In the "Books" section, you can purchase Ancestry publications—which include many of the best-selling titles in the genealogy field—as well as thousands of other books on genealogy, family history and related topics.

The "Books" category includes titles in the following areas: "Staff Favorites;" "Ancestry Magazine;" "Ancestry Publishing;" "Biography and Memoir;" "Custom Products;" "Family;" "Genealogy" books organized by geographic areas, ethnic groups and specific reference topics, including a large selection of how-to books for beginners; "Heritage Cookbooks;" "History" organized by geographic areas and special interests, including a large collection of military history books; and "Reference and Pictorial." Ancestry.com has taken extraordinary pains in evaluating and selecting books that address the interests of novice and advanced family historians and history buffs.

Records

Ancestry.com is not only the industry's leading provider of online content, but the company also provides many records on CD-ROMs and in other formats. The "Records" section provides access to a wide variety of products and services, including:

- **Census Records**—These CDs include indexes to records from colonial America, the United States, Great Britain, and other areas.

- **Church and Parish Records**—These CDs contain English county parish records of births, christenings, baptisms, burials, tombstone inscriptions, and more.

- **Immigration**—This group contains CDs and books of passenger lists, atlases, emigrant lists, and more.

- **Location**—This group consists of vital records, parish records, local and family histories, and other records organized by geographic areas.

- **Military**—You will find CDs with muster rolls from the American Revolutionary War, the War of 1812, the Civil War, World War II, and the Korean Conflict. In addition, there are military books concerning American, British, and Canadian military history and regiments.

- **Other**—This group includes reference library CDs and miscellaneous record types, including a Slave Narratives CD and the Biography and Genealogy Master Index (BGMI) on CD.

- **Trees**—These CD bundles include the family trees submitted for inclusion in the Ancestry World Family Tree.

- **Vital Records**—This group includes parish registers, primarily in book form, for many areas of England, along with Irish marriage registers and a selection of CDs containing U.S. states' vital records indexes.

- **Certificate Service**—VitalChek Express Certificate Service is a government-authorized service offering expedited delivery of certified copies of birth, death, marriage, and divorce certificates for you and your ancestors.

Software

The past decade has seen an explosion in genealogical database software products and in the development of utility software to complement your family history research. Ancestry.com has compiled an impressive collection of genealogy-related software for this category. its own *Family Tree Maker* software and bundles, *Legacy*, *Roots Magic*, *The Master Genealogist*, *Clooz*, *Personal Historian*, and *Family Atlas* are among the software titles. In addition, there are DVD training products in this collection to help you learn how to use the leading genealogy database software packages.

Photos

The past lives again in this magnificent collection of photographs. There are three groups of photos included in this category: "People, Places and Things;" "Ward and Conflict," which includes military photos from the U.S. Civil War forward; and "Staff Favorites" that you will recognize as classics, such as the image shown on the ordering page in figure 17-2.

Figure 17-2: One of the "Staff Favorites" shown on the ordering page.

Available in a number of sizes, each photograph is a silver-halide photo print using high quality, archival safe paper, suitable for gallery framing and display. These photos make a lovely gift or a treasured addition to your own collection.

Maps

Maps are essential for effective genealogical research, and Ancestry.com has compiled a collection of more than two thousand historical U.S. and international maps, including a large selection of railroad maps. All maps are available as high-quality silver-halide photo prints in a variety of sizes, ranging from ten to forty inches.

Gifts

The "Gifts" section presents suggestions to help you find the perfect gift for almost anyone: a custom book filled with fascinating facts about your friend's surname, a framed historic print or photograph from your relative's home town, a puzzle featuring the *New York Times* front page from your family member's birth date, a military history book for a veteran or war buff, an introductory genealogy book for a novice family historian, or a more advanced genealogy product for an experienced researcher. The "Gifts" section is refreshed often with products from the store's large store collection.

Figure 17-3: Expanded product information.

Ordering

When you click on a product, you will see a page with a larger product image, more descriptive text, and a price. Other related products are sometimes displayed for your consideration. See figure 17-3 for an example for the book, *They Became Americans*.

You may also see another small button labeled **More Information**. Click it and you will see the full product description and product specifications, such as is shown in figure 17-4 on the next page.

Anytime you see the orange button labeled **Add to Cart**, you can click to add this item to your order. When you do, your "Shopping Cart" page, shown in figure 17-5 on the next page, will be displayed. You can change the quantity of any item you have added to the cart, or you can click the check box in the "Remove" column to delete an item. When you are finished making changes, click the **Update** button and a refreshed, revised "Shopping Cart" page will be displayed.

You may now either click "Return to shopping" or click the orange **Checkout** button to complete your purchase. If you do the latter, you will be prompted to enter your shipping information, and then your billing and payment information.

Figure 17-4: Full product description and specifications.

You will then be taken to the "Review and Confirm" page, where, if necessary, you can change the quantities of your orders (or delete them by changing the quantity to "0"). If you make any changes, click the **Update** button. Otherwise, if everything looks good, click the orange **Complete Your Order** button. A confirmation page will appear that you can print for your reference.

You will also note that there is a "Customer Service" link at the top of The Ancestry Store pages. Here you will find contact information, policies, shipping options, and FAQs (Frequently Asked Questions).

Another link at the top of the page is labeled "My Account." This is the account

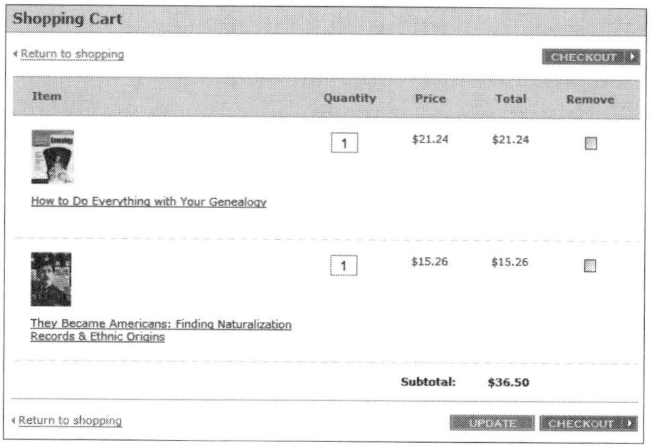

Figure 17-5: The "Shopping Cart" page.

information that you entered as you placed your order. You may also update your username and password, e-mail address, and mailing address and telephone number here.

Summary

As you have seen, The Ancestry Store has thousands of products that appeal to customers with varied interests and backgrounds. Regardless of your level of family history experience, you are sure to find products that will help you better understand and appreciate your heritage. The store's navigation makes it easy to browse or to search for specific products or services, and the ordering process could not be simpler. Take a tour to see what the store offers, and check back frequently for new products and features, promotions, and sales.

Chapter 18

Putting It All Together

We have covered a *lot* of material in this book. But then again, Ancestry.com is the largest genealogy site on the Web. You should now have a strong understanding of what kinds of information can be found at Ancestry.com, how to navigate the site, how to effectively search the site, how to create and use your Family Trees how to use the Ancestry Community facilities to extend your research and make contact with other members. The skills you have learned by reading this book, studying the examples within, and practicing your searching and research skills should have prepared you to be a much for effective user of Ancestry.com.

Remember, however, that Ancestry.com is not the only part of The Generations Network, Inc. There are the UK and Ireland site (Ancestry.co.uk), the Canadian site (Ancestry.ca), the Australian site (Ancestry.au), and the new German site (Ancestry.de). In addition, the other sites in the family of The Generations Network, Inc., also provide exceptional content.

The understanding you have gained for working with Ancestry.com is important because it has prepared you to succeed in working with the other sites, as well as having helped you develop your research thought processes to search the Internet and to work with other databases.

Traditional versus Electronic Evidence

Contrary to some people's perceptions, the electronic content found on the Internet has not replaced traditional documents and other genealogical evidence in our research. Likewise, not everything on the Internet is correct.

It is imperative that you *personally* verify the information you find on Ancestry.com for yourself. Remember, your detailed knowledge of your ancestors and their family members gives you the advantage of applying that knowledge to the assessment and interpretation of details on that original evidential document. Likewise, you cannot be sure that the quality and accuracy of another researcher's work is as accurate and reliable as what you would produce.

Ancestry.com has amassed more than 23,000 databases and titles containing more than 5 billion names. The company continues to acquire and add new content on a regular basis. There is a massive quantity of digitized original material available there to help further your research. You will, of course, evaluate that material, develop hypotheses, and reach conclusions based on that original content weighed against other evidence you uncover.

Other resources at Ancestry.com include indexes and transcribed records. You know that these materials are secondary evidentiary sources. They may contain inaccurate or incomplete information. Ancestry.com knows, too, that its indexes are not infallible. It is difficult to read old handwriting and dim original documents and microfilmed document images. Human indexers, despite the best intentions, may make typographical errors too. You will undoubtedly find indexing and transcription errors at Ancestry.com and in original documents as well. Remember that you can always report errors and omissions to Ancestry.com for correction, and doing so benefits everyone.

Using the Help Tool at Ancestry.com

Ancestry.com is committed to providing solid help to its users. In the upper right-hand corner of almost every page we've examined is a link labeled "Help." A click on that link takes you to the page shown in figure 18-1.

The Help tool is actually includes several services. The core piece is the Knowledge Base. A knowledge base is a special kind of database for knowledge management. It is the base for the collection of information and often FAQs. A knowledge base should have a carefully designed classification structure, content format and search engine, and the Knowledge Base at Ancestry.com is no exception.

In figure 18-1, you will notice that there are four tabs at the top of the "Help" page:

- **Ask Ancestry**—This is the core of the Knowledge Base, where questions and answers are stored, and which you can search by topic.

- **Email Ancestry Support**—This tab provides a formatted template that you can use

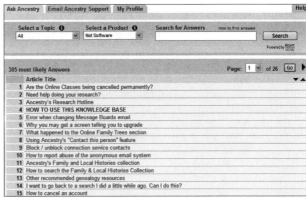

Figure 18- 1: The "Help" page.

to send a message or inquiry to the Ancestry.com customer support group.

- **My Profile**—This tab is different from the My Personal Profile that we have seen before. It provides assistance with logging in, notifying you of a forgotten password, and registering for the site.

- **Help**—This tab provides a brief summary of what the Ancestry.com Help tool is all about and how to use it.

Ask Ancestry

Figure 18-1 shows the Ancestry.com Help tool displaying, as it always does, the default **Ask Ancestry** tab. You certainly could browse through all the pages of the Knowledge Base, but it would be much easier to search for what you want to know.

There are three fields and a **Search** button above the numbered list of topics. Let's discuss how these work.

The first field, "Select a Topic," is a drop-down list of major subject areas in the Knowledge Base. If you click on a topic, another drop-down list will appear with sub-topics. You can select one of these sub-topics, and then click the **Search** button.

Your search will yield a list of possible articles that might answer your question. If I click on one, a page loads that contains the question, answer, and links to other areas where information may be found.

There is another way to get to the topical and sub-topical areas in the Knowledge Base. Beside the "Select a Topic" drop-down list is a dark blue circle with an "i" in it. This is an informational link and, when you click on it, another page will pop up. It allows you to view the entire hierarchical list of topics and sub-topics. Click on one of the links and you will immediately be presented with the same list as if you had used the topic and sub-topics from the drop-down lists.

The "Select a Product" drop-down list and information icon ("i") work identically to the "Select a Topic" list. Instead of containing topics, however, it contains a list of products about which you may have questions.

The "Search for Answers" field allows you to enter one or more terms and have the search engine locate responses for you. Here are some tips for using this search field.

- **Narrow Your Search**—Select topics and products from the drop-down menus to narrow your search.

- **Require Words**—Use a plus (+) symbol in front of words to require that documents contain those words *Example*: Type "+census +viewer" to find documents that contain both words "census" and "viewer."

- **Exclude Words**—Use a minus (-) symbol in front of words to exclude documents that contain those words. *Example*: Type "census -print" to find documents that contain the word "census" but not "print."

- **Use Uncommon Words**—Use uncommon words to retrieve documents with more focused results.

Email Ancestry Support

When you click on the **Email Ancestry Support** tab, the page shown in figure 18-2 is displayed. It is a formatted template you can use to send a message to the Ancestry.com customer support group. Use it only if you were unsuccessful in finding an answer to your

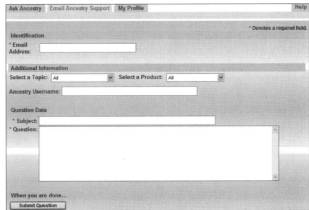

*Figure 18-2: The **Email Ancestry Support** tab.*

question using the **Ask Ancestry** tab. All fields indicated by the presence of a small red asterisk must be completed. You will note there are drop-down lists again on this page for "Select a Topic" and "Select a Product."

When you have completed the information in the fields, click **Submit Question**. Your message will be sent to the customer support group. You will receive an e-mail response, answering your question.

My Profile

The **My Profile** tab, when clicked, will look like figure 18-3 when it is displayed. There are three areas:

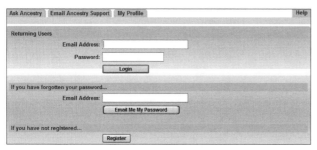

Figure 18-3: The My Profile tab.

1. **Returning Users**—If you are already registered or are a subscriber with Ancestry.com, you may log in here.

2. **Forgotten Password**—If you have already registered or subscribed but have forgotten your password, enter your e-mail address here and Ancestry.com will send you an e-mail with your password.

3. **Register**—If you are not a subscriber but still wish to use the free areas, you must register. Click the **Register** button and a form will be displayed allowing you to complete some basic registration information.

As you can see, the Ancestry.com Help tool and its Knowledge Base are easy to use and will provide you with a great deal of help information. In the meantime, you will want to keep this book handy too. Use the table of contents and the index to locate just what you need to know.

Now, get started on your genealogical odyssey and discover the wealth of great information available at Ancestry.com.

Happy hunting!

Index

Index

images (*continued*)

    saving, 65–66

    sharing with others, 66–67

    thumbnails of, 62–63

    viewing, 57–58

    zooming in and out of, 59–60

Image Viewer

    help for, 67

    overview, 63

    toolbar, 58

immigration, by surname, 138

immigration records. *See also* naturalization records

    overview, 185–87

    Passenger and Immigration Lists Index, 1590s–1900s, 193–95

    searching

        entire collection, 187–93

        individual databases, 195–200

Immigration Records Collection, 185–87

immigration year, by surname, 133–34

Ireland, Ancestry website for, 291

K

Knowledge Base, 293–95

L

land ownership maps, 241

land records, 201–10

Learning Center

    contents of, 245–48

    Family Facts, 131–39, 246

    guides to record collections, 248

    Today @ Ancestry.com, 246

Learning Center tab, 16–17, 245–52

Library

    contents of, 245–46

    searching, 248–52

life expectancy, by surname, 134

living relatives, in family trees, 74

local histories

    overview, 147–49

    searching, 142–45

localities, searching *PERSI* by, 237–38

logging in, 2–3

M

Map Collection, 239–42

maps

    buying in Ancestry Store, 287

    searching for, 35–38

marriage records

    overview, 116

    sample search, 123–24

Member Connections, 87–88, 279–80

Member Directory, 15, 256, 277–79

members, connecting with others, 87–88

message boards

    bookmarking favorites, 276

    browsing, 270–77

    creating posts, 264–68

    e-mail alerts for, 276

    Page Tools, 276

    searching, 268–70

middle names, searching with, 47–48

military records

    of Civil War, 216–19

    draft registration cards, WWI, 219–21

    of enlistment, WWII Army, 221–22

    of Revolutionary War, 213–16

Military Records Collection, 211–23

military service, evidence found in census records, 213

misspellings, correcting in index, 96–97

My Account, 3–4

My Ancestry tab, 10, 69–70

My Public Profile, 254–55, 257–64

My Site Preferences, 255, 263–64

About the Author

George G. Morgan

George G. Morgan has been working on his own family genealogy since he was ten years old in North Carolina, and he has traced his family lines across the southeastern United States to the UK, Scotland, and Ireland. His extremely popular and award-winning weekly genealogy column, *"Along Those Lines ..."*, appeared each Friday at Ancestry.com for more than eight years and now appears as a weekly blog at his company's website at <ahaseminars.com>. He is the author of five books, including *How to Do Everything with Your Genealogy*, which has become one of the fastest-selling genealogy books in the past twenty years. He is also the co-host, with Drew Smith, of "The Genealogy Guys Podcast" each week at <genealogyguys.com>.

George is a director of the Florida Genealogical Society of Tampa and is currently serving on the Marketing Committee of the Federation of Genealogical Societies (FGS). He is a member of the Association of Professional Genealogists (APG), the National Genealogical Society (NGS), and more than twenty other local, state, national, and international genealogical societies. He lives in Odessa, Florida, a suburb of Tampa.